The Future of Learning

The Future of Learning

Insights and Innovations from Executive Development

Edited By

Shirine Voller
Research Manager, Ashridge Business School

Eddie Blass
Senior Lecturer in Professional Education, University of Hertfordshire

Vicki Culpin
Research Director, Ashridge Business School

First published 2011 by
PALGRAVE MACMILLAN

Palgrave Macmillan in the UK is an imprint of Macmillan Publishers Limited, registered in England, company number 785998, of Houndmills, Basingstoke, Hampshire RG21 6XS.

Palgrave Macmillan in the US is a division of St Martin's Press LLC, 175 Fifth Avenue, New York, NY 10010.

Palgrave Macmillan is the global academic imprint of the above companies and has companies and representatives throughout the world.

Palgrave® and Macmillan® are registered trademarks in the United States, the United Kingdom, Europe and other countries

ISBN 978-0-230-24053-7   hardback

This book is printed on paper suitable for recycling and made from fully managed and sustained forest sources. Logging, pulping and manufacturing processes are expected to conform to the environmental regulations of the country of origin.

A catalogue record for this book is available from the British Library.

A catalog record for this book is available from the Library of Congress.

10   9   8   7   6   5   4   3   2   1
20   19   18   17   16   15   14   13   12   11

Transferred to Digital Printing in 2014

Contents

List of Tables and Figures

Tables

Figures

Notes on Contributors

Eddie Blass started her academic career lecturing in HRM after a period of time training in industry. She completed her Doctorate at Durham on 'The Future University' and combines her research interests in adult learning, HE and leadership development in her current job role at the University of Hertfordshire in the School of Education.

Dave Bond specialises in personal leadership development, using coaching dialogues, presence and narrative in change processes. He has an MSocSci in politics (Cape Town), an MA in language ecology (Stellenbosch) and is completing his MSc in Executive Coaching (Ashridge). Dave is currently both a leadership faculty member at Ashridge (UK) and works privately out of Cape Town.

Chris Breen took early retirement as Emeritus Associate Professor in mathematics education from the School of Education at the University of Cape Town in July 2008 after completing a three year term of office as President of the International Group for the Psychology of Mathematics Education. He currently consults and teaches topics such as Complexity and Diversity, Personal Leadership, Becoming More Aware and Decision-Making in the Moment.

John Burgoyne is Professor of Management Learning in the Department of Management Learning and Leadership at Lancaster University Management School. He is also an Associate at Ashridge and Henley Business School. In addition he is a Trustee of Brathay Trust, an outdoor development charity, and a fellow of the Leadership Foundation and the British Academy of Management. His interests are management, leadership and organisation development and the evaluation of initiatives in these areas. He has been interested in the Learning Organisation since the late 1980's and is currently working on network theory as applied to all these areas.

Ghislaine Caulat is Associate Business Director at Ashridge Consulting. She has been researching and working in the field of virtual working and virtual learning for the last seven years. She is currently finalising her Doctorate on Virtual Leadership (ADOC, the Ashridge Doctorate in Organisation Consulting in co-operation with Middlesex University). She also holds an MSc in Organisation Consulting from Ashridge and Middlesex University and an MA in English and Spanish Philology from the Johannes-

Gutenberg University in Mainz (Germany). Ghislaine combines over fifteen years of consulting practice with global organisations with several years of business management practice working for companies such as Beiersdorf (FMCG) and Daimler (Automotive).

Susan Coggan holds a Masters in Professional Education and Training from Deakin University. She has worked in primary and tertiary education; and was a learning and development consultant with CIPD, before becoming self employed as a L&D consultant. She previously worked in New Zealand at the Performance Improvement Centre.

Vicki Culpin studied Psychology at Manchester University, followed by an MPhil and PhD in Psychology from Lancaster University and an MSc in Applied Forensic Psychology from Leicester University. She spent nine years working in academia before moving to Ashridge Business School where she is Research Director.

Mollie Dickenson is an executive business coach and a research fellow at Henley Business School, University of Reading. Her research interests focus on: informal learning approaches, particularly action learning, coaching and mentoring; adapting such approaches to virtual environments; and embedding learning within an organisational culture.

Dave Duarte is Managing Director of Huddlemind Labs, a company that manages online learning for various multinational corporations. He is the programme director of Nomadic Marketing at UCT's Graduate School of Business, and lectures collaborative technologies for the Executive MBA programme. Other appointments include: Director of the Ogilvy Digital Marketing Academy; Public Lead for Creative Commons South Africa; Dean of the Digital Dream Faculty at the Maharishi Institute of Management; Partner in the SA Blog Awards, and judge in The Bees Global Social Media Awards.

Matthew Gitsham is Director of the Ashridge Centre for Business and Sustainability. The centre's research work is at the intersection of adult learning, leadership development, behavioural and organisational change, and the ways in which communities, societies and organisations innovate to adapt to major global trends such as sustainable development.

Ronan Gruenbaum studied Computational Science and Economics at Leeds University, followed by a Graduate Diploma in Law from the University of Westminster and an MBA from Ashridge. He teaches Social Media, Web 2.0 and Business 2.0 on qualification and customised executive education programmes, has presented at a number of international management education conferences and is a member of the European Foundation for Management Development External Relations Committee.

Sue Honoré has an MSc in Networked Learning from Lancaster University and a Bachelor's degree in Biological Sciences. She has worked in a variety of consultative roles in industry, more recently centred around learning. She was a Learning Consultant at Ashridge for six years and currently is a freelance Researcher and Consultant in business and learning.

Anne Jasman currently works at the University of Southern Queensland. She has over 35 years experience working in initial and continuing teacher education as researcher, university lecturer and policy adviser in universities and regulatory authorities in Australia, UK and US. Her research interests include professional learning, leadership, collaborative work and teaching standards. Her most recent work focuses on quality provision in professional education from a futures perspective.

Carina Paine Schofield has a first degree in Applied Psychology and Computing, a post graduate diploma in Psychology and a PhD in Psychology. She worked in academia for several years before moving to a market research company. She is currently a research fellow at Ashridge Business School.

Mike Pedler works with leadership, action learning, the learning organisation and network organising. He is Emeritus Professor at Henley Business School, University of Reading and co-edits the Journal: Action Learning: Research and Practice.

Ellen Pruyne has a Master's and Doctorate in Education from Harvard University and a Master's in Management from Northwestern University. She spent the early part of her career working to promote entrepreneurship and the development of micro and small businesses. In her current role as a Learning Consultant at Ashridge Business School, she supports faculty and clients in designing effective learning environments and experiences, optimising participant learning, and conducting learning assessments and impact evaluations.

Elaine Rumboll holds an MA and an MBA from the University of the Witwatersrand. She was appointed Director of Executive Education, UCT Graduate School of Business in 2005 after being Dean for Damelin Management School. Elaine is involved in the teaching and design of their customised Leadership interventions. She is the winner of the 2010 Business Women's Association Regional Business Achievement Awards in the Professional category, was granted a meritorious award as a finalist in the 2010 Most Influential Women in Business and Government in the Educational and Training category, and received a nomination for Top Businesswoman 2010 in the annual Top Women in Business and Government.

Steve Shelley is a Principal Lecturer in Human Resource Management at the Work and Employment Research Unit, University of Hertfordshire Business School. He teaches and researches on management strategies and development, work control, public sector management, skill, learning and training. Steve's earlier book 'Working in Universities: the realities from porter to professor', explores the way in which work is undertaken and managed in UK universities. From his studies of work in higher education he has previously published on the subjects of management decision-making, retirement, appraisal, performance-related pay and Investors in People in universities. His current research projects are an analysis of managerialism across public service organisations, and an examination of the outcomes of trade union learning and education.

Tom Short holds a MA in Human Resource Management from the University of Huddersfield and a PhD in Education from the University of South Australia. Prior to becoming an academic he was Director of the Performance Improvement Centre at the University of Auckland, has worked as a management consultant and before moving overseas was a senior human resources manager in a UK multi-national manufacturing organisation.

Shirine Voller holds an MA in Natural Sciences from Cambridge University and a Masters by Research from Cranfield University. She was the lead organiser of the 2009 Future of Learning Conference at Ashridge. She has worked in primary education, organisation consulting and grant management and is currently Research Manager at Ashridge Business School.

Preface

This book presents papers that originated from The Future of Learning conference held at Ashridge Business School in 2009. When the conference was conceived and the call for papers sent out, we didn't know what response we would get. We knew what we hoped to achieve – a creative space for practitioners and academics to talk together about the future of learning, focusing on executive education – but we were unsure about how our vision would 'land' with potential contributors and attendees. As it happened, the conference worked out even better than we could have hoped for.

The way this book has developed reflects the blend of intention and emergence that characterised the conference: We had not prescribed nor anticipated what the sections of the book would be, yet the contributions that made it through to final selection split naturally into three areas: the future context, the future of learning and the future learner. So this is how we have structured the book. On reflection, these areas make good sense: We need to understand the context and environment in which learning will take place in the future; this context will shape and be shaped by the processes by which learning occurs; and learners will respond to this environment and the means for learning available to them, and place demands on learning providers as they grow up in our future society and work in our future workplaces.

Bringing variety to the book is the international mix of authors: There are contributions from Europe, Africa and Australasia. Yet geographical distances are diminished by the proximity of the authors' informing experiences and visions of the future. It was also harmony that informed our choice of who to partner with for the conference: As lead organiser (Ashridge), we wanted to work with institutions that we felt were similarly forward-thinking and innovative and would be interested in addressing the future of learning in a non-traditional way. We approached the University of Cape Town Graduate School of Business Executive Education Unit and Mt Eliza Executive Education, Melbourne. Whilst miles apart physically, these were two highly reputed institutions with whom we felt a congruence of philosophy and mutual respect. The partnership worked brilliantly, and the next iteration of the conference is scheduled to take place in Melbourne in March 2011.

Clearly, what has been 'the future' at some point transitions to 'the present' and then merges with the wealth of experience and memories that is 'the past'. In this book we present ideas and practice that are, at the time of writing, toward the leading edge in executive education and beyond. We recognise and embrace the fact that some of the themes will drift into the mainstream, while others might never fully develop, because something else comes along in their place. Regardless, we are confident that the quality of thinking that informs each chapter will pique the reader's interest and stimulate ideas and action.

Shirine Voller
Eddie Blass
Vicki Culpin

Part I
Future Context

1
Future Context: Section Editorial

Vicki Culpin

The future of learning must consider the individual learner and the research that is shaping how we see the learner operate within and interacting with the learning environment. Interaction with the learning environment is also where the role of tools, techniques and technology may play a significant role in the future. A third aspect of the future of learning that should be considered, and the first section of this book, is around context; the political, environmental, social and technological changes that we face now and may face in the future.

Context is so important in the interpretation of events and understanding of communication (hence the phrase 'that was taken out of context' to explain a misunderstanding) and in appreciating intention. In a recent event at Ashridge I spoke about the importance of context in memory. For example, the cognitive interview is a technique employed by Police Officers when eliciting statements from witnesses and victims of crime. The cognitive interview is an interview process but it has been specifically designed with memory research in mind, to ensure that questions are asked in the appropriate way to maximise the accuracy of the statement being given. One of the methods used in the cognitive interview is the reinstatement of the context during the time of the crime. That is why crime reconstructions can be so successful in triggering previously forgotten information. Often the context is stored at the same time as the memory, so retrieving the context can help individuals to recall the previously forgotten information.

If context is important in memory, then context must be critical in learning. Pruyne and Bond, in their chapter, consider that the context in which we live and work is experienced by individuals as unstable, complex and 'messy'. They note that one of the biggest challenges facing leaders at the present time is contending with rising levels of fear and anxiety in the population, with the UK in particular becoming more fearful as a nation. They go on to argue that this individual level of anxiety is mirrored at an organisational level with widespread feelings of disorientation and identity loss.

The central tenet for Pruyne and Bond is that in an increasingly complex and unpredictable world there is a need for people to learn how to comprehend, adapt and respond in the face of challenges that have both organisational and personal consequences. In relation to leadership specifically, they argue that leaders must learn how to acknowledge and embrace this increasingly complex and messy world. Pruyne and Bond advocate the use of both storytelling and improvisation to help individuals learn how to become '21st Century Leaders'.

Research has consistently shown that negative affect can compromise decision-making, problem solving and rational processing, whereas developing 'psychological capital', positive mood and emotions, allow individuals to respond to challenges in a pro-active and more effective way. Pruyne and Bond suggest that storytelling and improvisation are two vehicles that will help develop resilient individuals and more effective leaders. What is important here, in relation to the future of learning, is not the methodology, which is not new, but the context. They claim that storytelling and improvisation is successful because of their capacity to be integrated and applied in ways which successfully meet the challenges of complexity and uncertainty that leaders of the future will face.

Gitsham, in the second chapter of this section, also considers context to be important for developing leaders of the future. Gitsham, like Pruyne and Bond, sees that the fundamental issue for leaders of tomorrow is the expectation to understand and respond to a far broader range of social, political, cultural and environmental issues and trends than any generation before them. For Gitsham, the key issue is not just the individual learner, as it is for Pruyne and Bond, but the necessity of organisations to recognise these issues as important and respond to the challenges in a pro-active manner.

Gitsham outlines a study led by Ashridge Business School, co-coordinated by EABIS, which sought to understand what the shifting landscape of global challenges means for leadership development and executive education. Key findings from the research include the fact that 76 per cent of CEO's and senior executives believe it is important to have the necessary knowledge and skills to respond to the challenges and opportunities of the 21st century, but fewer than 8 per cent see this knowledge and skills being developed effectively within organisations. For Gitsham, if there is a fundamental need to address these issues in the future, a need which is currently not being met, then the question is 'What qualities need to be fostered to meet this demand and develop leaders of the future?'

The research conducted by Gitsham and colleagues found that three prominent qualities emerged: context; complexity; and connectedness. Context is seen as the need to understand the changing business context; complexity is the ability to lead in the face of complex and ambiguous situations; and connectedness describes the ability to understand the actors in the wider political landscape and the need to build relationships within and across organisations. Gitsham concludes by emphasising the need for both business leaders and educators to remember that the new world they operate within, the context they work in, has real implications for leadership development and executive education.

The final chapter of this section also considers the future of executive education, but rather than the organisational context taken by Gitsham, Blass, Jasman and Shelley consider the future of executive education within the context of Higher Education.

Blass, Jasman and Shelley start by noting that within the context of a global recession, and the move of the MBA from the pinnacle of executive education to a mass delivery graduate conversion course for business, the future of executive education provision within the HE sector is under scrutiny. They suggest that universities must start to question what they can offer organisations that the organisations themselves are unable or unwilling to provide. With the future of HE within the executive education arena uncertain, Blass and colleagues have undertaken a futures study to examine this sector in 25 years time.

Five 'future' scenarios were developed by Blass, Jasman and Shelley. The first two focus on the nature of knowledge: The first in terms of the sector leading knowledge creation; and the second on the nature of knowledge in response to knowledge needs from external stakeholders. The third scenario considers the organisation of work and the need for collaboration, and the final two hypothesise a significant funding cut in the HE sector by the government. In scenario four the funding cut is maintained, whereas in scenario five the funding is re-established after ten years to rebuild the sector.

For Blass and colleagues, all five of these scenarios have significant implications for executive education, with some relating to what they label as the supply side of education, such as the academic workforce drawing on corporate managers for part-time teaching. Others relate to the demand side and include delivery through the internet and niche specialist provisions. Blass, Jasman and Shelley discuss in detail the implications of the scenarios within this supply and demand framework, and conclude by arguing that regardless of what the future of HE may look like, and how accurate the five scenarios are, a number of issues must be considered: the radical shift in the executive qualifications market; the move to corporate universities for academics, and the undertaking of part-time teaching in traditional universities by executives; and the increased digitalisation of learning.

All three chapters in this section consider the importance of context within the future of learning. This context may be at the individual level, the organisational level or at the sectoral level, but the interplay between learning in the future, the learner of the future and the future context cannot be ignored.

2
Learning to Lead in Uncertain Times through Storytelling and Improvisation

Ellen Pruyne and Dave Bond

The leadership learning challenge

The second decade of the 21st century confronts us with seemingly intract-able global challenges, such as climate change, the global financial crisis and the war on terror. Yet, our leaders in government and industry often disappoint with inadequate solutions and self-interested or even corrupt actions.[1] One could even add 'credible global leadership' as one of the 21st century challenges. Increasingly, our clients in the private, public and charitable sectors express unease and distrust in national and international leadership at the same time as they are forced to face the fallout of these global challenges at the organisational level. To them, and us, the world feels increasingly complex, uncertain and 'messy'; the contexts in which we live and work are experienced as unstable and constantly shifting under our very feet. Our concern in this paper is with ordinary, everyday leaders (see Binney et al., 2009) who are called upon to do extraordinary things to help keep their organisations on a viable course in these turbulent times.

One of the challenges faced by these leaders is contending with the rising levels of fear and anxiety in the population at large (Halliwell, 2009), including their own workers and clients/customers. In a recent survey, the Mental Health Foundation (MHF) found that 37 per cent of UK respon-dents reported being more frightened and anxious than they used to be, 77 per cent considered the world a more frightening place than it was ten years ago, and 77 per cent believed that people have become more fright-ened and anxious in general (*ibid*, 2009). The MHF contends that the UK is

---

[1] In the UK alone, 2009 saw weeks of media coverage on MPs' abuse of expenses fol-lowing months of public dismay at the factors which had contributed to the global financial meltdown. In 2010 there continues an extensive inquiry into the veracity and legality of UK government claims made to justify the Iraq war. It remains uncer-tain whether the billions pumped into the banking system will bring about a 'correc-tion' or that the Iraq war will contribute to peace in the region.

becoming more fearful as a nation and that this fear and anxiety is linked to significant increases in depression and anxiety disorders as documented in government surveys of psychiatric morbidity (*ibid*, 2009). This contention has received direct support from a survey of family physicians and their patients in which a direct link between fears and anxieties about the economy and increasing levels of stress and depression was found (MHF, 2010). Approximately 17 per cent of UK adults and 10 per cent of children are known to suffer from mental health problems (although true prevalence may be higher), with mixed anxiety and depression being the most common problem. In the US about 18 per cent of the adult population is known to suffer from an anxiety disorder, with a direct cost to the society of about $42 billion (ADAA, 2009). Worldwide the number is similar – approximately 17 per cent (Somers et al., 2006).

Research at the organisational level portrays a similar picture. When Day (2007) investigated five large UK organisations undergoing considerable change, he found evidence of widespread feelings of disorientation and identity loss. Painful emotions such as anger and fear were evident, as were tension, fragmentation and hostility amongst groups and individuals. People were engaged in heightened political behaviour and responded to ongoing and persistent change with manic activity and 'fire-fighting'. The findings were not all negative, however; there was also evidence of people responding with heightened energy, creativity and personal development. A common factor in these more constructive responses was that individuals were concentrating on local spheres of impact, where they had some semblance of control, rather than fixating on issues well beyond their influence (Day, 2007). The value of finding some sense of personal power, a stepping stone in the turbulent waters, is one we will return to below.

What these findings at the population and organisational levels signal to us is that, more than ever, there is a need for people to learn how to comprehend, adapt and respond in the face of seemingly intractable challenges that have both organisational and personal consequences. We call this 'learning how to learn in real-time'. There is also the critical need to learn how to lead at all levels of society. This is leadership that acknowledges and recognises the uncertain nature of the challenges we face as a human community and the messiness of the situations in which we increasingly find ourselves in our organisations. This, we contend, is the current 'cutting-edge' in the areas of learning and leadership development. In this chapter we will introduce an approach which combines storytelling and improvisation to help individuals learn how to be 21st century learners and leaders. It is important to note here that the methodologies we will be exploring are not new. What makes them so pertinent, however, is their capacity to be integrated and applied in ways which seem particularly powerful in meeting the challenges of complexity and uncertainty that we have described.

Developing psychological capital

The good news is that the human brain has actually been designed to solve problems in the midst of action as a means for survival in an unstable environment (Medina, 2008). It would therefore seem that people should be able to thrive in the unstable and perplexing environments we face today. However, the generalised fear, anxiety and/or depression that are afflicting more and more people tend to interfere with this capacity to engage in problem-solving by initiating and sustaining an emotionally aroused state of mind in which rational processing is compromised (Ledoux, 2002). Individuals suffering from such prolonged mental and emotional stress find it more difficult to take in new information, adapt and learn in real-time, solve problems and form memories (Medina, 2008; Ledoux, 1996; Blakemore and Frith, 2005; Picard et al., 2004). Positive mood and emotions tend to have the opposite effect: under their influence, we tend to be more flexible and creative in our thinking, more efficient and thorough in our problem-solving, and more motivated to decide and act upon our circumstances no matter how challenging they might be (Picard et al., 2004; Kringelbach, 2009). Having positive mood and emotions on an ongoing basis is what is referred to in the psychological and management literature as 'psychological capital' (Luthans et al., 2006; Peterson et al., 2008), its hallmarks being hope, optimism, confidence and resilience.

Until recently it was believed that each individual was born with a certain disposition that remained unchanged throughout life (Diener and Biswas-Diener, 2008). There was nothing to be done if you were born a pessimist or had a depressive personality. We now know that individuals are born with an emotional or happiness set point but that this set point can be changed through 'sustained effort to modify the ways [we] think and behave' (*ibid*: 162). We can learn to transform fear and anxiety into optimism and hope. Although talking therapies and anti-depressant medications that affect serotonin and norepinephrine levels in the brain have perhaps been the most common approaches for bringing about lasting emotional change, research is now demonstrating that other avenues such as cognitive behavioural therapy (CBT) (Burns, 1999), meditation (Lutz et al., 2009) and training in emotional intelligence (Goleman, 1996, 1999; Boyatzis et al., 2002; Slaski and Cartwright, 2003) can be equally effective in developing psychological capital. The research on happiness suggests that ongoing engagement in a religious or spiritual practice tends to lead to higher levels of mental health and wellbeing as well (Diener and Biswas-Diener, 2008). People can learn how to manage potentially debilitating emotions and respond in a more proactive way to an uncertain and challenging environment. As we explain below, we believe that we have identified yet another approach to help bring about such cognitive reframing and emotional change.

Very recently, Day and Powers (2009) found numerous examples of the capacity to effect this kind of shift at the organisational level despite a turbulent context. Their research included interviews with 50 executives and senior managers around the world asking how they were experiencing the global economic crisis. Amidst stories of anxiety, fragmentation and confusion, they found that even in the recent turbulence and change, leadership can create and sustain an environment of hope, confidence and resilience within organisations. They argue that leadership development and learning for the future will have to take into account even greater levels of uncertainty and ambiguity. Two of the capacities they see as needed for future leadership include the ability to...

> *engage in sense making as an emergent and collaborative process and... manage acute anxiety states so as to provide the energy for creativity and adaptive responses. This represents a paradigm shift for how many of us think about leadership in organisations. Such a shift cannot be taught to leaders in the traditional way; rather it can only be developed through hard won experience and experiential learning that confront leaders about their 'deepest' assumptions about the world and challenge them to access, and make use of, their own emotions and feelings* (2009: 25).

More specifically, leaders of the future will need to engage in a variety of specific activities, such as providing direction to 'contain' anxiety, relating to people and showing concern for them even when the news is bad, adhering and appealing to the core values of the organisation, and staying 'in conversation' and constant communication with customers and key stakeholders. To put this into our own words, effective leadership in times of uncertainty, instability and complexity requires the courage and capacity to be present with 'what is', to sustain messy conversations, and to co-craft stories that can lead to a better future.

Like Day and Power, we argue that this requires leaders to be reflective, to tap into their own feelings and emotions, and to work with their anxieties, assumptions and hopes, in ways which will sustain them amidst the challenges they and their organisations will face. Improvisation and storytelling integrate powerfully to provide a means of reflecting, reframing and experiencing in ways which promote these kinds of leadership qualities.

Developing the capacity to learn and lead in uncertain times

In our view, the crux of the approach for developing psychological capital should be learning how to transform our perception and experience of challenging problems and messy situations. It involves moving from a framing of the situation that provokes fear and anxiety and makes us feel overwhelmed and inadequate to a story of opportunity and the possibility of a better future, a story that engenders feelings of agency and hope. The power of framing and reframing is long established in the leadership and organisational development literature (see, for example, Morgan, 1997, and Bolman and Deal, 1997), as is the potential in appreciative framing (Seligman and Csikszentmihalyi, 2000; Cooperrider and Whitney, 2005). We believe that the development of the ability to reframe the scary present into the reassuring and beckoning future requires that we learn how to live in current reality and future aspiration at the same time. We need to craft the desired future while learning and adapting to current events and situations in real-time and in a congruent, authentic and courageous manner. In particular, this combined 'future-backwards' and 'present-forward' approach involves learning two critical and complementary skills: storytelling and improvisation.

Storytelling is essentially generating a guiding narrative of who we are over time – where we have come from, where we are now, and where we wish to go. Over recent decades, there have been a number of studies on the role of narrative and sense-making in organisational learning, organisational development, teamwork and leadership (Weick, 1995; Grant et al., 2004) More recently, Denning (2007) has argued that a skilled grasp of narrative is an essential leadership competency for influencing and inspiring action. One example is the shift in public perception of Al Gore as US vice-president to Al Gore, the Nobel prize-winner.

Although there are merits in Denning's categorisation of key elements for successful leadership narrative, it risks ignoring some of the psychological depth required for sustainable leadership. There are two kinds of stories we need to learn to tell. The 'big story' is the story of who we are across time – a story of identity and purpose. The 'little story' is the narrative arc in the moment as we encounter the moment-to-moment challenges of our lives and make moral choices of consequence. In living the big story, we ask 'who are we?' and 'what is the meaning of our lives?'. In living the little story, we ask 'what is happening?' and 'how do I wish to respond?' in this particular moment. Many people fail to define a big story of who they are and why they are here, allowing the little stories of their everyday lives to accumulate into a general sense of self. Resilient individuals and effective leaders, on the other hand, deliberately create a grand narrative within which all of the little stories acquire broader sense and significance. As the Jungian therapist, James Hollis (2003: 54), argues, we would do well to heed William Blake's provocation that if we don't create our own myth, we will be enslaved to that of another or, one could add, that which has emerged without us noticing. Hollis is talking of the potential for individuation within all of us. In our work, we have found that the crafting of a deep personal narrative is a vital component of leadership sense-making and empowerment. It helps provide an authentic compass for navigating the turbulence of our times and the emotional volatility of our anxious colleagues (as well as ourselves).

Resilient leaders, then, develop a coherent narrative for the past, present and intended future, which they use to guide their actions and to inspire and influence the human communities in which they endeavour to lead. It is this big story of meaning and purpose that guides their actions in the moment, rather than the little story of that specific moment being allowed to take them in the direction of some unspecified and perhaps unintended and even undesirable future. For those wishing to explore this further, Hollis' work (2003, 1995, 1993) is an excellent guide on ways to plumb the depths of our patterns to reveal the implicit personal story we are living. By following rigorous and systematic processes of inquiry, of ourself and our practices, we can move beyond the accumulation of 'small events' to develop a fresh and more authentic story (see also Mason, 2002, and Kegan and Lahey, 2009).

Religious and spiritual practices are at least in part linked to resilience and happiness because they tend to be situated within a narrative that provides this bigger story of meaning, purpose and intention (see, for example, Boldt, 1999; Carroll, 2007; Kornfield, 1994; Scharmer, 2007; Zohar and Marshall, 2005). Such narratives are powerful avenues for individual sense-making. In essence, we are seeing storytelling, in a multitude of guises, as a means for meaning making in such a personally coherent way that it can provide leaders with (a) an antidote to their own crippling anxiety or flight, (b) a convincing discourse for being present to others through turmoil, and (c) a creative and energising form for crafting new stories of possibility within organisations.

Improvisation, on the other hand, is the equally critical skill of being able to adapt and respond skilfully in the current moment no matter the situation or challenge facing us. In a sense, it is the complementary capacity to operate where there is no coherent story, to craft a dynamic storyline which shifts with every engagement and participant. Jazz music and musicians hold valuable analogies here (see, for example, Barrett, 1998). For this reason, accomplished jazz musicians are increasingly regular guest speakers and performers on some of our leadership development programmes. Jazz has also been the inspiration for some highly innovative work by some of our colleagues. They have woven an experientially rich process through which leaders in the consultancy field can expand their understanding and their capacity to respond creatively in the midst of organisational uncertainty and complexity.[2]

Improvisational skill can be developed in a number of ways, e.g. participating in live cases or online games. Our focus for this paper is the use of improvisational exercises from the theatre world. These exercises in pure or adapted form originated in the work of Keith Johnstone (1979) and Viola Spolin (1999). Working independently in the UK and the US respectively, Johnstone and Spolin created improvisational acting exercises to help child and adult actors become less stilted and mechanical and more spontaneous and authentic in the moment as they acted on stage. Johnstone contended that improvisation taps into the unconscious, which '...will lead you to

[2]Dave's thanks to Caryn Vanstone and Kathleen King for inviting me to participate in one of these workshops in their MSc in Organisational Consulting, Ashridge Business School.

places you never dreamed of, and produce results more "original" than anything you could achieve by aiming at originality' (Johnstone, 1979: 10). Spolin believed that the point of 'education is to train for crisis, to reach intuition and self' (Spolin, 1999: xv), and that 'with intuitive awareness comes a feeling of certainty' (p.xiii). In other words, their approach was designed to help individuals learn to operate from their intuition rather than the part of the mind that prefers to analyse and plan ahead. By trusting their intuition, people learn how to stay in the present moment rather than living in fears and anxieties carried forward from the past and projected into the imagined future. In other words, they learn to be present and mindful. Perhaps even more importantly, they learn to be skilful in adapting and responding in real-time to whatever the moment brings, and thus learn to trust themselves to be courageous and true in the heat of any particular circumstance or moment.

Example of an exercise

There are many storytelling and improvisation exercises that can be used to develop the individual capacity to learn and lead in uncertain times. In this section we introduce one of the exercises that we have developed and used. The appendix provides a list of resources in which other approaches and exercises can be found, as well as the website address for the Applied Improvisation Network, an organisation devoted to using improvisation in organisational life.

The exercise we are sharing here is a guided visualisation that taps into both the storytelling and the intuitive parts of our minds. It is based on some recent research about the power of creating psychological distance by projecting ourselves into the future (Shapira and Liberman, 2009). Psychological distancing allows us to gain a different perspective on our situation and creates the 'space' necessary for us to make sense or meaning of our situation and to conceive of a different way of being or responding.

This exercise has been used within tailored and open senior leadership development programmes and individual executive coaching sessions, as well as in a conference workshop. It usually arises in the context of exploring elements of Stacey's model of complexity and the participants' responses to uncertainty in their leadership domains. In particular, we draw on it when a client or participant is experiencing a high degree of anxiety and confusion. To help leaders distance themselves from such feelings, they are invited to cast their minds forward in order to look back on the present as if it had already occurred.[3]

---

[3]This approach is an adaptation based on the observation of one of our Ashridge colleagues, Hugh Pidgeon, that we make choices about the present on the basis of the stories we believe about the future. Hence, our 'paralysis' in the present moment, derives from our fear of what may happen in the future, or our refusal to change may derive from our belief that our current life and world is sustainable. It is also inspired by an approach called timeline therapy developed by Tad James (1989).

In this visualisation exercise we invite participants to scroll backwards in time to a specific time when they encountered a difficult problem or challenge and came through it with flying colours. We have them remember exactly how it felt to encounter the problem and challenge – what they saw, heard and felt – and then how it felt when they successfully resolved the challenge. This part of the visualisation allows them to get in touch with their own resilience and capacity to engage with and overcome a challenge. We then have them scroll forward into the present and allow a leadership (or other) problem or challenge they are currently grappling with to come into mind. Again we ask them to remember exactly how it has been feeling to encounter that challenge – what they see, hear and feel. Then we ask them to scroll forward into the future to a time when they are an older, wiser person. In effect we are allowing them to locate themselves in a safe future point where they have the luxury of looking back and gaining perspective on what they are going through in the present. Having done this, they are invited to 'imagine the story you would like to be telling yourself and others about how you led now, through this current period'. This often generates a fresh capacity to touch into their core values of personal leadership and to conceive of new possibilities for action (cf. Zander and Zander, 2000). We invite them to share these stories with one another.

Next we move into an improvisation exercise in which the participants are invited to 'step into the light' of the leadership they wish for themselves, and to inhabit and speak from this new 'sense of being'. They are invited to mingle amongst the other participants and interact with one another as these future leadership selves they have imagined in the guided visualisation. Rather than consciously acting in this role, they are encouraged to embody the leadership being they have imagined and maintain a sense of curiosity about what they will say and do as this being. We extend the invitation in this way to give them the opportunity to play with this new sense of perspective and to explore more fully how it actually feels to speak and act as the leader they imagined themselves to be when they projected into the future. We also intend that the physical act of stepping into this role and speaking from this perspective will help the individual to form memories that they can draw upon in their efforts to 'live into' this imagined leadership approach in the future.

The responses to this exercise have indicated that, at least for some participants, it does help them to gain psychological distance on a particular leadership problem and get beyond the fear and anxiety that are immobilising them. It also helps some participants to re-imagine themselves in terms of their capacity to lead and to get a nominal sense of what it actually feels like to speak and act in that capacity. In our experience no single exercise works for everyone, but this exercise appears to help some participants to gain a measure of hope and a sense of possibility about a specific leadership challenge of their choosing.

Conclusion

As we work with storytelling and improvisation, we have found that these approaches can begin to develop new perspectives and skills that lead to an enhanced capacity to lead in times of unsettling change and uncertainty. We have found that they can help individuals learn how to be more fully present in the moment and to operate with an open heart and mind. In particular, leaders can learn to:

- be fully present with 'what is'
- see things differently from their usual lens or frame
- generate a range of options
- realise there does not have to be a foregone conclusion
- enjoy experimenting and making mistakes.

These approaches are also intended to help individuals grow their personal reserves of psychological capital. Part of these reserves consists of more optimistic and trusting beliefs and attitudes about one's self in relationship to the world. In particular, storytelling and improvisation are designed to help an individual understand the importance of the following:

- Acting from an inner knowing that they have everything they need in the moment to be with and respond to what comes
- Allowing answers and solutions to emerge from the inter-*play* with others
- Co-creating an emerging future
- Operating from faith, hope and love rather than fear, anxiety and control.

As leaders or simply as individuals, we believe that we *can* overcome fear and anxiety in the face of the daunting challenges that increasingly face us, summon internal reserves of resilience, and engender hope and optimism in ourselves and those around us. And we believe that an approach that combines storytelling and improvisation is one powerful way to learn how to do this.

References

ADAA, 'Statistics and facts about anxiety disorders' (2009). Available at: www.adaa.org/AboutADAA/PressRoom/Stats&Facts.asp. Accessed: 17 August 2009.

F.J. Barrett, 'Creativity and improvisation in jazz and organisations: Implications for organisational learning', *Organization Science*, Vol. 9, No. 5, September–October (1998), 605–622.

G. Binney, G. Wilke and C. Williams, *Living Leadership: A Practical Guide for Ordinary Heroes*, 2nd edn. (Prentice Hall: Financial Times, 2009).

S. Blakemore, and U. Frith, *The Learning Brain: Lessons for Education* (Oxford: Blackwell Publishing, 2005).

D. Burns, *The Feeling Good Handbook* (NY: Plume, 1999).

L.G. Boldt, *The Tao of Abundance. Eight Ancient Principles for Abundant Living* (New York: Penguin Compass, 1999).

L. Bolman and T. Deal, *Reframing Organizations*, 2nd edn. (San Francisco: Jossey-Bass, 1997).

R.E. Boyatzis, E.C. Stubbs and S.N. Taylor, 'Learning cognitive and emotional intelligence competencies through graduate management education', *Academy of Management Learning and Education*, Vol. 1, No. 2 (2002), 150–162.

M. Carroll, 'The Mindful Leader. Ten principles for bringing out the best in ourselves and others', *Trumpeter* (2007).

D. Cooperrider and D. Whitney, *Appreciative Inquiry: A Positive Revolution in Change* (Berrett-Koehler, 2005).

A. Day, 'Living in uncertain times: Organisation dynamics in response to uncertainty', *360° The Ashridge Journal*, Autumn (2007), 29–34.

A. Day and K. Powers, 'Developing leaders for a world of uncertainty, complexity and ambiguity', *360° The Ashridge Journal*, Winter (2009), 20–25.

S. Denning, *The Secret Language of Leadership: How Leaders Inspire Action Through Narrative* (San Francisco: Jossey-Bass, 2007).

E. Diener and R. Biswas-Diener, *Happiness: Unlocking the Mysteries of Psychological Wealth*, M.A. Malden ed. (Oxford: Blackwell Publishing, 2008).

M. Gitsham, 'Developing the global leader of tomorrow', Draft Report, *1st Global Forum for Responsible Management Education, United Nations, New York*, Berkhamsted, Ashridge (2008).

D. Goleman, *Emotional Intelligence* (London: Bloomsbury Publishing PLC, 1996).

D. Goleman, *Working with Emotional Intelligence* (London: Bloomsbury Publishing PLC, 1999).

D. Grant, C. Hardy, C. Oswick and L. Putnam, *The Sage Handbook of Organizational Discourse* (London: Sage, 2004).

E. Halliwell, *In the Face of Fear: How Fear and Anxiety Affect Our Health and Society, and What We Can Do About It* (London: Mental Health Foundation, 2009).

J. Hollis, *On This Journey We Call Life. Living the Questions* (Toronto: Inner City Books, 2003).

J. Hollis, *Tracking the Gods: The Place of Myth in Modern Life* (Toronto: Inner City Books, 1995).

J. Hollis, *The Middle Passage: From Misery to Meaning in Midlife* (Toronto: Inner City Books, 1993).

T. Jame and W. Woodsmall, *Time Line Therapy* (Capitola, CA: Meta Publications, 1989).

K. Johnstone, *Impro: Improvisation and the Theatre* (New York: Routledge, 1979).

J. Ledoux, *The Emotional Brain* (New York: Simon and Schuster, 1996).

J. Ledoux, *Synaptic Self: How Our Brains Become Who We Are* (New York: Vicinity, 2002).

F. Luthans, J. Avrey, B. Avolio, S. Norman and G. Combs, 'Psychological capital development: Toward a micro-intervention', *Journal of Organisational Behavior*, 27 (2006) 387–393.

Kegan and Lahey, *Immunity to Change* (Boston, Mass.: Harvard University Press, 2009).

J. Kornfield, *A Path with Heart* (London: Rider, 1994).

M.L. Kringelbach, *The Pleasure Center* (New York: Oxford University Press, 2009).

A. Lutz, H. Slagter, N. Rawling, S.A. Francis, L. Greischar and R. Davidson, 'Mental training enhances attentional stability: Neural and behavioural evidence', *Journal of Neuroscience*, Vol. 29, No. 42 (2009), 13418–13427.

J. Mason, *Researching Your Own Practice. The Discipline of Noticing* (London: Routledge, 2002).

J. Medina, *Brain Rules* (Seattle, AW: Pear Press, 2008).

Merriam-Webster's Online (2009). http://www.merriam-webster.com/dictionary/courage.

G. Morgan, *Images of Organization*, 2nd edn. (Beverley Hills: Sage, 1997).

S.J. Peterson, D.A. Waldman, P.A. Balthazard et al. 'Are the brains of optimistic, hopeful, confident, and resilient leaders different?', *Organizational Dynamics* Vol. 37, No. 4 (2008), 342–353.

R.W. Picard, S. Papert, W. Bender et al. 'Affective learning – a manifesto', *BT Technology Journal*, Vol. 22, No. 4 (2004), 253–269.

O. Scharmer, *Theory U. Leading from the Future as it Emerges* (Cambridge: SoL, 2007).

P. Seligman and M. Csikszentmihalyi, 'Positive psychology. An introduction', *American Psychologist*, Vol. 55, No. 1 (2000), 5–14.

O. Shapira, and N. Liberman, 'An easy way to increase creativity', *Scientific American Mind*, July 21 (2009).

M. Slaski and S. Cartwright, 'Emotional intelligence training and its implications for stress, health and performance', *Stress and Health*, Vol. 19, No. 4 (2003), 233–239.

J.M. Somers, E.M. Goldner, P. Waraich et al., 'Prevalence and incidence studies of anxiety disorders: A systematic review of the literature', *Canadian Journal of Psychiatry*, Vol. 51, No. 2, February (2006), 100–103.

V. Spolin, *Improvisation for the Theater*, 3rd edn. (Evanston, IL: Northwestern University Press, 1963/1999).

R. Stacey, *Strategic Management & Organisational Dynamics. The Challenge of Complexity* (Harlow, Essex: FT/Prentice-Hall, 2000).

Weick, *Sensemaking in Organisations* (London: Sage, 1995).

R.S. Zander and B. Zander, *The Art of Possibility* (Mass, USA: Harvard Business School Press, 2000).

D. Zohar and I. Marshall, *Spiritual Capital. Wealth We Can Live By* (San Francisco: Berrett-Koehler, 2005).

Some additional resources

Useful addresses

The Applied Improv Network (AIN) http://appliedimprov.ning.com

Books with more exercises

K. Johnstone, *Impro: Improvisation and the Theatre* (New York: Routledge, 1979).

V. Spolin, *Improvisation for the Theater*, 3rd edn. (Evanston, IL: Northwestern University Press, 1963/1999).

3

The Shifting Landscape of Global Challenges in the 21st Century, What This Means for What Businesses Want From Tomorrow's Leaders, and the Implications for Management Learning

Matthew Gitsham

A global mining conglomerate contemplates a major new development in a remote region in Southeast Asia and has to navigate diverse expectations from host governments, project finance partners, local communities and global NGOs. An auto manufacturer hammered by the credit crunch needs to avoid being eclipsed by competitors who invested earlier in environmentally friendly technologies. A major clothing retailer struggles to work out how to improve its purchasing practices to improve labour standards across a complex global supply chain and avoid another front-page exposé of worker abuses by a Central American subcontractor. An airline grapples with the triple dilemma of managing to stay afloat, satisfying consumer demand for more and cheaper air travel and regulatory pressure to include aviation in the European Emissions Trading Scheme. Big pharma wonders how it can innovate to respond to pressure from regulators and investors over access to medicines in developing countries. New start-ups look for the right kind of talent to innovate to create value from business ideas that help us move to a low carbon economy.

Leaders across our organisations have over the past decade or more found themselves expected to understand and respond to a far broader range of social, political, cultural and environmental issues and trends than the generation before them, as these examples illustrate. There are specific developments that account for this change: globalisation and the opening up of global markets through the 1980s, increasing certainty in the scientific evidence around the causes and impacts of environmental degradation, the increasing influence of globally connected social movements and NGOs, unprecedented advances in global communications technologies. These global mega-trends will continue to shape the business context for the next decade and beyond.

When our major global corporations first began to find themselves on the back foot around these new kinds of issues and trends in the 1990s, many CEOs and senior teams responded defensively. But after a decade of dialogue, innovative partnerships and learning, more and more CEOs increasingly recognise that these issues are important – that it is not only right for organisations to be responding proactively, but in most cases there is a compelling business case for doing so, both in terms of value protection and value creation.

Dexter Dunphy and Simon Zadek have both developed frameworks that help us understand some of the phases organisations have been through on this journey (Dunphy et al., 2003; Zadek, 2004). Early 'defensive' responses included little more than PR and greenwashing. 'Compliance', 'efficiency' and 'managerial' responses have included formulating new policies and codes

Table 3.1   **Phases in the development of corporate sustainability (adapted from Dunphy et al., 2003)**

1. Rejection:	*Hostile to sustainability issues; no responsibility for sustainability impact, no steps to address impacts; sustainability action seen as a threat to the organisation; the environment is there to exploit.*
2. Non-responsiveness:	*Sustainability is not a relevant strategic or operational factor in decision making with financial and technical factors dominant; sustainability impacts and resource use taken for granted; sustainability risks, costs and opportunities seen as irrelevant or not perceived.*
3. Compliance:	*Financial and technical factors still dominate strategies, but managers try to comply with sustainability laws; focus on minimising sustainability liabilities and litigation and on avoiding reputational damage; being seen to do the right thing, and match wider cultural and societal expectations becomes important.*
4. Efficiency:	*Poor sustainability practice is seen as source of avoidable costs; focus on reducing costs and inefficiencies associated with sustainability impacts; sustainability issues are ignored if they are not seen as generating avoidable costs, or increasing efficiencies.*
5. Strategic Proactivity:	*Proactive sustainability strategies seen as source of strategic competitive advantage. Product redesign reduces material throughput. New products and processes developed to replace damaging ones and to address wider sustainability issues. Organisation seeks competitive leadership through spearheading sustainability-friendly products and processes.*
6. The Sustaining Corporation:	*Organisation becomes active promoter of ecological sustainability values seeking to influence key industry and societal participants. Organisation tries to assist society to be sustainable and uses its entire range of products and services to this end. Organisation influences policy in government and the restructuring of markets to facilitate the emergence of a sustainable society. Nature valued for its own sake.*

of conduct, setting up environmental management systems and processes for non-financial reporting. 'Strategic' and 'civil' responses have more recently seen organisations innovating in their products, processes and business models, and engaging in cross-sector and multi-stakeholder initiatives and partnerships to negotiate collective responses to the most difficult issues.

As CEOs have progressed along this journey, they have increasingly found that one of the biggest challenges in ensuring their organisations are fit to survive and thrive in tomorrow's new global economy is building in their organisations both the right kinds of capabilities and skills to enable this, and the broader mindsets and culture underpinning these. This is what lies behind the challenge to management educators issued by Unilever's then CEO Patrick Cescau to the Business as an Agent of World Benefit Global Forum convened by the Academy of Management, the United Nations and Case Western Reserve University in October 2006:

> *The challenges of doing business in the 21st century...will require business managers with the skills and capabilities needed to benefit from the new opportunities... In the world that we are now entering, it is not only the mindset of multinational businesses that needs to change, but the skillset of the people we employ... Corporate social responsibility, having a positive impact on society – are no longer optional add-ons. They are an integral part of business strategy and business practice... Today, and increasingly in the future, we need people with an innate and profound understanding of business's social and environmental impacts and potential... In our view, management education has a key role to play... New skills are required, new understandings. We, business, need managers and leaders with a much broader set of capabilities. You have the task to provide them.*

In response to this challenge, Ashridge recently led a study conducted with a group of leading business schools coordinated by the European Academy for Business in Society (EABIS) for the United Nations Global Compact Principles of Responsible Management Education (PRME).[1]

The question at the heart of our inquiry was: what does this shifting landscape of global challenges mean for leadership, leadership development, and management education?

People have been reflecting on the nature of leadership for thousands of years, and, more recently, also reflecting on how leaders might most effectively

---

[1]The study was sponsored by Unilever, IBM, Shell, Johnson & Johnson, and Microsoft, the founding corporate partners of EABIS. The partner business schools included EGADE at Tecnológico de Monterrey in Mexico, the Graduate School of Business at the University of Cape Town, China Europe International Business School (CEIBS), Weatherhead School of Management at Case Western Reserve University and the Center for Creative Leadership in the US, INSEAD, IESE and IEDC-Bled in Europe, and the University of Waikato in New Zealand.

be developed and educated. One of the big shifts in contemporary thinking about leadership has been from thinking about the leader as 'the great man', charismatic, in control and issuing commands which are obeyed like pulling levers of a machine – to recognising organisations are networks of people, patterns of relationships and influence, where each individual has opportunities to exercise leadership and no individual is 'in control' (Raelin, 2003; Stacey et al., 2000; Rost, 1991). This has led to notions of shared leadership and distributed leadership (Bradford and Cohen, 1998; Chaleff, 1995; Mintzberg, 2009), and placed more of a primacy on 'emotional intelligence' (Goleman, 1996) and authenticity (George, 2004), and leaders as servants (Greenleaf, 1970) and educators (Heifetz, 1994). Many have also been reflecting on the implications for leadership of changing patterns of work and the revolution in information and communications technologies, in particular, for example, asking what the growth in complex virtual teams working together but remotely in globalised matrix organisations means for the practice of leadership (Davison and Ward, 1999; Fisher and Fisher, 2001; Jones, 2007; Gobillott, 2009).

Recent thinking in leadership development has been influenced by new understandings about the relationship between learning and how the brain works, emphasising the importance of emotional experiences as much as rational argument, and the immeasurable value in understanding yourself and your own strengths, vulnerabilities and psychological preferences as much as a body of knowledge about technical organisational 'know-how' (Medina, 2008). Another major theme has been a growing belief in the importance of reflecting on personal experience and your own context as much as someone else's case study (Parks, 2005; Tate, 2009).

Within the context of these broader debates, we wanted to ask the question, does this change in the external context – this change in the kinds of activities that leaders in our organisation are having to lead in the context of – have any implications for our notions of leadership, and in particular, how we might develop leaders?

In particular we wanted to:

- Check how widely CEOs and senior executives agree with Cescau's view
- Understand CEO perspectives on precisely what kinds of capabilities and skills are required – what kind of leaders are today's CEOs looking for?
- Explore what kinds of experiences might be most valuable for developing these kinds of capabilities and skills

The research, based on an extensive global survey of CEOs and senior executives conducted in September and October 2008,[2] presents a stark message.

---

[2] 194 individuals responded to the global survey representing organisations from a cross-section of different industry sectors and regions globally. Full details about the demographics of survey respondents can be found at http://www.ashridge.org.uk/globalleaders

Seventy-six per cent of CEOs and senior executives polled say it is important that senior executives have the necessary knowledge and skills to respond to the challenges and opportunities of the 21st century – trends like climate change, resource scarcity and doing business in emerging markets marked by poverty, corruption and human rights violations, for example.

However, fewer than 8 per cent believe that these knowledge and skills are currently being developed very effectively in their own organisations. Tellingly, fewer than 8 per cent also believe business schools have very effective responses in place either.

So what kinds of qualities emerged as valuable to look for, foster, develop and value in today's and tomorrow's leaders? A number of potential qualities were identified through a series of more than 30 interviews with managers and professionals in the fields of human resources, learning and development, and sustainability. CEOs and senior executives were then asked for their perspectives through the survey. Researchers grouped the most prominent qualities into three clusters, which the researchers coined as 'context', 'complexity' and 'connectedness'.

Context

CEOs and senior executives believe, according to the survey, that the global leader of tomorrow needs to understand the changing business context – 82 per cent of those polled say senior executives need to understand the business risks and opportunities of social, political, cultural and environmental trends. And they need to know how their sector and other stakeholders (regulators, customers, suppliers, investors, NGOs) are responding. Global warming, for example, has become a strategic issue for organisations: not just because of direct implications for organisations and their assets and business models from changes to the climate, but more significantly because of the way customers, investors and most importantly regulators and competitors are responding.

As Michael Porter noted in the *Harvard Business Review* in 2007, '*Climate change is now a fact of political life and is playing a growing role in business competition. Greenhouse gas emissions will be increasingly scrutinized, regulated and priced. While individual managers can disagree about how immediate and significant the impacts of climate change will be, companies need to take action now.*' (Porter and Reinhardt, 2007: 22)

Senior executives also need the skills to respond to this information – 70 per cent say that global leaders need to be able to integrate social and environmental trends into strategic decision-making. This can mean knowing how to use tools for horizon scanning, scenario building and risk management, for example.

FMCG giant Unilever, through its in-house Marketing Academy, has introduced the Brand Imprint process to help build the skills of its brand directors to factor opinion leader and consumer attitudes about social and environmental issues into the development of its top brands in order to build customer loyalty, differentiate and capture value. Brand teams seek new opportunities by conducting a 360° scan of the social, economic and environmental impact that their brand has on the world, taking into account consumer attitudes as well as the views of external stakeholders, NGOs and opinion formers, and market forces driving the brand's success. The learning experience revolves around developing skills to identify business-relevant social and environmental issues and factor this information into product and brand development to improve the bottom line. The first four brands to go through the Brand Imprint process were four of Unilever's most successful brands: Lipton Tea, Dove, Lifebuoy and Flora/Becel. Many other brands within Unilever are now undertaking the process as well.

Leaders need to be able to introduce environmental and social criteria into strategic decision making from the start – not doing this is worse than stupid, it's reckless.

André van Heemstra, Global Board Member and Global Head of HR, Unilever 2000–2006 (Gitsham et al., 2009: 14)

Complexity

The second cluster of knowledge and skills is around the ability to lead in the face of **complexity and ambiguity**. The challenges and opportunities these issues and trends present tend, by definition, to be complex – there is often little certainty and little agreement about both their precise nature and the response that is required. Leadership in these circumstances requires a range of discrete skills: 88 per cent of those polled say senior executives need the ability to be flexible and responsive to change; 91 per cent, the ability to find creative, innovative and original ways of solving problems; 90 per cent, the ability to learn from mistakes; and 77 per cent, the ability to balance shorter- and longer-term considerations.

The global leader of tomorrow needs to be able to understand the interdependency of actions and the range of global implications that local level decisions can have. For example, buyers for food and textile companies in Europe and North America are often unaware of the potential impact that last minute changes to orders can have on workers in factories in distant emerging markets. Increasing or varying orders at short notice can mean vulnerable workers being intimidated into working excessive forced overtime. Cancelling orders on the other hand frequently results in workers being sent home early and not getting paid fully for hours already worked (Ethical Trading Initiative, 2007).

Sixty-one per cent of those polled say that understanding that business decisions are not always driven by rational quantitative analysis, but often by feelings, emotions, values and intuition is important. According to our interviews, many believe this can be particularly relevant in organisations in sectors dominated by professionals from a scientific and engineering background, who tend to be groomed with a mindset that ranks rational analysis over more emotional and intuitive interpretations (Critchley et al., 2007; Brown, 2002).

There are echoes here of the work of Stubbings, drawing on that of Stacey and colleagues at the University of Hertfordshire (Gitsham and Stubbings, 2009). In situations of low certainty and agreement, it can be more productive for leaders to pursue strategies that include increasing awareness of context, fostering diversity, challenging habits and patterns, provoking and encouraging contention, encouraging 'positive deviants', and supporting emerging ideas and innovation. This is in contrast to the kinds of strategies frequently pursued, but more effective in times of high agreement and high certainty – designing formal structures, planning and budgeting and formalising established practices in codes of conduct and performance management systems.

Connectedness

The final cluster of knowledge and skills is around **connectedness** – the ability to understand the actors in the wider political landscape and to engage and build effective relationships with new kinds of external partners. For different businesses this can mean regulators, competitors, NGOs or local communities. The mindset with which our current leaders are groomed does not encourage productive engagement with partners outside the organisation. Leaders receive plenty of training in negotiation skills, for example, but on the whole, lack the skills for engaging in effective dialogue and partnership. To survive and thrive, 73 per cent of senior executives say people in senior leadership positions need to be able to identify key stakeholders that have an influence on the organisation and 74 per cent say they need to understand how the organisation impacts on these stakeholders, both positively and negatively. Seventy-five per cent say senior executives need to have the ability to engage in effective dialogue and 80 per cent say they need to have the ability to build partnerships with internal and external stakeholders.

Engaging with local communities can be increasingly important for a variety of companies, for example, especially those in the oil, gas and mining sectors, where the expectations of governments, institutions providing project finance, and NGOs, not to mention local communities themselves, are rising. This means moving from a mindset in which local communities are viewed as a nuisance that must be managed, to a strategic partner where constructive relationships are central to value protection and value creation. This means more than financial donations for community projects – it means a real focus on relationships.

The ability to engage and contribute to public policy is another specific example of the skill of building partnerships and engaging in effective dialogue. This has become particularly important in the context of negotiations over a successor to the Kyoto Protocol and the second phase of the European Emissions Trading scheme. By 2012, the European Union will make decisions on the future distribution of permits that could be worth up to €3 billion for the airline industry (Enkvist et al., 2008): there is clearly a lot at stake. Companies need to work closely with regulators to ensure that the new rules do not have unintended consequences, but work in the best possible way. For many business leaders, this engagement will require enhanced skills.

A need for diverse learning approaches

If these are the kinds of qualities and skills that might be increasingly valuable, how can they best be developed? CEOs and senior executives seem to be clearly of the view that traditional 'lecture-style knowledge transfer' approaches are not enough: a broad range of learning approaches are required. Because the issues are complex, senior executives believe the most effective learning and skills development comes through practical experience, whether the learning is on-the-job, project-based or experiential. These learning experiences can be enhanced by structured reflection through coaching or Appreciative Inquiry. Learning directly from the experience of others is also valued as important – through mentoring, or communities of practice and other formal and informal learning networks.

Although learning approaches like e-learning and lecture-style learning are less rated by executives, these are likely to still have a role where more straightforward knowledge transfer and basic awareness raising is required. But learning programmes that rely heavily on a lecture-based format are not fit for purpose.

CEO perspectives on learning approaches here echo surprisingly clearly well established thinking among learning and development professionals about what makes for effective learning and development generally. There are strong resonances, for example, with the 70:20:10 rule described by McCall and colleagues at the Center for Creative Leadership in the 1980s, which suggests that 70 per cent of learning occurs through on-the-job experience, 20 per cent through learning directly from others and 10 per cent from formal 'training' interventions (McCall et al., 1988). There are also clear echoes of Kolb's learning cycle, with learning occurring through a cycle of experience, reflection, theorising and active experimentation (Kolb, 1984). This implies that business schools interested in creating powerful learning experiences around sustainability will need to innovate in learning approach as much as content.

Individuals need to seek out their own opportunities to learn and refine the skills they need. HR and Learning and Development Directors also have a responsibility to ensure that the organisational learning agenda supports the development of appropriate skills. Leadership development programmes can play a valuable role in supporting this process.

The following examples of innovative leadership development programmes from Unilever, IBM, and InterfaceFLOR illustrate many of these ideas being put into practice. For example, all of these leadership development programmes involve learning about sustainability issues, how other actors are responding, and the business implications. Many also involve learning through building relationships with individuals and organisations that participants do not usually come into contact with, and cycles of action and reflection with experiential learning and learning through projects combined with coaching and other forms of reflection.

Unilever

Unilever is a global Anglo-Dutch-based manufacturer of leading brands in foods, home care and personal care.

Leadership development programmes for high potentials – emerging markets strategy

Unilever organises a variety of integrated programmes for employees who have been recognised as having high potential for senior leadership positions. One of these programmes is designed around Unilever's emerging/development markets strategy.

The challenge for participants is to develop an overall strategy for Unilever for emerging and developing markets so that Unilever can obtain a disproportionate share of this market as it develops. This requires that participants understand a variety of socio-economic trends.

The programme involves 28 participants taking part in two residential modules working with CK Prahalad of the University of Michigan and author of *The Fortune at the Bottom of the Pyramid*, a seminal work highlighting the potential of new business models that deliberately target the poorest people in emerging markets.

Between these two residential modules, participants conduct a number of field visits over a two month period in 'next practice' organisations in emerging and developing markets. 'Next practice' organisations include 'price-performance disruptors' (organisations able to offer significantly reduced price for products and services such as cars, hotels and heart operations), NGOs and multi-lateral organisations (including WWF, WRI, WHO, WFP), social entrepreneurial organisations and micro-finance organisations.

'The premise is that Unilever will find success by "folding the future in", rather than just incrementally extending current best practices – the organisation needs to look at where it wants to be in 2015, and fold that picture in now.'
Robin Blass, Global Leadership Development Director, Unilever

Social and environmental trends that have emerged as business-relevant include:

- water usage and other environmental trends such as consumer concern over packaging
- the implications of population growth
- urbanisation and the growth of slums
- the growth in more affluent middle classes in emerging markets
- the benefits of digitisation
- personalising and co-creating between suppliers and consumers.

The learning from these experiences is brought into the second residential module, where project teams develop business proposals and make a presentation to the Unilever Executive Board who join the programme on the final day. Successful proposals are then taken forward and implemented.

Learning objectives

The objectives of the programme are to:

- Evolve Unilever's strategy around emerging/developing markets in a way that 'brings the outside in' – a discovery-based learning process where the participants themselves conduct research to identify relevant social and environmental trends, what the business implications are and how the business should respond.
- Build participants' ability to engage in a meaningful way with people and organisations that they are unlikely to come into contact with otherwise.
- Create new connections among the future leaders of the organisation and between future leaders and the existing leadership.

IBM

IBM is a globally integrated enterprise, headquartered in Armonk, New York, USA. Its business includes the creation, development and manufacture of advanced information technologies, consulting, and IT services.

The Corporate Service Corps development programme

IBM's Corporate Citizenship and Human Resources teams have collaborated to develop a leadership development programme designed for IBM's top talent – individuals identified as potential future leaders of the organisation. The origins of the programme lie in an exercise undertaken by the corporate citizenship team to audit the organisation's current corporate citizenship strategy and identify whether there were any gaps in relation to core business strategy.

The programme is designed to build knowledge and skills that a team of 30 people from IBM's top management during 2007 identified as core to the profile of future leaders. This team found that, while in the past for top leaders it was enough to know about business, now they also need to know and understand the wider political landscape. They found that IBM's future global leaders need:

- A deep understanding of the business, economic, and political landscape of emerging markets
- The ability to develop relationships with the social sector, local government, NGOs and other influencers
- Sensitivity towards different cultures and customs
- The ability to work within and lead multi-cultural teams
- Awareness of core societal, educational and environmental challenges impacting the way the organisation does business in the 21st century
- To understand and maintain the highest global integrity standards.

The programme also meets another critical business need: building greater connectivity between talented employees embedded within different functions and regions globally.

Participants work in project teams of eight to ten in project destinations in emerging markets. The participants are individuals from different countries and business units grouped together, outside of office structure.

These employees build relationships and work on some of the world's toughest problems, such as global economic opportunity, environmental challenges, and access to education resources.

The six-month Service Corps experience includes:

- Three months' pre-work, including online, wiki-enabled learning, to familiarise participants with language, culture, socioeconomic and political climate of the destination country; team building and leadership development workshops; online learning modules on cultural awareness; international development; corporate responsibility; facilitated phone conversations.
- One month embedded in the emerging market. This phase comprises team-based work focused on core societal, educational and environmental challenges working with local NGOs, SMEs or public bodies.
- Two months' post-service work (plus ongoing sharing upon return), including synthesising lessons learned and structured activities to share experiences and transfer knowledge and relationships gained with local IBM teams. Participants are encouraged to share the Service Corps experience with colleagues, family, friends and their home community and to connect to IBM's business development process.

'We are sending some of IBM's best emerging leaders. Individuals will get the skills needed to compete, IBM will get a group of leaders able to lead in a Globally Integrated Enterprise, and the organisations where they are working will get a team of highly skilled problem solvers whose efforts will support economic growth in the developing world.'

Stanley Litow, VP, Corporate Citizenship & Corporate Affairs and President, IBM Foundation.

IBM believes that the value of sending participants away to experience social and environmental issues first hand, rather than discussing them in the classroom, generates an emotional response and therefore a deeper learning experience.

When the programme was launched, it was intended that 200 people would participate per year. After the programme received more than 5,000 applications, the programme has been expanded to cater for 500 individuals per year, with the expectation that it will grow further.

InterfaceFLOR Europe, Middle East, Africa and India (EMEAI)

InterfaceFLOR designs, produces and sells modular flooring systems, and is a division of Interface Inc, headquartered in Atlanta, USA. Manufacturing locations are on four continents and offices in more than 100 countries. Interface's vision is to become the world's first environmentally restorative company by 2020.

Fast Forward to 2020 development programme

InterfaceFLOR EMEAI has developed a comprehensive education programme to support InterfaceFLOR's vision of becoming an environmentally restorative company by 2020. This programme has been running since 2004. It comprises three different levels and involves employees at all levels across the organisation in the EMEAI region.

Individuals must have participated in certain levels of the programme, and where appropriate passed a graded assessment, to be eligible to be considered for promotion to more senior roles in the organisation.

The Fast Forward to 2020 programme is complemented by an 'Ambassadors' programme, which is an internal network of champions who facilitate learning and change.

Ambassadors

The Ambassador network of sustainability champions is drawn from across all business functions and regions. Individuals choose to become ambassadors and they are motivated to learn more and do more about furthering the company's vision to be an environmentally restorative organisation by 2020. Their role is to act as change agents within the organisation and the network is organised to support learning by participants sharing between themselves and raising awareness further among other colleagues and managers across the organisation. Ambassadors are offered three to four inspirational sessions per year, projects they can participate in, coaching on developing their own idea and are supported by an internal communications platform where they stay posted on the action in the programme.

Fast Forward to 2020: Level 1

Level 1 of the Fast Forward programme is for all employees. All existing employees have been through the programme and it forms part of the induction process for all new employees. The short programme introduces key issues around sustainability, InterfaceFLOR's strategy and approach, and the rationale behind this.

Fast Forward to 2020: Level 2

After completing the induction programme, individuals can apply to go onto Level 2 of the Fast Forward programme. Around 50 per cent of individuals in the company have participated in Level 2, including all team leaders, all senior management, all sales, marketing and communications executives and all Ambassadors.

Level 2 is a one day programme and functionally specific – there are customised Level 2 programmes for marketers, sales, operations and human resources for example. Individual experts from a variety of different backgrounds and organisations are brought in to contribute to the programme as appropriate. The focus of the programme is on building knowledge around sustainable development and what it means for the business. Participants focus on the personal question: 'How do I contribute InterfaceFLOR's vision of being the world's first environmentally restorative company by 2020 as an individual? What does this mean for my part of the business and my role?'

To pass the Level 2 programme, participants must pass a test and complete an assignment which takes the form of a personal action plan describing an initiative that contributes to making InterfaceFLOR an environmentally restorative company. Participants whose assignments do not meet the grade are coached until their assignment is judged to be eligible for a pass. These assignments have generated several excellent proposals, many of which have been implemented by the company.

Fast Forward to 2020: Level 3

This advanced programme runs for two days. Around 10 per cent of employees participate in this programme. Individuals are specially selected to participate – all members of the senior management team have participated, as have all of Interface's Ambassadors.

Participants undertake their own research into future trends that will impact the business. The programme builds further understanding around complex issues and how other organisations are responding. It also builds skills in critical analysis. Participants' ability to debate complex issues and argue for and against is developed. This is important where there is low agreement around controversial issues: for example nuclear power, bio-fuels, and the role of business in alleviating poverty.

To successfully pass Level 3, participants must again complete an assignment similar to that required at Level 2. They must also pass an assessed mock television interview. For this exercise, external journalists are brought into the programme and participants are required to prepare for and participate in a filmed interview with a challenging interviewer. Preparation for this interview requires participants to undertake their own research to raise their own knowledge to the required levels.

So what?

Business leaders are increasingly recognising that the new world they operate in has real implications for mindsets and skills, and therefore for leadership development and management education. This study explored business leader perspectives on the specific skills they see as being increasingly important, and what they see as the most effective learning approaches for developing them. Clusters of qualities around context, complexity and connectedness emerged as increasingly valuable, as did learning approaches that relied heavily on supporting individuals and teams to learn from experimentation through cycles of action and reflection, rather than being dependent on more conventional knowledge transfer and content input. A number of organisations have already put together learning programmes to support the development of these orientations and skills employing the kinds of learning approaches described in this study, as evidenced by the case examples from Unilever, IBM and InterfaceFLOR.

So what are the implications? These findings raise a number of questions to consider, whether you are in a senior leadership position or a learning professional. We hope the findings from this study can help stimulate your own responses.

If you are in a senior leadership position in your organisation, ask yourself:

- What kind of people are we looking for in our organisation?
- What kind of mindsets and qualities should we be valuing when recruiting, building teams, thinking about talent management and succession planning, or designing learning programmes?
- What are the most effective methods of developing these qualities and ways of thinking in our context?
- Have we got things broadly right at the moment, or should we be experimenting with some new ideas?

If you are a business school dean or teaching faculty, or a human resources or learning and development professional ask yourself:

- What kinds of qualities, knowledge, skills and ways of thinking should we be seeking to develop in the people we work with?
- What are the most effective learning approaches for doing this? Have we got things broadly right at the moment, or should we be experimenting with some new ideas?

If you are an aspiring leader, ask yourself which qualities, skills and orientations you think are important to develop in yourself for the future, and seek a broad range of different learning opportunities to take this forward. If you are considering MBA and executive programmes offered by business schools, you should certainly be asking the question 'Which schools are doing the most to help me build the leadership qualities and skills I need for the future?'

If you have found this work stimulating and would be interested to learn more or be involved in further research, please contact globalleaders@ashridge.org.uk. Further information and the full research report is available from www.ashridge. org.uk/globalleaders

References

D.L. Bradford and A.R. Cohen, *Power Up: Transforming Organisations Through Shared Leadership* (New York: John Wiley, 1998).

M. Brown, 'Working with complexity', *Directions – The Ashridge Journal*, Ashridge (2002).

I. Chaleff, *The Courageous Follower: Standing Up, To and For Our Leaders* (San Francisco: Bennet-Koehler Publishers, 1995).

B. Critchley, K. King and J. Higgins, *Organisational Consulting: A Relational Perspective* (Middlesex: Middlesex University Press, 2007).

S.C. Davison and K. Ward, *Leading International Teams* (New York: McGraw-Hill, 1999).

D. Dunphy, A. Griffiths and S. Benn, *Organisational Change for Corporate Sustainability* (London: Routledge, 2003).

P. Enkvist, T. Nauclér and J.M. Oppenheim, 'Business strategies for climate change', *The McKinsey Quarterly*, April (2008).

Ethical Trading Initiative, *Purchasing Practices: Case Studies to Address Impacts of Purchasing Practices on Working Conditions*, Ethical Trading Initiative (2008).

K. Fisher and M.D. Fisher, *The Distance Manager: A Hands-on Guide to Managing Offsite Employees and Virtual Teams* (New York: McGraw-Hill, 2001).

B. George, *Authentic Leadership: Rediscovering the Secrets to Creating Lasting Value* (San Francisco: Jossey-Bass, 2004).

M. Gitsham and A. Stubbings, 'Leading organisations of tomorrow: Sustainability, leadership development and organisational change', presentation to the Conference Board, Brussels, October (2009).

M. Gitsham, G. Lenssen and N. Roome, 'Leadership qualities and management competencies for corporate responsibility', presentation to the Conference Board, Brussels, June (2007).

E. Gobillot, *Leadershift: Reinventing Leadership for the Age of Mass Collaboration* (London: Kogan Page, 2009).

D. Goleman, *Emotional Intelligence: Why It Can Matter More than IQ* (London: Bloomsbury, 1996).

R.F. Greenleaf, *The Servant as Leader* (Mahwah, NJ, USA: Paulist Press, 1970).

R.A. Heifetz, *Leadership Without Easy Answers* (Cambridge, Mass: Harvard University Press, 1994).

P. Jones, *Managing for Performance: Delivering Results Through Others* (London: Prentice Hall, 2007).

D. Kolb, *Experiential Learning: Experience as the Source of Learning and Development* (London: Prentice-Hall, 1984).

M.W. Jr. McCall, M.M. Lombardo and A.M. Morrison, *The Lessons of Experience: How Successful Executives Develop on the Job* (New York: The Free Press, 1988).

J. Medina, *Brain Rules: Twelve Principles for Surviving and Thriving at Work, Home and School* (Seattle: Pear Press, 2008).

H. Mintzberg, *Managing* (London: FT Prentice Hall, 2009).

M.E. Porter and F.L. Reinhardt, 'A strategic approach to climate change', *Harvard Business Review*, October (2007): 22.

S.D. Parks, *Leadership Can Be Taught: A Bold Approach for a Complex World* (Boston, Mass: Harvard Business School Press, 2005).

J.A. Raelin, *Leaderful Organisations: How to Bring Out Leadership in Everyone* (San Francisco: Berrett-Koehler Publishers, 2003).

J.C. Rost, *Leadership for the Twentieth-first Century* (Westport, Connecticut: Praeger Publishers, 1991).

W. Tate, *The Search for Leadership: An Organisational Perspective* (Axminster, Devon: Triarchy Press, 2009).

S. Zadek, 'The path to corporate responsibility', *Harvard Business Review*, Vol. 82, No. 12 (2004).

4

The Future of HE: What Will the Sector Look Like in 25 Years Time and What Does This Mean for Executive Education?

Eddie Blass, Anne Jasman and Steve Shelley

Introduction

The concept of 'university' has been around for centuries and yet the majority of British Universities have yet to reach their 50th birthday. The higher education (HE) sector has been through extensive change over a relatively short period of time and this is likely to continue in the future. With regard to Executive Education, the HE sector has been the provider of a range of qualification programmes, most notably the MBA and now it's Doctoral upstep, the DBA; as well as short course provisions and accreditation of in-house training programmes. Individual HE institutions partner organisations to provide bespoke, tailored qualification programmes, sometimes linked to the organisation's Corporate University (Blass, 2001). As the MBA shifts from being the pinnacle of executive education to a mass delivery graduate conversion course in business (Blass and Weight, 2005a), and organisations are experiencing the impact of a global recession and the 'credit crunch', the future of executive education provisions within HE is questionable. Universities need to be identifying exactly what it is that they can offer organisations, that are 'better' than the organisations can provide themselves. Simple accreditation of programmes is not going to be enough in the medium to long term as the Privy Council is demonstrating willingness to offer corporate entities degree awarding powers. The market for short course provision is becoming increasingly competitive and specialised, and expenditure on executive education is being reined in as the impact of the recession takes its toll on organisations. The current debates governing the future of HE centre on the issues of globalisation, use of ICT and the internet, and the knowledge economy.

Current debates in higher education

In today's knowledge economy, the role of higher education is being redefined – not simply tweaked and fine-tuned. Participation in the open source movement is breaking down monopolistic practices and preventing the sector becoming over commercialised (Hilton, 2006). Knowledge economy policies are currently very powerful drivers of change in contemporary university approaches to research. They typically orientate universities to a national innovation system which both positions knowledge as the key factor of economic growth and sees the main purpose of knowledge as contributing to such growth (Kenway et al., 2004). However, it is not just research that is the focus of government policy; teaching is also under scrutiny. Creating the right skills culture requires a collective effort – over 70 per cent of the 2020 workforce is already adult (Department for Innovation, 2007). Demand led development rather than supply driven is key, hence a suggestion of changes in funding mechanisms to fund HEIs based on their results with engaging with business rather than intake numbers (Leitch, 2006). The proportion of the population with graduate qualifications and the percentage of GDP invested in the education sector as a whole is lower in the UK than in many other countries including USA, Canada, Sweden and South Korea. Leitch suggests that we have over-targeted young people at the expense of engaging with employer and work-based qualifications, favouring full-time undergraduate students with funding rather than part-time students who are also employees. He notes that we are unlikely to grow the graduate population within the current framework and provision. This suggests that we need a policy shift away from 'traditional' undergraduate education towards a more work-based and 'executive' provision.

This need for a shift in education is echoed by the Chartered Management Institute. Tomorrow's workforce will be increasingly individualistic, older, mobile, international, ethnically varied and far more demanding of their employers (CMI, 2008). There is doubt as to whether the education system can produce the right number of people at the right skills level in the future. Over 20 per cent of UK nationals with a degree live in other OECD countries while immigration to the UK tends to be by unskilled or low skilled workers. By 2010, fewer than 20 per cent of the full-time workforce will be white, able bodied men under the age of 45 – the historic core of the workforce (*ibid*).

Much of the debate about the type of person the education system should be producing has been framed within a national context (Lauder et al., 2006) rather than a global context. The knowledge base that underpins global development is vast. It includes cultural knowledge, cognitive skills, languages, ICT skills and the ability to relate to people who hold a different set of assumptions to your own. Much has been written on globalisation, and the CMI/ Ashridge Talent Management Research (Blass, 2009) showed that international assignments were a key development requirement for senior management roles, and yet was one of the least favoured development opportunities of young managers in the UK. In terms of potential global competitiveness, this is particularly bad news for UK PLC and good news for the rest of Europe whose populations are much more open to international travel and placement.

The role of ICT is another issue currently dominating educational futures debates. Until the internet boom, Higher Education was mainly offered in three formats; full-time, part-time and a traditional form of distance learning involving self-directed study around paper-based guides (with telephone tutor support), supplemented with residential blocks and summer schools providing an interactive element. There were also some bespoke corporate programmes being provided but these were delivered in the form of a combination of the above. E-learning differs from the other forms of delivery because it changes the element of tutor: student and student: student interaction such that it occurs through computer-mediated technology, rather than face to face or even over the telephone. Margules (2002: 3) argues that 'like it or not, the storage and distribution of information and the associated teaching and learning pedagogy aided by technology, is now undermining the more traditional methods of teaching, learning and research.' Given the focus on knowledge transfer at the expense of behavioural skills currently being witnessed in e-learning qualifications (Birchall and Smith, 2002), there is a danger that a proliferation of such qualifications will result in a form of social de-skilling in the workplace. This could lead to a new *niche* area of e-learning provision for executive education providers, or indeed a new means of delivering executive education.

HE providers (specifically those Higher Education Institutions that are funded through public funds by the Higher Education Funding Councils for England, Wales or Scotland) engage in Executive Education provision as a means of boosting their income generation, usually through provision of short courses, accreditation of in-house corporate provisions or provision of executive qualifications such as the MBA. They compete in this market against specialist providers, particularly in the short course arena; consultancies, particularly with regard to bespoke learning solution design; and the growth area of Corporate Universities, the in-house provision of large organisations that may or may not seek degree awarding powers in the future. If the latter is to happen, then HE providers will no longer hold the monopoly on qualification provision and the market for this lucrative provision may diminish.

This chapter looks much further into the future than these debates address, it is considering the sector in 25 years time. It is based on a research project commissioned by HEFCE to consider the higher education workforce in the future, but has been developed further to specifically identify the issues and innovations that will be relevant to the executive education market. The study is essentially a 'futures study' and the approach adopted in this paper stems from this field.

Methodology

An extensive review of the literature was carried out which was then taken forwards through a scenario development process resulting in five scenarios for the future of the Higher Education sector in the UK. Literature was drawn on from a number of fields including and beyond the field of HE in order to understand what the world is likely to be like in 25 years time, from which the scenarios were developed regarding what the HE sector would be like in 25 years time. The key elements that were examined in order to gain a fuller picture of the future HE sector were demographics, economics, social and political trends, educational context, business process analysis and futures studies relating to the worlds of work and education. The process of selection of the literature to review was based on searching academic databases, relevant government department websites, and various futures journals and publications using the terms 'future', 'HE' and 'University'. The literature provides an overview of what the future might look like from which the scenario building team draw down the features that they view as being important for each scenario. This is not as random a process as it might appear. It involves a process of discussion and sharing expertise, to highlight the factors most impactful in each of the areas of expertise, looking for synergies, overlaps and areas of conflict. The discussion of the literature takes the form of making sense of the ideas stemming from the literature in the respective areas of expertise and working through how these then impact on the future of the sector. A process of exploring the factors underlying the issues in the literature, in search of the drivers for the changes suggested, gradually filters through to a limited number of issues to take forwards into the scenarios for the HE sector itself.

These scenarios differ from other work that has been carried out in the field (see, for example, UUK, 2008a; UUK, 2008b; Vincent-Lancrin, 2004) as they are sectoral scenarios rather than institutional scenarios. As such they take many of the issues that are used to determine institutional scenarios as given assumptions for the whole sector, namely the knowledge economy, ICT and globalisation. These are factors that will allow institutions to differentiate within the sector, but will be applicable across the sector as unavoidable issues. Hence they do not come in to play in sectoral scenarios, but would at an institutional level. Sectoral scenarios set the vision for the whole HE sector within which institutions will differentiate. Institutional scenarios offer a range of forms that individual institutions may take in the future within the sector itself.

The basis for developing the scenarios is asking what the world of work will look like in 25 years time, who will the students be, what will be the nature of academic work and what will be the role of Higher Education in 25 years time. From these scenarios, the development team worked through a process of visioning and mapping back to what the ten year stepping stone would be in order to provide a set of ten and 25 year pictures for the future of the sector.

Five scenarios were developed as each drew on a unique set of drivers and assumptive circumstances. None of the five emerged as polar opposites and none were developed from the 'business as usual' position which often underpins a futures study, taking forward the situation of 'no change'. We do not see 'no change' as a feasible future for Higher Education in the UK as the *status quo* cannot be maintained from a funding or an organisational perspective according to analysis of HEFCE returns. The first scenario developed focuses on the 'nature of knowledge' and the sector leading knowledge creation; the second focuses on the 'nature of knowledge' and the sector responding to knowledge needs from external stakeholders; the third scenario focuses on the organisation of work and the need for regional collaboration; the fourth scenario focuses on the funding base being reduced by government and the final scenario follows the fourth scenario up to the ten year mark and then sees a change in policy to renewed government funding to re-establish the sector.

Presenting the scenarios

In brief, the five scenarios developed as possible futures for the HE sector in the UK are presented below. All of them are possible; none of them are intended to be more probable than others; any of them can be prevented through changes in policy and action now; and none of them represent a position of 'no change'. The scenarios are presented in short summary form as the implications of the scenarios are of more benefit to the reader than the scenarios themselves, although it helps to have an understanding of the scenarios in order to place the implications in some context.

1. *'Leading knowledge creation'* in which the credit crunch results in a societal paradigm shift to debt aversion in future generations. The full-time undergraduate market diminishes in favour of part-time offerings in Further Education, and Higher Education focuses on post-graduate offerings only. The sector shrinks back to 'Ancients' and 'Red-Bricks'. A new 'professional' academic role develops alongside 'traditional' academic roles to manage knowledge transfer interface and secure funding. The sector is concerned with leading innovation and contribution to policy, offering high level, conceptual development in an increasingly specialised manner.

2. *'Responsive knowledge creation'* in which disciplines divide as corporate sector development leads to a funding stream for professional activity and then the higher education sector divides. Part of the sector will be 'Pure' providers who are funded by research councils, undertaking Mode 1, 'just in case' knowledge production, and amounting to 20 per cent of the sector's workforce and 10 per cent of students; and the remainder will be the 'Applied' providers who will have strong links with industry and will engage in practice-based research and qualifications, and Mode 2, 'just in time' knowledge production. Differential contracts and terms between pure and applied providers develop and there is some movement of staff within the sector from pure to applied but not the other way round.

3. *'Regional conglomerates'* in which funding cuts necessitate savings in core services. The key driver here is the continuing increase in the non-academic workforce from the current level of 55 per cent of the HE sector workforce. Regional universities exist, dispersed across a range of campuses, providing education at all levels to anyone who is beyond school age. Institutions are mutually dependent, and movement is between teams and institutions within the region. The role of the academic is lower status and there is less specialisation than is currently the case. Harmonisation of terms and conditions exist across the sector. Competition in the labour market only occurs inter-regionally, not intra-regionally.

4. *'No government funding'* in which we see the economy continuing in recession to the point that government funding of students in HE sector is withdrawn and students are expected to fund themselves. A small, privatised sector remains solvent in a highly competitive market place. Academics expected to generate enough income to sustain their position in order to remain in employment and a 'celebrity' culture develops. The student body and workforce are both largely part-time and institutions are internally competitive. Networking is key. Academics have personalised contracts based on the minimum required to secure their services/ employment.

5. *'Full government funding'* in which societal unrest arises in response to the decline of the education system, and this results in a 2 per cent National Education Tax (as an alternative to a VAT rise) which gives everyone an entitlement to free undergraduate education. The sector expands, is largely modularised and is the envy of other nations. The concepts of quality and student satisfaction converge. National bargaining equalises employment around the country. Competition ceases and collaborative working dominates, but the sector is not homogenous. Long-term career structures develop with a multitude of opportunities in lifelong learning and wider curriculum activities.

The implications of the scenarios for executive education are many and varied. Some relate to the supply side of education, and others relate to the demand side.

Implications for executive education

The implications are presented in terms of implications with regard to the provision of executive education, the role of academics in the future of executive education, the future of delivery of executive education, and the future role of qualifications within executive education. A summary is provided in Table 4.1 before each element is discussed more fully.

Table 4.1 Summary of future changes likely in Executive Education provision by HE

Demand-side	Supply-side
Provision of general executive education qualifications in decline; short course provision in specialist niche	Sector split into mass provisions of graduate conversion course and specialist niche provision
Academics shifting between traditional and corporate markets as corporate demand increases and public demand decreases	Academic workforce drawing on corporate managers for part-time teaching
Delivery through internet and niche specialist provisions	Competition emerging from players outside of the training/consultancy field
Qualifications need to be more flexible, adaptable, and 'just in time' curriculum rather than 'just in case'	Corporate universities with degree awarding powers pose threat to provision within HE sector

The demand-side of the equation for provision – It is possible that in the regional conglomerate and the full government funding scenarios, we see demand for general executive education provision through qualifications expanding, but in the other scenarios, the funding of the sector is likely to mean a squeeze on provision such that the cost of providing executive education courses becomes prohibitive and the MBA returns to being the 'elite' qualification it was once considered to be. In terms of short course provision, expansion may be possible within the leading knowledge creation scenario as those elite institutions remaining within the sector will be producing ideas and innovations that will be leading and challenging management practice, and hence will be sought after by the corporate market. Otherwise, the short course intervention market is likely to subside as more specialist expert players emerge within the training and consultancy *niche* markets. More weight is also likely to be placed on the development of staff through job rotation and international placements, where support is provided in-house rather than through external providers. As in-house corporate universities become more established and embedded in their organisations, it will only be a matter of time before they start to apply for degree awarding powers themselves, and this will then create a whole new market of qualifications within the sector.

The demand-side of the equation for academics – As the corporate universities gain degree awarding powers and increasing numbers of global organisations provide their own suite of executive education qualifications, a new labour market will emerge for the 'corporate academic'. This is likely to offer higher rewards than the public funded sector, without the same pressures for research outputs within set parameters for outcomes. Whether this will result in the part-time Prof, working half their time for the public sector and half their time within corporate universities, or a shift of academic talent to the corporate sector is unknown, and it is likely to be dependent on the culture and ethos of the sector at the time. The part-time option may be more attractive in the regional and full-funded scenarios, while the opportunity to move to a more comfortable working environment may be more appealing to those at the pinnacle of their careers in the no government funding, knowledge leading and knowledge responding scenarios.

The demand-side of the equation for delivery – While ICT is not going to dominate any one particular scenario, the embeddedness of ICT in all of our lives is not something that can be ignored, especially when we are considering the future. The internet has already become the first source for information for young people with their studies and also for social networking/meeting new people and downloading music which now exceeds sales in shops (Williams and Rowlands, 2007). By 2035, it is likely to be the natural choice for learning, with young people only seeking out additional support if they cannot learn what they need online. Hence some areas of executive education may continue as face-to-face delivery, but much of it will be provided online. Whether the HE sector is best placed to provide this is yet to be seen; and it may require significant investment now that no single institution can afford to spend. This again will open the door to private, *niche* providers.

The demand-side of the equation for qualifications – A report on measuring and reporting student achievement has already concluded that while the UK honours degree is robust and a highly valued qualification, the classification system itself is no longer fit for purpose (Burgess, 2007). It cannot do full justice to the range of skills, knowledge, attributes and experience of a graduate in the 21st century and acts as a summative, simple numerical indicator which is at odds with lifelong learning. Burgess recommends a Higher Education Achievement Record along similar lines to the European Diploma Supplement along with an academic transcript. The Quality Assurance Agency offer broad guidance in the form of a framework and table of comparators of credits across different systems and CAT points, clarifying that institutional freedom will be maintained in terms of approach to learning, learning outcomes, module credit size, assessment and so forth (QAA, 2008). We also have the Bologna agreement which stretches across Europe, endeavouring to allow qualifications to be transferable throughout Europe. The value of any single qualification itself is likely to be questionable by 2035, particularly within executive education. As the government targets 50 per cent intake into higher education, the value of the undergraduate degree has diminished and more and more people are undertaking postgraduate and professional qualifications to give themselves an edge in the marketplace. As qualifications become in-house provisions through corporate universities, the market value of any single qualification will change, and the balance of qualifications and experience is likely to be more important. Organisations are less likely to be concerned with what you know as what you can do. This could result in a decrease in demand for HE provisions within executive education, since the HE sector is more often associated with creating and disseminating theoretical knowledge 'just in case' rather than a practice-based improvement agenda developed 'just in time'.

The supply-side of the equation for provision – In the leading knowledge creation scenario the university is well placed to be a strong provider of executive education, as they will be specialist institutions providing a restricted experience to the elite than can afford to engage with it. This scenario offers a small HE sector in the future, but one from which executive education could benefit. All the other scenarios are less positive. The responsive knowledge creation and no government funding scenarios see smaller sectors fighting to remain viable, much in need of corporate funding but not really providing a service that corporate providers can't better themselves. In the regional conglomerates and full government funding scenarios the sector has expanded, but in doing so is providing much of the same, and while organisations will engage with the mass education to a basic level of knowledge and skill for many element of the provision, they will be seeking the expert specialist provision within these types of institutions. This will essentially split the executive education market into a mass low level provision of generalist professional qualifications, and a specialist *niche* market for providers who focus on specific expertise.

The supply-side of the equation for academics – Recent research has shown that many professionals who are past the mid-point of their careers would actually quite like to undertake some lecturing (Blass and Randle, 2008), either as a means of giving something back (for the altruistic), as a means of adding something new to their CV (for those who are still career minded), or as a means of bringing new challenge to their job (for those who are stuck in a rut). This offers an interesting opportunity to both the HE sector and organisations. Organisations are likely to see their executives rejuvenated in the workplace as they are motivated by their new activity, and they are also likely to see an improvement in their work performance as well. It is well known that you learn something best when you have to teach it, so by releasing executives to undertake part-time lecturing, they are likely to get even better at what they are doing as they are teaching it. The HE sector benefits by having a willingly available part-time workforce to draw on with a wealth of expertise in the workplace. This part-time labour force may be particularly welcome in the no government funding scenario and the responsive knowledge creation scenario, and may also be needed in the regional conglomerate and full government funding scenarios as demand may outstrip supply as the sector expands.

The supply-side of the equation for delivery – There is only one scenario which clearly sees the HE sector expanding and that is full government funding. The regional conglomerate scenario may result in expansion, particularly at lower levels of provision. The other three scenarios result in a shrinking HE sector from what we have today. While the economy is unlikely to be in a permanent recession, the HE sector may not be able to recover in order to provide an executive education provision that is truly competitive across the market. The Leitch report (Leitch, 2006) clearly set the government agenda towards skills development in a manner that requires the HE sector to become bipolar. On the one hand they have to adapt to the market needs for higher skills levels in graduates resulting in a curriculum shift towards work-based education; while on the other hand they require top international research and knowledge creation. The two do not sit easily together, particularly as practice-based research is not well recognised amongst the research funding councils or within the research assessment exercise at the present time. As the HE sector struggles to resolve this dichotomy, other players are likely to emerge in the market to fill the gap. This may move executive education out of the HE sector itself into the consultancy market, possibly with the large consultancy firms offering their own corporate university provisions. This is particularly likely within the ICT market where the 'games' companies are the hubs of expertise for engaging people in online activity for hours on end. If this expertise could be transformed into executive education online, the market could change considerably. Wii developers are already breaking into new markets where you are physically as well as intellectually engaged.

The supply-side of the equation for qualifications – The HE sector will not be the sole provider of academic qualifications in the future. Academic qualifications may not even be the most appropriate for executive education in the future. So how will universities respond? Perhaps they will have to stick to doing what they do best, because they will be out-paced by organisations that are superior in areas that universities are poorer in. Basic Darwinist principles of survival of the fittest (or most adaptable) will allow those who are truly expert at executive education to continue dominating this market, while those who are tinkering on the edge will fall off. The MBA is now so heavily regulated by the various accrediting bodies that there is little room in the curriculum for any provider to teach anything particularly innovative, insightful or new (Blass and Weight, 2005b). Perhaps it is time for the executive education qualifications to be replaced, perhaps with newer, more appropriate practice-based research qualifications that allow executives to explore and enquire into their own practice. In many ways this is what the DBA (Doctorate in Business Administration) seeks to achieve but that is at the highest level of qualification only.

Conclusions: Innovations and insights for the future of executive education

The five scenarios all present very different futures for the HE sector in the UK, yet there are common themes emerging from them for the future of executive education provisions. These in turn provide us with a range of insights and innovations for the future of executive education.

Firstly, we will see the executive qualification market shift radically. The value of a qualification which is available on the mass market will diminish as the market reaches saturation point and then declines. Ultimately the MBA will return to being the elite leadership qualification it once was as it will only remain viable within universities with specialist, leading edge management centres.

A new range of qualifications will ultimately emerge which are experience-based qualifications based around the paradigm of practice-based research. These will allow executives to develop their insight, self-awareness and authenticity through the exploration of their own practice and enquiry into their impact on their workplace. This is currently available under the guise of some DBA courses, but will develop further at lower levels of qualification also.

Lastly, in the area of qualifications, we will see corporate universities developing their own in-house qualifications which they will award themselves with their newly granted degree awarding powers. This will change the face of the HE sector generally, and specifically wipe out a large element of university business school custom. Given that most universities' business schools are their most profitable element, this will present a further funding crisis within the sector.

In terms of academics, there will be two shifts in patterns. Firstly we will see 'traditional' academics shifting to the corporate university provision, either on a part-time basis or as a full-time step down towards retirement. The terms and conditions of employment will be more favourable in the corporate sector and the job will be less pressured than in the future HE sector. At the same time, we will see executives undertaking part-time lecturing in 'traditional' universities as a means of gaining further personal development and job enrichment. This in turn will act as a means of executive development for this tranche of managers.

Finally, attention needs to be paid to the provision. As we move through the generations we will see increasing digitalisation of learning habits such that the future executive will anticipate learning online first. Whether the

HE sector can respond adequately to generate such a provision remains to be seen, but the games companies could probably mobilise a response relatively quickly and in a suitably engaging manner. Short courses will still occur but will be provided by *niche* experts in the field, be they in universities or the consulting sector.

Many challenges lie ahead for the HE sector, not just in the UK but globally as Universities are no longer local entities. These may at first appearance appear negative, as we are wedded to the historical idea of the university, but if you reframe them as positive there are many opportunities to exploit. Universities should be working now to establish partnerships with corporate universities so that when they gain their own degree awarding powers, they are in a strong position to partner with them further. Universities should be exploring developing their curriculum through online gaming and alternative means of engaging young people in learning activities. They should also be identifying the specialist niches and investing in these to bring them to a point where they can exploit the market and corner the *niche*. It is time for universities to become smarter at focussing their provision. They need to decide what they can offer in the field of executive education that they can sustain as a *niche*, expert area rather than offering generalist provisions in line with all their competitors. They also need to start developing expertise in practice-based research and developing qualifications based on this paradigm. There will always be a market for people wanting to understand what they do better – it is human nature to enquire into our own practice. In a knowledge economy this can become the most innovative and entrepreneurial approach to research and development particularly when this occurs collaboratively as well as individually.

Whichever scenario ultimately represents the future of the HE sector, the sector needs to make some changes now. Attention needs to be paid to developing *niche* areas of expertise; qualifications need to be reviewed; partnerships need to be established; and new ways of working need to be considered. Universities are renowned for their bureaucracy and lack of flexibility. This will need to change if they are to continue operating in the executive education market in the future.

References

D. Birchall and M. Smith, *Scope and Scale of E-Learning Delivery Amongst UK Business Schools* (London: CEML, 2002).

E. Blass, 'What's in a name? A comparative analysis of the traditional public university and the Corporate University', *Human Resource Development International*, Vol. 4, No. 1 (2001).

E. Blass (ed.), *Talent Management* (Basingstoke: Palgrave Macmillan, 2009).

E. Blass and K. Randle, 'Developing industry/university relationships: A study of industry perceptions of "the university"', *SRHE Annual Conference*, 9–11 December, Liverpool (2008).

E. Blass and P. Weight, 'The MBA is dead: Part 1 – God save the MBA!' *On The Horizon*, Vol. 13, No. 4 (2005a), 229–240.

E. Blass and P. Weight, 'The MBA is dead: Part 2 – Long live the MBL!' *On The Horizon*, Vol. 13, No. 4 (2005b), 241–248.

R. Burgess, 'Beyond the honours degree classification', *The Burgess Group Final Report*, (Universities UK, 2007).

CMI, *Environmental Scanning: Trends Affecting the World of Work in 2018* (London: Chartered Management Institute, 2008).

Department for Innovation, U.A.S. (2007) 'World class skills: Implementing the Leitch Review of skills in England', in Dius (ed.), Norwich: HMSO.

J. Hilton, 'The Future for Higher Education: Sunrise or Perfect Storm?', *Educause Review*, 41 (2006), 58–71.

J. Kenway, E. Bullen and S. Robb, 'The knowledge economy, the technopreneur and the problematic future of the university', *Policy Futures in Education*, Vol. 2 (2004), 330–350.

H. Lauder, P. Brown, J. Dillabough, et al., *Introduction: The Prospects for Education: Individualization, Globalization, and Social Change*, in H. Lauder, P. Brown, J. Dillabough and A. Halsey (eds), *Education, Globalization & Social Change* (Oxford: Oxford University Press, 2006).

S. Leitch, *Prosperity for All in the Global Economy – World Class Skills*, in H. Treasury (ed.) (Norwich: HMSO, 2006).

D. Margules, *University Teaching and Learning: Why a More Flexible Approach?* (2002) http://www.ioe.ac.uk/schools/leid/oet%20html%20docs/Margules_D.htm

QAA, *Higher Education Credit Framework for England: Guidance on Academic Credit Arrangements in Higher Education in England* (London: Quality Assurance Agency, 2008).

UUK, *The Future Size and Shape of the Higher Education Sector in the UK: Threats and Opportunities* (London: Universities UK, 2008a).

UUK, *Patterns of Higher Education Institutions in the UK*: Eighth Report (London: Universities UK, 2008b).

S. Vincent-Lancrin, 'Building future scenarios for universities and higher education: An international approach', *Policy Futures in Education*, Vol. 2 (2004), 245–263.

P. Williams and I. Rowlands, 'The literature on young people and the information behaviour', *Information Behaviour of the Researcher of the Future* (London: JISC & British Library, 2007).

Part II
Future Learning

5
Future Learning: Section Editorial

Shirine Voller

While the world changes, so learning tools, techniques and approaches change too. However, there is a tension between what is possible through technological advancement and the extent to which we as individuals are able and willing to adapt. The chapters in this section explore how future learning might look, examining both emerging learning media and the characteristics of the learner, and the demands these place on how new technology is adopted and used. What I find most interesting is not the technology *per se*, but how it reflects, allows for, and stretches the ways in which we learn.

Gruenbaum interrogates the broad arena of technology, including web 2.0 and social media in his chapter, *When the classroom is no longer a room*; Caulat and Dickenson et al. in two complementary chapters, *Virtual Action Learning: a new genre for powerful learning* and *Virtual Action Learning: a new frontier?* focus specifically on the practice and theory of Virtual Action Learning; and Schofield and Honoré describe the characteristics of Generation Y, the latest generation to be entering our workplace, in *The impact of Generation Y on learning*.

In the context of learning, technology could be seen to do two things: first, it speeds up and/or makes easier, learning processes that we would have used anyway; and second, it can change the way in which we think. Gruenbaum argues that over the past 600 years, technological innovation in education has been limited to the former – progress that tinkered around the edges of existing norms. Indeed, even in the second half of the twentieth century, the traditional paradigm of teacher to student in a one-to-many didactic situation prevailed. Gruenbaum reminds us of how recently the World-Wide Web and our dependence on communications technology have emerged, their overwhelming, blanket impact belying their newness. Part of this impact is the shift, at least to some degree, away from the 'oracle to subjects' model of education, towards co-creation of knowledge, the challenge of the notion of 'expert' and the rise of the collective voice, through tools such as blogs and wikis.

According to Gruenbaum, engagement in the virtual space currently follows an 'extended' Pareto principle, whereby rather than the 80:20 rule applying, in social media it is 90:9:1, i.e. 90 per cent of users engage passively with web content, whilst 9 per cent comment on what the 1 per cent have written. It will be interesting to see if this shifts over time once familiarity with blogs and wikis grows. But what it does demonstrate even now is that there will always be leaders and laggards; individuals in front of, on and behind the curve. The same applies at the organisational level: some organisations will jump 'both feet in' to new technologies, to help them do what they do better, and to enable them to start doing things very differently to achieve competitive advantage.

Gruenbaum also talks about how virtual worlds – graphical, three-dimensional online spaces, where avatars are created as representations of individuals – can support learning. Whilst the advantages of being able to simulate a delicate medical procedure or emergency rescue operation are clear, there are fascinating questions about how to transfer and adapt rules, norms and etiquette from 'real life' into a parallel one. The interplay between technological advances and the consequences for the real human beings behind our virtual puppets is important, and evolving.

The role of the human in technology-enabled learning processes comes to the fore again in Caulat's work. She describes how she and colleagues have developed and adapted the well-established practice of Action Learning into two new variants: Virtual and Audio Action Learning. Virtual Action Learning is dealt with also by Dickenson et al., from a theoretical perspective, and the two chapters on this topic provide a helpful complement to one another.

What is striking is the advocacy which Caulat brings to her choices: her clarity on when to use audio only and when to use a combined audio-visual approach comes from a deep understanding of human interaction combined with experimentation. It demonstrates the skill required to navigate successfully through a range of technological possibilities, to identify the one that will work best in a particular context and for a particular purpose and to understand why that is.

Virtual/Audio Action Learning is a case-in-point demonstration of how technology can provide not only salient advantages over traditional learning formats in terms of saving travel costs and time and in expanding the potential market, but also in its unique characteristics. Caulat explains that it is easier to form diverse groups virtually – in terms of roles, genders, functions and cultures – and higher diversity has been shown to link with better learning outcomes. It seems also that the quality of listening is higher when participants work virtually. Dickenson et al. identify similar benefits, emphasising also the time for reflection that is built in to asynchronous forms of Virtual Action Learning, the advantages of the slower pace in general (compared with face-to-face) and the necessary turn-taking discipline which encourages participation by all members of a group.

Caulat discusses the factors essential for Virtual/Audio Action Learning to work well. It is not simply a case of transferring the face-to-face practice lock-stock-and-barrel across to a virtual format, and – echoed in Dickenson et al. – the facilitator plays a crucial role. Caulat explains the re-conceptualisation required to see it as a process and not just a session, the challenges of working against teleconferencing etiquette, how to work with silence, the difference between group dynamics in the virtual and physical space and the nature of developing trust virtually. The perhaps paradoxical idea, that trust may actually be quicker to build when participants retain a degree of anonymity becomes apparent also in Gruenbaum's work when he discusses the much less inhibited ways in which people interact through their avatars in virtual worlds, such as 'Second Life' (which has been used to support Action Learning).

Virtual/Audio Action Learning, as in the case of any technology-enabled learning process, places specific demands on the learner and the facilitator, or tutor. There are arguments for using simple technology so as to minimise opportunities for distraction from the main event – the learning. However, these days simplicity is not necessarily correlated with ease-of-use: the secret of success for major players in the virtual space seems to be the ability to hide highly sophisticated processes and programming behind a simple, user-friendly interface that allows impressive functionality with minimal user effort. Not all learners are sophisticated, and this applies equally to younger generations as it does to older ones.

Schofield and Honoré's chapter on Generation Y sets out to debunk some of the media-fuelled stereotypes of this group, those born after 1982. It sits within this section not because of the popularly assumed link between Gen Y and technological wizardry, but because of the importance of understanding the strengths, weaknesses, similarities and differences of this generation as they begin to enter the workforce and how this might impact on future learning.

According to Schofield and Honoré, Gen Y are heavily influenced by their family, their education, the media, world events and the socio-political landscape. For example, our education system, at least in the UK, engenders a consumerist attitude whereby students demand more of their teachers and hold educators accountable for their success. The media often portrays Gen Y in a negative light, and presents them with information in ever shorter segments on the basis of an assumption that they have shorter concentration spans – potentially a self-fulfilling prophecy?

Whilst Gen Y are seen to have a range of positive character attributes, there is evidence to suggest that they may be missing skills in their ability to handle difficult conversations, self-awareness, and understanding their impact on others. Perhaps this ties in with increasing use of text-based messaging where 'conversations' are happening in real time, or with only a slight time-lag, but are in shorthand with no cues other than the written text. Schofield and Honoré suspect that Gen Y may also have an under-developed sense of personal and professional risk, and are poor at critical analysis. Given the volume of information available at our fingertips, the ability to make judicious choices and scrutinise information is crucial, particularly if connected to an under-developed understanding of risk.

On entering the workplace, Gen Y's adaptability tempered by their honesty, demanding nature and vociferousness will ensure that there is a corresponding adaptation of the workplace to their expectations. Such 'co-evolution' is mutually beneficial, though there will always be abrasion between 'old' and 'new', in any context.

All four chapters in this section infer implications for the future of executive development: the importance of being at least 'on the curve' in respect of using technology, and making strategic decisions as to where it might be a competitive advantage to lead the field; the new, often high level skills required to facilitate learning in a different medium; the importance of matching available learning technologies with the needs and competence of the learner; and the insight to spot where a technological solution is making an existing job easier, and where it is fundamentally changing the way we connect and learn. Technology will feature largely for all levels of learning, but it must be driven by human preferences and capabilities if it is to be successful.

6
When the Classroom is No Longer a Room

Ronan Gruenbaum

Old classrooms, old technology

Education, by its very nature, has always existed. We have all learned from our parents, our elders and our communities. Formal education was well established 3,000 years ago in ancient Greece (Cubberley, 2004) and China (Encyclopaedia Britannica, 2009a); and the Bible encouraged education around 1500BC (The Bible, Bible Researcher, 2009). The three paradigms that have dominated education systems for all age groups since then are those of *expert* as teacher; the *one* teaching the *many* (Woodill, 2009); and the classroom being the main location of that teaching.

The *monitorial* system, as devised by Joseph Lancaster, became common-place from the early 19th century (Encyclopaedia Britannica, 2009) with one teacher instructing a few older children, or *monitors*, who would then teach the younger ones and help instil discipline. There were developments in educational theory, such as Pestalozzi's (1894) suggestion in the mid-18th century that children would learn better through what we now think of as *experiential learning* rather than learning by rote, but the technology, such as it was, extended to some chalk and slate for writing on. It certainly didn't extend to teaching anyone outside the room. If someone wanted private lessons, they would need the teacher to physically come to them – and only the wealthy could afford such attention.

Gutenberg's development of the printing press using movable type in the mid-15th century meant that information could finally travel through time and space (Briggs and Burke, 2002) (for Europe – China and Japan had enjoyed block printing as far back as the 8th century). You no longer needed to physically be in a room listening to the teacher explain a subject, you could read it when you wanted, where you wanted (assuming you were able to read). Within 50 years of Gutenberg there were an estimated 13 million books in print; and by the 16th century scholars complained of being unable to find the information they needed and differentiate between the wealth of books now available (Briggs and Burke, 2002).

The growth of literacy fuelled by the growth of publishing was not completely welcome, with the church wary of the common classes being able to read the Bible and similar texts for themselves (Briggs and Burke, 2002: 18) and it wasn't until the mid-19th century that an *illiterate* underclass was seen as more of a danger than a *literate* one (Cook-Gumperz, 2006).

That, however, was the sum total of technological innovation in education spanning the past 600 years (Saettler, 1968). Blackboards gave way to whiteboards, slate gave way to paper, and chalk gave way to pencil, pen and ink.

Old classrooms, new technology

From the second-half of the 20th century, visual aids have been introduced (such as slides, films, overhead projectors and interactive whiteboards) but these developments have not affected the fundamental way that knowledge is imparted and learning takes place, that is, in the classroom with one teacher and many students. This has been the case in all levels of education from kindergarten to executive education; and since the first business school, *École Supérieure de Commerce de Paris*, opened its doors in 1819, to the present day.

Whilst most students, whether in undergraduate, postgraduate or professional education, now have personal computers, it is easy to forget how quickly this has come about. At the end of the 80s, very few students could afford the new (and very slow) PCs that were available; it wasn't common for people to have a home computer, and not every office worker had a desktop as the main focus of their desk. The idea that we would all carry mobile phones was inconceivable just 30 years ago when Japan launched the first commercial cellular network (Agar, 2004).

The internet, whilst having existed for 40 years as a method of communicating between universities, only entered most people's lives in the 90s, thanks to the efforts of Sir Tim Berners-Lee at the nuclear research organisation, CERN, and the birth of the World-Wide Web.

Connection speeds from those early days have risen from a tortuously slow dial-up rate of 7Kbps (Kilobits per second) to broadband speeds in the developed world of 100MBps (Megabits per second) and more (an increase in the order of one million percent) although average speeds still vary widely from city to rural areas; from country to country; and from the developed to the developing world (OECD Directorate for Science, Technology and Industry, 2008).

It is worth remembering that the electronic calculator only began to replace the slide-rule in the 70s; and the developments of personal computing – and the access to information made possible through the internet and the growth of the mobile phone – have only impacted on individuals in the past 15 years.

Technology, quite simply, is not here to stay. It is here momentarily before being superseded ever quicker by smaller, faster, more powerful tools that hadn't been dreamt of a decade earlier.

Social technology

When the World-Wide Web was born, communication was very one-sided. It was not dissimilar to the traditional view of the classroom, with large dominant organisations passing information to 'the many'...the users... the general public...the 'students'.

This first phase of the web evolved over time to allow the end-users more and more interaction with each other. People with some technical ability were able to create their own websites from the very beginning of the World-Wide Web, and therefore be published without the need of a large organisation to help with distribution. Online chats and forums allowed users to talk to each other either in real-time or asynchronously over days, weeks or months. Shortly after launching online in 1995, *Amazon.com* started to allow readers to rate the books they had read and leave comments about them; thereby creating a system where customers would recommend books to other customers; making assumptions that if two customers liked the same book, the second customer might also like the other books purchased by the first. *Ebay.com*, the auction site also founded in 1995, allowed anyone to set up an online shop with no technical knowledge at all, where buyers would recommend sellers through aggregated feedback.

In 2003, Tim O'Reilly of O'Reilly Media, a US consultancy, labelled this 'new' type of internet, where people were able to communicate *with* each other, as 'Web 2.0'. The first Web 2.0 conference was held in 2004 and, whilst debate continues as to the exact meaning of the term, and what 'Web 3.0' will look like, broadly speaking if Web 1.0 was *them* talking to *us*, Web 2.0 is *us* the users, talking to *each other*.

This is an important innovation as, for the first time, the power of knowledge has largely been wrested from the hands of large institutions. Knowledge can now be transmitted and shared amongst people the world over. This is not, however, a democratisation of knowledge. The source of knowledge is now more important than ever, and the ways in which knowledge is verified and quality-checked have changed. If someone creates a website to explain their theories of management behaviour, are those theories as valid as those expounded in the *Harvard Business Review*? If business schools conduct surveys and hundreds of interviews to arrive at a conclusion that can, in theory, be applied to other organisations, is that 'better' than a theory based on a person's own experience and expounded on their blog? Who decides that the individual, or the organisation, is an 'expert'? When seeking information on the web, how can one be sure that it is reliable? Is an expert someone who knows a lot about their particular specialisation and has published extensively in the academic arena, or is it someone who has a lot of 'followers' on the internet, either via Twitter or a personal blog?

The answer to all these questions must ultimately be the stock answer that all MBA students learn at the start of the course: *'It depends'*. Traditional academic notions of quality assurance rail against suggestions that the 'crowd' can provide valuable learning; and yet much executive education in business schools is based around case studies of real-life examples and comparing and contrasting the approaches of different organisations – and *not* providing theory for the students to learn by rote and telling them that 'this approach is right and that way is wrong'.

The 'wisdom of crowds' does not mean that someone with a large following is therefore wise; yet the views of celebrities are held up in the media as having more validity purely by virtue of the fact that they are in the media. Successful business leaders, for example, are given a status hitherto unheard-of due to their appearance on reality TV programmes. Despite it being easy to dismiss information from the 'crowd' as being unreliable, it has become the first point of call for many when seeking clarification or information on a particular subject.

Encyclopaedia Britannica famously missed the boat on embracing new technology when ignoring the danger posed by the new CD-ROMs of the early 1990s, assuming that everyone who wanted encyclopaedic information would choose the print-only options that *Encyclopaedia Britannica* offered at that time (and at great expense – the full volume edition costing over £1,000).

When Microsoft released *Encarta*, their encyclopaedia on a disc, in 1993, it almost ended *Encyclopaedia Britannica*'s 200-year domination of the information market. *Encyclopaedia Britannica* didn't realise that the majority of people would rather get something for nothing, even if it meant there was a reduction in the amount of information available at their fingertips.

Encarta has also found itself displaced by the free online encyclopaedia created by thousands of unpaid volunteers: *Wikipedia*. The concept behind a 'Wiki', such as *Wikipedia*, is that anyone can edit it with no knowledge of website programming and no pre-authorisation. Whilst this has resulted in famous examples of erroneous and often malicious entries appearing in *Wikipedia* (incorrectly announcing the deaths of US Senators Edward Kennedy and Robert Byrd, and Apple CEO Steve Jobs (Pershing, 2009), to name but a few),the idea is that with the 'Power of Many', the majority of editors will ensure that the mistakes and malicious entries created by a few will be corrected.

In a study of 42 articles by the journal *Nature* in 2005 (Giles, 2005), *Encyclopaedia Britannica* was shown to be more accurate than *Wikipedia* (with 2.9 errors per article compared to Wikipedia's 3.9) but had no articles, from the sample tested, that were completely error free, whereas *Wikipedia* had four. *Encyclopaedia Britannica* refutes these findings (Encyclopaedia Britannica, Inc., 2006), but *Wikipedia* is still sufficiently accurate often enough to be the primary source of information for many.

The internet in general has proved to be the primary source of research for students in many disciplines, benefitting from the generosity of others in detailing issues or explaining concepts. Sources are not restricted to *Wikipedia* either, 'Wikiversity' is a '*Wikimedia Foundation project devoted to learning resources, learning projects, and research for use in all levels, types, and styles of education from pre-school to university, including professional training and informal learning*' (Wikiversity, 2009a). The 'open learning community' has its own School of Business (Wikiversity, 2009b) with learning resources on a wide range of topics, including specific qualifications' curricula such as for an MBA (Wikiversity, 2009c), which either provides open source content for free or links to pages on that content on the main *Wikipedia* site or other pages through the *WikiMedia Foundation* (WikiMedia Foundation, 2009).

The vision of the *WikiMedia Foundation* is '*...a world in which every single human being can freely share in the sum of all knowledge*'. The open-source projects, besides *Wikipedia* and *Wikiversity*, include *Wiktionary* (a dictionary and thesaurus) and *Wikisource* (a free-content library).

The *Open Source Initiative*, another non-profit organisation, is founded on the idea that knowledge, such as that held as programming code in software, should be free for all to improve upon and develop; and for the benefit of everyone. Programmers can still sell their programs, but others must have access to the code to further develop it (rather than reinventing the wheel every time).

The idea of 'setting knowledge free' permeates the new era of online collaboration. It is the ethos behind peer-to-peer sharing of copyright music and film; it is the tenet upon which the *Guardian* newspaper is campaigning for all UK government data to be freely available (*Guardian*, 2009; Free Our Data, 2009).

As well as the *Wikiversity Business School*, websites such as *PersonalMBA* offer reading lists that help users self-educate, rather than '*mortgaging your life to go to business school*' (PersonalMBA, 2009). These websites should make academic institutions examine their purpose in society. Are they there to produce qualifications for people to obtain and append to their name and CV and thereby step up the career ladder? Or are they there to help people learn? If the answer is 'to produce qualifications', then business schools can rest easy. Wiki sites will not, any time soon, find a way of assessing and awarding certificates to those who have studied from the many. If, however, business schools believe their purpose is to help people learn, then they are likely to face stiff competition from the abundance of free learning and tutorials that exist online.

Wikirooms

As discussed above, the tool behind *Wikipedia*, *Wikiversity* and so on, the 'Wiki', is simply a website that anyone can edit. In the case of *Wikipedia* and *Wikiversity*, 'anyone' means just that – anyone in the world with access to the internet. However, *wikis* are also useful when used by closed groups, teams or courses; allowing members to collaborate on texts without the need to send change-tracked Word documents from one person to another hoping that what one person is working on is the latest version and hasn't been updated since by another member of the team.

Ashridge Business School, for example, has used wikis on the Executive MBA programme to encourage collaboration on revision topics by the whole class; as an extension of the long-standing 'Learning Support Groups' where students are formally placed into small groups to encourage them to support each other's study when they are away from the residential modules at Ashridge. They, and others (Roushan, 2009), have also used them for students to collaborate on joint projects and assignments.

The *Pareto Principle* (or the *80–20 Rule*) applies to wikis specifically and social media in general. However, rather than 80 per cent of the content and contributions to the wikis being written by 20 per cent of the users, the Social Media *Pareto principle* follows the ratio: 90:9:1, that is that 1 per cent of the users actually write the content. This could mean they write blogs or contribute to wikis. They post links to interesting articles on the internet and create podcasts. Nine per cent of the users then comment on those blogs, forward links and podcasts to friends and perhaps add to the wikis. The remaining majority, 90 per cent, simply read, observe and 'use' the content.

In *Groundswell* (Li and Bernoff, 2008), the authors described six levels of engagement with social media: Creator, Critic, Collector, Joiner, Spectator and Inactive (quite simply, not engaging)...where 'Spectators' are the largest group across all demographics, and 'Creators' the smallest (Forrester Research, 2009). Whilst this may, for some, prove to be an argument against using social media tools for education, as not everyone engages in the creation of the content, the same problem exists in every classroom. There are those that prefer to sit quietly at the back and never raise their hand or ask questions, but benefit from the discussions of those around them and, undoubtedly, learn – if exam and assignment results are anything to go by. In short, the differential between the creators and the spectators is no argument for not using social media tools for learning virtually.

Blogs are also increasingly used in education, though in a different way. For many schools they are used by faculty members to publish opinion and thought pieces without the need to have peer-reviewed research in place and then going through the rigmarole of getting published in an academic journal. They can also be used by teams (to blog on a particular subject, such as 'Leadership') and, of course, allow for audio and video content to be uploaded, and for the Critics (according to Forrester's nomenclature) to debate with the authors on particular topics. Furthermore, in the same way that faculty blogs can be valuable publications when the formality of peer-reviewed journals is not required, so can student blogs be used to assess progress and learning when the formality of exams and assignments is unnecessary. Distance learners at Bournemouth University Business School, for example, are expected to keep a learning journal in a blog format, to 'ensure individual reflection as part of the performance development planning process is captured' (Roushan, 2009).

Virtual engagement

Perhaps the biggest tool in what marketers refer to as the 'social media toolbox' is the Social Network. The most famous networks, such as *Facebook* and *MySpace*, have a reputation as being easy ways to waste time (Millard, 2008), with no discernible benefit, although the problem of employees wasting company time existed long before the creation of online social networks (Adams, 2007). Many businesses block access to social networks, fearing that employees will be less productive and waste their time chatting to friends online rather than doing work; despite the fact that the benefits of online recreation for employees have been identified for many years (Oravec, 1999) – and when management does not trust employees to act responsibly, a damaging parent-child dynamic may emerge.

Furthermore, a study in 2008 showed that three-quarters of employees who used social networks such as *Facebook*, *MySpace* and *LinkedIn*, did so for business purposes (Awareness, 2008); and whilst a third of companies either have, or are planning, internal corporate social networks (taking the traditional intranet directory onto a level that allows knowledge sharing and collaboration), 49 per cent said that they allowed their employees to express themselves freely on the corporate social networking platforms.

The disparity between those organisations that are already embracing the power of social networks in the workplace and those who block access mirrors the usual diffusion of new technologies as described by Rogers (Rogers, 2003) and shows a progression from *innovators*, through *early adopters*, *early majority*, *late majority* and *laggards*. Some organisations are innovators and early adopters; and others tend to be laggards.

All organisations, including business schools, should think carefully about where they want to position themselves on that spectrum. Will being an early adopter give them some competitive advantage and, in the specific case of executive education, if organisations are changing the way they communicate and operate through new technology, surely business schools need to examine what they are teaching and see if it is still relevant?

Companies are beginning to understand that encouraging a culture of collaboration in the workplace makes business sense...but universities and business schools often lag behind. The open-source Learning Management System, *Moodle*, doesn't include social networking facilities. For those, business schools have to bolt on *Elgg*, also an open-source system. Despite modern education at all levels moving towards group work, discussion and collaboration in the learning process, most business schools are wary, or ignorant, of the potential learning benefits available through a social network and rely, instead, on learning objects and other online content.

Virtual broadcasting

The Open University started broadcasting late-night lectures on BBC 2 to UK distance learners in 1971; and with the proliferation of VHS video in the late 70s and 80s, most education institutions incorporated video content into the classroom in one form or other, with a variety of specialist companies sprouting up to produce learning videos for management education.

The technology now available to all institutions (let alone individuals) has placed the technical ability to produce audio and video content within the grasp of all; and yet podcasts (audio and video distributed over the internet) produced by business schools are still predominantly used to market programmes, not for learning. To broadcast (or 'stream') live videos of lectures over the internet to enhance distance learning, all that is needed is a domestic video camera and a laptop with an internet connection, yet it is still the case that students who are unable to attend physical classrooms tend to have to rely on course colleagues to provide them with notes on the class they missed.

Podcasts have, however, changed education in three areas. The first, on websites such as *YouTube* and *iTunes*, is when individuals and institutions decide to share their knowledge and create podcasts that explain specific issues, both practical (360Feedback Expert, 2008) and theoretical (IIT Kharagpur, 2009) on a variety of subjects (University of Warwick, 2009). *YouTube* has even created a specific channel to cater for education videos (YouTube, 2009), as has *iTunes* (Apple Inc, 2009). The videos are not usually completely altruistic in nature – they are used to promote programmes, courses or institutions – but are nevertheless available for all to access.

The second area where podcasts have changed education and training is as an additional learning resource, for example, to instruct engineers in the field of the requirements of a particular machine or to allow students to catch up on lectures they have missed. In the case of executive education, busy managers will often find it easier to listen to subject-specific podcasts or entire audiobooks on the daily commute than reading the equivalent articles and books.

A third innovative use of podcasts is to provide feedback to students, where the teacher records (using screen-capture software that records the computer screen and a voice-over commentary) the actual process of marking an assignment. Russell Stannard, from the University of Westminster, claims that the comments and feedback the teacher is able to provide during the marking process tends to be of far more use to the student than comments scribbled in red pen at the end (Tobin, 2009).

Virtual environments

The Open University has always been innovative in using technology to reach its students and overcome physical distances, from broadcast TV in the early seventies to the current use of Multi-User Virtual Environments (MUVEs). These environments, often referred to as 'Virtual Worlds', are graphical three-dimensional online spaces where users can interact with each other. Rather than seeing a photo of the person one is talking to online (via text-chat or VoIP[1]) one sees their 'Avatar', a graphical three-dimensional representation of them, which may be an accurate reflection of their real-life body (in size, shape, skin tone, gender, hair and so on) or may be a fantasy figure (be it of a different gender, or even a different species to their real-life). The users, through their avatars, are able to move, 'touch', build objects and fly. In some of the MUVEs, users can buy and sell virtual land, property (including objects they have built) and earn a real-life income from their virtual world activities.

An important difference between MUVEs and Massively Multi-player Online Role-Playing Games (MMORPGs) is that MUVEs are not intended to be games. There is, to a large extent, no 'purpose' to a user in that environment, other than to interact with people they find there and to use the options available in the virtual space that are not possible, or practical in the real world.

An example of this is where paramedics learn how to assess and treat patients in different scenarios that could prove expensive, or even life-threatening, if carried out in the real world. St George's, University of London, have developed a range of scenarios to aid in training paramedic students who are able to interact with each other, the tutors, and importantly, the patients, in the virtual space (Medical News Today, 2008).

The NHS has created a variety of 'ideal hospitals' of the future in *Second Life*, the most famous MUVE, to 'illustrate what healthcare in the future could look like' (NHS, 2009). They have also, along with the Department of Biosurgery and Surgical Technology at Imperial College London, used the virtual environment for training, such as how to manage patients and treat clinical emergencies, or obtaining informed consent from patients with learning difficulties (in conjunction with University of Brighton, Sussex Partnership NHS Foundation Trust and Grace Eyre Foundation) (Medical Media and Design Laboratory, 2009).

---

[1]Voice over the Internet Protocol: telephony service over the Internet.

In 2004, UC Davis created a 'Hallucinations Building' in *Second Life*, to help educate healthcare professionals, caregivers and the general public about the auditory and visual hallucinations experienced by people with schizophrenia (Cook, 2004). In this environment, created in consultation with schizophrenia sufferers, users experience, through their avatars, the distorted reality and negative voices that are typical of the condition.

Other examples of education in *Second Life* involve visualisations of abstract or complex subjects, such as viewing DNA in 3-D, going inside microscopic organisms or using scales to show how changes on a balance sheet can affect other accounts (Ryan, 2008). Kaplan University have created Maslow's *Hierarchy of Needs* as a 'physical' space in *Second Life*, where students are able to explore each of the nine levels in turn (Gerstein, 2009). The social needs, for example, are, represented by a native American community meeting space, reflecting the sizeable community in that area.

The inherent role-playing opportunities in *Second Life* also make it useful for teaching negotiation skills (Jankowski, 2010); languages (Sobkowiak, 2009) and for teaching how to spot and gather evidence for law enforcement, child advocacy and social services (Stafford, 2009).

It is noteworthy that secondary and higher education are better represented in *Second Life* than management development. Perhaps business schools are wary of experimenting too much with new technology, preferring to play safe with tried and tested methodologies, though this is not the case for all. The Open University is using its six islands on *Second Life* for a variety of teaching. In addition to the examples already given, architecture, design, archaeology and, perhaps unsurprisingly, computer science, have also been taught in Second Life, embracing the features of this virtual space that set it apart from other online tools (Kirriemuir, 2009).

For those interested in experimenting with *Second Life* and bringing the teaching out of the classroom, there are whole communities of educators who share experiences and help each other to develop ideas; whilst *Second Life* itself encourages educators and universities to use the MUVE through a mailing list, SLED (LindenLabs, 2009), that puts together over 5,000 teachers and researchers from kindergarten through to post-graduate and executive education. For a more permanent resource, SimTeach (SimTeach, 2009) is a wiki set up by *Second Life* educators for *Second Life* educators. Organisations such as the Educational Support Management Group (ESMG) also provide virtual classroom facilities for schools and companies that want to experiment with education in the virtual space (Virtuosity Magazine, 2009).

Virtual obstacles

There are, it must be stressed, many obstacles to overcome before exchanging one's real life for a second one. Not least of these obstacles are the technical ones. *Second Life* requires users to download a program to their computers, and the computers themselves require high quality graphics cards and a fast broadband connection. Many students all over the world cannot rely on consistent internet connections (it is impossible to connect to *Second Life* with a dial-up connection) and have computers that are better suited to text and internet surfing rather than 'gaming'. Even in businesses, where the technical specifications are easy to meet, corporate IT policies often prohibit users from downloading and installing software to individual machines and block access to certain sites.

It remains to be seen to what extent those IT policies and anxiety about adopting new technology in organisations inhibits growth. For example, it is worth considering how early adopters of the internet, such as Amazon.com, quickly grew to dominate markets that already had many large, well-established companies that suffered by being slow to create an online presence. Conversely, the dot-com boom-and-bust at the turn of the century also shows how many organisations suffered in turn by jumping on the bandwagon too early and over-investing.

If organisations decide to embrace virtual worlds to encourage virtual learning amongst the staff (and thereby sanction general access to *Second Life*), the users themselves may still find themselves frustrated by the experience. When many people, or avatars, gather in the same space in *Second Life* and try to interact with each other (as one would hope for in a teaching scenario) the *Second Life* systems (run by LindenLabs – the creators of *Second Life*) are often found to grind to a halt (Warburton, 2008).

This sluggish response of virtual worlds is not unlike the slow connection speeds that made surfing the internet a hit-and-miss affair in the early-to-mid nineties, whilst the number of users online at that time meant that many sound business models failed by simply being too quick to market and not achieving a critical mass of customers. Only time will tell if the business schools that are early adopters of virtual world teaching will dominate the future of executive education; or merely show the way for late-adopters to follow...learning from the mistakes of the early-adopters and innovators.

Virtual universe

Second Life is by far the best known virtual world at present. At the time of writing it has over 19 million registered users, with over one million logging in every 30 days, and over 500,000 a week (Second Life, 2009a). The largest number of concurrent users so far at any one time on *Second Life* is just over 80,000. In 2008, *Second Life* had over US$100 million bought and sold on the *LindeX* (the virtual currency exchange for buying Linden dollars – which are used 'in world') (Second Life, 2009b). This pales in comparison, however, with the environment built by another

MUVE company, MindArk, who were contracted in 2007 by the Chinese Government to build a virtual world capable of having seven million concurrent users and of sustaining a US$1 million per day real-currency economy.

According to virtual worlds consultancy, Kzero, there are over 70 different MUVEs in existence at this time or in 'beta' development (that is, being used by a reduced group of users before being opened to the general public). Of those MUVEs, there are only a handful (such as Utherverse, Twinity, HiPiHi and GeoSim) aimed at the over-30s. By comparison, according to Kzero's research (Kzero, 2009) Stardoll has over 34 million registered users with an average age just under 15. Habbo is just under that age group, with 135 million registered users and Poptropica, for the under-tens, has over 76 million users.

What is clear is that virtual worlds are not a passing fad. In the same way that Generation X grew up with television, and Generation Y grew up with the internet, the next (millennial) generation are growing up with virtual worlds. When one adds to this the developments in creating electronic interfaces that can control characters in virtual worlds through real-world movements – such as an electronic glove (Hanlon, 2009) – and the creation of microchips that can be implanted in the human body, or brain, and transmit thoughts and movements to computers (Warwick, 2005) and that can equally transmit information back (telling your brain, for example, that you've been touched when it happens in the virtual world), it is no longer science fiction to consider a time when we will be able to interact physically in virtual worlds, and 'feel' the movements that occur. When we get to that stage, there is the danger that we may find ourselves as characters in EM Forster's '*The Machine Stops*', living in cocoons with all human interaction occurring through the machine. However, fear of reaching that dystopia should not dissuade us from enjoying a greater level of virtual interaction now.

One of the benefits of new technology is that tutors will soon be able to create their own virtual robot that will run classes, as their virtual self, in the virtual space without the need to be connected at that time (Dyson, 2009), allowing for a more interactive delivery of online sessions than is available through podcasts and learning objects.

One should not, furthermore, disregard the learning potential of MMORPGs. *World of Warcraft*, from Blizzard Entertainment, for example, is an online role-playing game, set in a fantasy world of quests and monsters, heroes and heroines, guilds and guild-masters (Blizzard Entertainment, 2009). It is massively multi-player in that it has over ten million members, with thousands playing together, online, in the virtual space. It is easy to dismiss games as 'games', but the interaction with real-people (through their character avatars); the need to work together to achieve goals; and the need to influence others to work together, make it a surprisingly useful training ground for many of the attributes and 'soft-skills' business schools seek to engender. Players do not come from a specific demographic either, being spread internationally, of all ages, of both genders; and recruiters are already rewarding the leadership skills required to become a top guild master (Wired, 2006).

Virtual identities

Whether in a virtual world, in a MMPORG or on a social network, does it matter how an employee behaves? Is their online private life still private, or will the fact that they are connected to clients or colleagues in the virtual space mean that they have forfeited their right to privacy online?

Before the urbanisation of the west, when the population still generally lived in small communities, everyone knew everyone's business in the village. If someone misbehaved on a Saturday night, the chances are their employer would learn about it. As transport links have improved, however, it has become more common for people to live away from their place of work, with a daily commute separating them from their boss and from their clients. In addition, globalisation means that one's clients are spread far and wide and are unlikely to share a social life with that particular person.

The growth of social media has begun to shrink the world once more to 'local communities'. It is not uncommon for business contacts to be connected through social networks such as *Facebook* or *LinkedIn*. Does it matter, therefore, if an employee's private life spills into their professional one? Should employees ensure that clients and colleagues are unable to see photographs of them online with their friends, misbehaving on a Saturday night? Should organisations discipline an employee for bringing the organisation into disrepute through their private online persona, or should they only concentrate on what the employee does in their working hours?

If, during one's working hours, one represents one's organisation in a virtual world, should one ensure that the avatar approximately resembles the real person? Should employees on company business be restricted to having an avatar of human form, of the same gender, of the same ethnicity? Should those avatars be 'appropriately' dressed? Organisations are already drawing up guidelines on such issues (Goodwin, 2009); but all educators need to think about online etiquette and whether they need to expand their syllabus to include issues of management, leadership, motivation and corporate responsibility in the virtual space.

For example, within the educational context, should students on a discussion forum be taught how to communicate in a suitable manner? Where written text cannot easily reflect the tone of the discourse, should the use of *emoticons* (such as 'smiley faces' created from punctuation: ☺) be encouraged, or is formal language use preferable? Should there be sanctions for inappropriate behaviour, and when is 'bluntness' considered inappropriate? Should tutors ensure their personal profiles on social networking sites are 'professional' – in case their students find out what they get up to in their private lives? Should lecturers be able to charge expenses for buying 'professional' clothing for their avatar? Should the institution disassociate itself from tutors' blogs, even though it encourages blogging and the blogs are hosted on the organisation's servers? Should tutors be forced to create an online presence, or should it be left to their own preference? If a tutor refuses to use online learning systems (even quite simple ones such as discussion forums) should they be disciplined or should they be allowed to only teach offline? Should online engagement, such as blogging or interacting with students through social networks and virtual worlds be rewarded in the same way as getting published in a traditional publication and holding seminars in real classrooms? Should the compensation and rewards be greater if they are able to manage hundreds of students *online* rather than dozens *offline* in the same amount of time?

Once more, it depends, and educators will have to find their own answers to these questions and more. Some of them, even in this global economy, will be culture-specific, and executive educators may find that they need to change the rules according to the participants and the sponsoring organisations.

The future of executive education

'It's hard to make predictions, especially about the future.'
Robert Storm Petersen

Executive education will probably always exist, in that executives and managers will probably always need help in improving themselves, their teams and their organisations. What is not clear is what form that education will take, but business schools and faculties will need to adapt if they are to survive.

By 2013, 80 per cent of the world's population is expected to have access to a mobile phone (PortioResearch, 2009), giving access not only to the global phone network, but increasingly to the internet. Kurzweil's *Law of Accelerating Returns* (Kurzweil, 2001), meanwhile, explains how the development of new technology will increase exponentially with the result that the 100 years of progress expected in the 21st century would be experienced as 20,000 years at today's rate; and become closer to the 'singularity' – where technological change is so fast that, according to Kurzweil, it *'represents a rupture in the fabric of human history'*.

Given such growth, can we make any sensible predictions of the state of executive education in ten years, let alone 50? Is the existing paradigm of students travelling to business schools for residential courses sustainable; both in terms of the environmental impact of business travel but also in terms of the cost to the organisation? Can businesses continue to allow managers to be away from the office for days or weeks at a time with the subsequent impact on both budgets and productivity?

With the pressure on reducing expenses and carbon footprints, more and more organisations are cutting back on business travel (PhoCusWright, 2009). There are three possible consequences for business schools: firstly, that they become 'hyper-local' institutions only serving their immediate geographic area; secondly, that faculty go to where the clients are, rather than having the clients travel to the school; and thirdly, that business schools move increasingly to provide their services online.

The coming decades are likely to see business schools differentiating themselves along these three lines; with some meeting the needs of their local community and not chasing the international, or even national students; some business schools (as already happens) specialising in travelling to where their clients are and keeping only administrative offices in a central location; and others will specialise in providing distance learning through online platforms. It is still worth remembering, however, that the online tools available through social media can be utilised across all of these scenarios – social media is not aimed solely at distance learners.

With distance learning, business schools will struggle to provide a premium service, and charge a premium price, when so much information and so many learning materials are available for free or at marginal cost (Anderson, 2009). It may well be that business schools will find themselves teaching less and providing more 'accreditation' through exams or other assessment. Business schools may need to decide whether they are in the business of educating executives and managers, or whether they are in the business of providing qualifications that will improve the CVs for those executives. These two aims are not mutually exclusive, but it is possible to do one without the other – and that choice may prove essential for some institutions.

For schools and educators who are thinking about how they can jump on the bandwagon of new technology, there is plenty of help available on the internet through social networks of like-minded learning professionals who are embracing new tools to share knowledge, tips and experiences (Hargadon, 2009). Any individual who wants to use technology in education clearly has to become comfortable with that technology first. And whilst there are plenty of potential pitfalls in engaging with students online, there are also huge potential benefits – the bandwagon is large and trundling inexorably forward. Educators and organisations have to decide not *whether* to jump on it, but *when* and *how*.

The three paradigms of education discussed at the beginning of this chapter (the *expert* as teacher; the *one* teaching the *many*; and the classroom being the main location of that teaching) are therefore in flux. Whereas we have traditionally assumed the expert to be the teacher, who now decides who the expert is? Is the teacher the '*sage on the stage*', the '*guide on the side*' or, in fact, the '*crowd in the cloud*' – where there is no one expert, but a communal consensus?

Many internet users already find it more valuable to have the consensus of a million free opinions, than pay to hear from the expert. Rather than the *one* teaching the *many*, we now have the *many* teaching the *many* – and business schools need to think about whether they intend to fight that trend over the coming decades, or embrace it and find new ways of reaching their students. After all, the classroom is no longer a room: it is wherever the student decides that they want to learn.

References

360FeedbackExpert, *What are 360 Degree Feedback Surveys and How do They Work?* Available at: http://www.youtube.com/watch?v=OXJkP13xACg Accessed: 13 October 2009 (2008).

J. Adams, 'Keeping employees from wasting company time', *Bank Technology News* 20, Vol. 5, No. 17, *Business Source Premier*, EBSCO*host* (2007).

J. Agar, *Constant Touch: A Global History of the Mobile Phone* (Cambridge: Icon Books Ltd, 2004).

C. Anderson, *Free: The Future of a Radical Price: The Economics of Abundance and Why Zero Pricing is Changing the Face of Business* (London: Random House, 2009).

Apple Inc, *Education: Mobile Learning*, Available at: http://www.apple.com/education/mobile-learning/ Accessed: 13 October 2009 (2009).

Awareness, *Whitepaper: Trends and Best Practices in Adopting Web 2.0*, Available from: http://www.awarenessnetworks.com/resources/AWN_WP_2008Trends.pdf Accessed: 13 October 2009 (2008).

Bible Researcher, *A Chronology of Scripture* Available at: http://www.bible-researcher. com/history1.html Accessed: 20 October 2009 (2009).

Blizzard Entertainment, *General FAQ* Available at: http://www.worldofwarcraft. com/info/faq/general.html Accessed: 12 October 2009 (2009).

A. Briggs, and P. Burke, *A Social History of the Media: From Gutenburg to the Internet* (Cambridge: Blackwell Publishing, 2002).

J. Cook, *Accessing Virtual Hallucinations*, Available at: http://www.ucdmc.ucdavis. edu/ais/virtualhallucinations/ Accessed: 13 October 2009 (2004).

J. Cook-Gumperz, *The Social Construction of Literacy*, 2nd edn. (Cambridge: Cambridge University Press, 2006).

E.P. Cubberley, *The History of Education* (Montana: Kessinger Publishing, 2004).

T. Dyson, *Pods and Blogs*, [Podcast: 24 November 2009] Available at: http://down-loads. bbc.co.uk/podcasts/fivelive/pods/pods_20091124-0335a.mp3 or http://www. ibot2000.com (2009).

Encyclopaedia Britannica, Inc., *Fatally Flawed: Refuting the Recent Study on Encyclopaedic Accuracy by the Journal Nature*, Available at: http://corporate.britannica.com/ britannica_nature_response.pdf Accessed: 10 October 2009 (2006).

Encyclopaedia Britannica, *Ancient China* Available at: http://www.britannica.com/ EBchecked/topic/179408/education/47455/Ancient-China Accessed: 20 October 2009 (2009a).

Encyclopaedia Britannica, *Monitorial System* [Website] Available at: http://www. britannica.com/eb/article-9053367/monitorial-system Accessed: 20 October 2009 (2009b).

Forrester Research, *Consumer Profile Tool* Available at: http://www.forrester.com/ Groundswell/ladder.html Accessed: 13 October 2009 (2009).

Free our data, *Free Our Data: Make Taxpayers' Data Available to Them* available at: http://www.freeourdata.org.uk/ accessed: 20 October 2009 (2009).

J. Gerstein, Personal email and Second Life interview. Jackie Gerstein, *Online Faculty for Departments of Education*, Kaplan University, 2 July 2009 (2009).

B. Goodwin, 'Employers should have dress code for avatars says Gartner', *Computer Weekly*, 7 October (2009). Available at: http://www.personneltoday.com/articles/2009/10/09/52489/online-dress-codes-for-avatars-should-be-enforced-by.html Accessed: 14 October 2009 (2009).

Guardian, Free Our Data Available at: http://www.guardian.co.uk/technology/free-our-data Accessed: 13 October 2009 (2009).

S. Hargadon, *Classroom 2.0* Available at: http://www.classroom20.com Accessed: 7 December 2009 (2009).

M. Hanlon, *The AcceleGlove – Capturing Hand Gestures in Virtual Reality* Available at: http://www.gizmag.com/go/2134/ Accessed: 12 October 2009 (2009).

IIT Kharagpur, *Lec-1 Introduction to Artificial Neural Networks* Available at: http://www.youtube.com/watch?v=xbYgKoG4x2g Accessed: 13 October 2009 (2009).

M. Jankowski, Personal email, Co-Founder and President, *Shapiro Negotiations*, 11 January 2010 (2010).

Kzero, *Research* Available at: http://www.kzero.co.uk/blog/?page_id=2092 Accessed: 13 October 2009 (2009).

J. Kirriemuir, 'Early summer 2009 Virtual World Watch snapshot of virtual world activity in UK HE and FE' Published by Eduserv and Virtual World Watch. Available at: http://virtualworldwatch.net/wordpress/wp-content/uploads/2009/06/snapshot-six.pdf Accessed: 18 August 2009 (2009).

R. Kurzweil, *The Law of Accelerating Returns* Available at: http://www. kurzweilai.net/ articles/art0134.html?printable=1 Accessed: 20 January 2008 (2001).

C. Li and J. Bernoff, *Groundswell: Winning in a World Transformed by Social Technologies* (Boston: Harvard Business School Press, 2008).

LindenLabs, *Educators – SL Educators (The SLED List)* Available at: https://lists.secondlife.com/cgi-bin/mailman/listinfo/educators Accessed 20 September 2009 (2009).

Medical Media and Design Laboratory, *About MMDL at Imperial College London* Available at: http://medmedia.wordpress.com/ Accessed: 13 October 2009 (2009).

Medical News Today, 'First Paramedic Course To Use Second Life', *Medical News Today*, 13 October (2008). Available at: http://www.medicalnewstoday.com/articles/125259.php Accessed: 13 October 2009.

S. Millard, 'Managing Web 2.0 Technologies in the Workplace', Roundtable discussion, London, UK, November 20 (2007). *Strategic HR Review*, Vol. 7, No. 2 (2008) 54. Retrieved from Business Source Premier database.

J. Giles, 'Internet encyclopaedias go head to head', *Nature*, Vol. 438 (2005) 900–901.

NHS, *Welcome to Second Health Hospital* Available at: http://slurl.com/secondlife/National%20Health%20Service/140/99/26 Accessed: 13 October 2009 (2009).

OECD Directorate for Science, Technology and Industry (2008) *Average Advertised Download Speeds, by Country*, September (2008) Available at: http://www.oecd.org/document/54/0,3343,en_2649_34225_38690102_1_1_1,00.html Accessed: 7 October 2009.

J.A. Oravec, 'Working hard and playing hard: Constructive uses of online recreation', *Journal of General Management (UK)*, Spring, Vol. 24, No. 3 (1999).

B. Pershing, *Kennedy, Byrd the Latest Victims of Wikipedia Errors* (Washington Post, 21 January 2009) Available at: http://voices.washingtonpost.com/capitol-briefing/2009/01/kennedy_the_latest_victim_of_w.html?hpid=topnews Accessed: 10 October 2009.

PersonalMBA, *PersonalMBA Manifesto* (2009). Available at: http://personalmba.com/ Accessed: 13 October 2009.

J.H. Pestalozzi, *How Gertrude Teaches Her Children: An Attempt to Help Mothers to Teach Their Own Children and an Account of the Method*. Translated by L.E. Holland, and F.C. Turner (London: S. Sonnenschein, 1894).

PhoCusWright, *Seven Major Trends Reshaping the U.S. Corporate Travel Landscape* (2009). [Website: 4 August 2009] Available at: http://connect.phocuswright.com/ 2009/08/seven-major-trends-reshaping-the-us-corporate-travel-landscape/ Accessed: 19 November 2009.

PortioResearch, *Mobile Industry Continues to Boom Despite Turmoil in World Financial Markets* (2009). Available at: http://www.portioresearch.com/WWMF09-13_ press. html Accessed: 27 November 2009.

E.M. Rogers, *Diffusion of Innovations*, 5th edn (New York: The Free Press, 2003).

G. Roushan, 'Senior Academic at Bournemouth University Business School', Personal email interview 13 October (2009).

M. Ryan, *16 Ways to use Second Life in your Classroom: Pedagogical Approaches and Virtual Assignments* Available at: http://www.lancs.ac.uk/postgrad/ryanm2/ SLEDcc08_ryan_paper.pdf Accessed: 18 August 2009 (2008).

P. Saettler, *A History of Instructional Technology* (New York: McGraw-Hill Book Company, 1968).

Second Life, *Raw Statistics* Available at: http://secondlife.com/statistics/economy-data.php Accessed: 13 October 2009 (2009a).

Second Life, *The Marketplace* Available at: http://secondlife.com/whatis/market-place.php Accessed: 13 October 2009 (2009b).

SimTeach, *SimTeach: Main Page* Available at: http://www.simteach.com/wiki/index. php?title=Main_Page Accessed: 10 October 2009 (2009).

W. Sobkowiak, 'Personal email interview', Professor at School of English, Adam Mickiewicz University, 24 June (2009).

J. Stafford, 'Personal email interview', R&D Coordinator, Teaching & Learning Technology, Winona State University, 23 June (2009).

The Bible. *Deuteronomy* 6:6–9.

L. Tobin, 'A whole new world of studying', *Guardian Newspaper*, 21 April (2009), Available at: http://www.guardian.co.uk/education/2009/apr/21/elearning-university-of-london Accessed: 13 October 2009.

University of Warwick, *Understanding Shakespeare's Sonnets* (2009) Available at: http://www.youtube.com/watch?v=LqOrZItROxs Accessed: 13 October 2009.

Virtuosity Magazine, Home Page Available at: http://www.virtualworlded.com Accessed: 29 September (2009).

Voice over the Internet Protocol: telephony service over the Internet.

S. Warburton, *Herding Cats* (2008) Available at: http://warburton.typepad.com/ liquidlearning/2008/11/herding-cats.html Accessed: 19 December 2008.

K. Warwick, *The Next Step Towards True Cyborgs?* (2005) Available at: http://www. kevinwarwick.com/Cyborg2.htm Accessed: 12 October 2009.

WikiMedia Foundation *Home* (2009). Available at: http://wikimediafoundation.org/ wiki/Home Accessed: 12 October 2009.

Wikiversity, *Welcome to Wikiversity* (2009a). Available at:http://en.wikiversity.org/ wiki/Wikiversity:Main_Page Accessed: 12 October 2009.

Wikiversity, *Wikiversity School of Business* (2009b). Available at: http://en.wikiversity. org/wiki/Business_school Accessed: 12 October 2009.

Wikiversity, *Master of Business Administration* (2009c). Available at: http://en.wiki-versity.org/wiki/MBA Accessed: 12 October 2009.

Wired *You Play World of Warcraft? You're Hired!* (2006) Available at: http://www.wired.com/wired/archive/14.04/learn.html Accessed: 26 September 2007.

G. Woodill, *Webinar: The History of Classrooms as a Learning Technology* (2009) [Blog entry: 10 August 2009] Available at: http://brandon-hall.com/garywoodill/?p=177 Accessed: 20 October 2009.

YouTube *YouTube Education* (2009) Available at: http://www.youtube.com/edu Accessed: 13 October 2009.

7

Virtual Action Learning: A New Genre for Powerful Learning

Ghislaine Caulat

Background

Over the last four years the practice of Action Learning at Ashridge Consulting has gone through a considerable change, namely a significant amount of Action Learning sessions are now delivered virtually. Since 2005 we have worked with more than 12 global organisations and more than 1,200 participants. Action Learning has in itself a long, successful tradition. Originated by Professor Reginald Revans in the United Kingdom in the 1940s this learning format enables groups of up to six managers to present their respective 'issues' (an issue can be, for example, a strategic decision that one needs to take, a challenging operational problem, or an interpersonal difficulty with a colleague) and through a process of questioning and feedback by peers the 'issue holder' (the person presenting the issue) obtains useful challenge and support to develop a deeper understanding of the issue at hand, which often results in finding a different approach to address it. The process is usually facilitated by an experienced process consultant. In some cases Action Learning groups carry on for several years and self-facilitate.

Generally, people's first reaction when one mentions the possibility of attending an Audio or Virtual Action Learning[1] session is one of scepticism. The sheer idea that this can happen virtually is in most people's view simply not possible:

> *But I need to see people in the eyes to get a sense of how they react to my question!, How can I work well if I don't see people's body language?* and so on...

---

[1]We will explain later on in this chapter the difference that we make at Ashridge Consulting between Audio and Virtual action Learning.

However, experience is showing us that once people have engaged with Audio or Virtual Action Learning they soon embrace it and see its advantages. A typical reaction of a participant would be:

> *It was a very good experience. I have got out of it more than I expected. It was a most positive surprise to me that it works.*

Being successful in the virtual space requires that the Audio/Virtual Action Learning sessions are facilitated in a professional and adequate fashion, which is in some critical aspects different from the face-to-face variant. Before exploring the key parameters of successful Virtual Action Learning facilitation and what this means for the role of the Audio/Virtual Action Learning facilitator, we would like to offer a few examples of Audio/Virtual Action Learning work that we have done with clients.

Examples of use of Audio/Virtual Action Learning

The most common use of Audio Action Learning is between face-to-face modules. In a recent case, I and three colleagues delivered four Audio Action Learning sessions as a complementary intervention interspersed with three face-to-face modules in the context of a Leadership programme for new talents in a multinational. Figure 7.1 below shows the structure of the work.

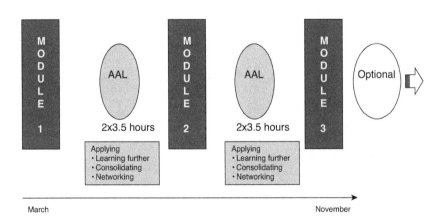

Figure 7.1 An example of how Audio Action Learning is interwoven into a traditional development programme and helps to ensure learning application and consolidation in the workplace

The above example represents a rather typical case where the Audio Action Learning sessions happen between modules and serve a purpose of transferring the learning from the classroom into the manager's day-to-day reality, developing and strengthening a learning network in-between the face-to-face modules. Participants are often very enthused when they learn theoretical models in a workshop because they develop a sense of how these could help them with their work. However on returning to work, reality kicks in and it is often difficult to apply the learning: their good intentions succumb to day-to-day priorities. With Audio or Virtual Action Learning support, participants are reminded on a regular basis to apply their learning and are asked to reflect on their learning in the group afterwards. Peer pressure combined with the virtual process of Action Learning offers a 'just in time' challenge and support function, helping participants consolidate and use their learning from the workshops. Audio/Virtual Action Learning also helps to develop sustainable learning structures. The idea is that after programme completion the Audio Action Learning sets have developed into learning networks that are sufficiently robust to continue, at the participants' wish, for as long as they want through the organisation. Practice shows that while this doesn't always happen mainly for reasons of prioritisation, we have several cases in which sets are continuing to meet virtually and discuss their issues on a regular basis for an unlimited timeframe.

In another example of Audio Action Learning, we worked with the HR managers of a major global engineering company, supporting them in their transition from a traditional HR role into an HR Business Partnering role and in strengthening their newly acquired skills and capabilities (learned during the HR programme at Ashridge) while applying them on the job (see Figure 7.2 below). Audio Action Learning provided a platform for them to continue practicing their consulting skills on and with each other. The

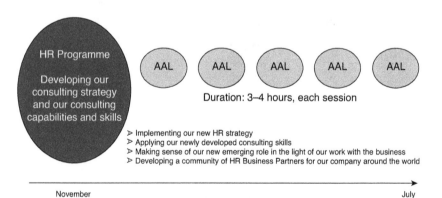

Figure 7.2   An example of how Audio Action Learning became the platform to implement a new strategy

aim was to establish several learning groups of HR Business Partners who would develop into a networked community of HR practitioners across the organisation.

When is Audio Action Learning and when is Virtual Action learning appropriate?

We deliver Audio Action Learning sessions using a teleconferencing platform that we have carefully selected for the quality of the phone lines over an extended amount of time (our session may last up to four hours) and across different locations and time zones. In some of our Audio Action Learning work we involve people in the most remote and least connected countries, including Kazakhstan, Uzbekistan and parts of Africa. We have opted for synchronous delivery (all participants work at the same time) because we feel that this is the most appropriate medium in which to practice Action Learning virtually (as opposed to asynchronous, where participants work in their own time, for example in the form of emails or web-based exchange). Nevertheless we have learnt that the choice of the medium is critical even when working synchronously.

Experience has shown us that the most appropriate platform for Action Learning work where participants bring a personal issue to work on is a teleconferencing setting when people have only the audio channel to connect and work with each other: we call this Audio Action Learning. On the other hand, we have learnt that when people choose Action Learning to work on a project common to the team, it is best to use a web-based platform in addition to the audio connection so that people can at the same time view and work together on documents: we call this Virtual Action Learning. We have had cases where we colluded with the client's wish to use a web-based platform for participants to work on personal issues and we experienced that the platform became more a distracter than an enabler and people were less focused on their peers' issues. On the other hand, we have tried to help several teams of a financial services client which, due to extremely strict security regulation, didn't want to use a web-based platform and preferred to stick to an audio-only environment. The teams were all working on a specific project and the lack of document support and reliance on audio alone hindered the team members' efforts to connect and think together on the subject matter. In other words, we have learnt over the years that choosing the right communication media and ensuring highest quality of the line are critical success factors.

The benefits of Audio/Virtual Action Learning

There are some obvious benefits to Audio/Virtual Action Learning due to the simple fact that the work happens virtually: savings in terms of carbon footprint, travel and accommodation costs and time spent NOT travelling (which often proves to be the most significant saving, particularly for extremely busy managers and leaders).

There are further obvious benefits. For example, given the fact that work can happen across geographies it is easier to form and work with highly diverse groups (in terms of roles, genders, functions and cultures), which we would always privilege as we know that the higher the diversity in the group the better the learning outcomes.

Be heard but not seen: Connecting with others at a deeper level

There are other benefits of Audio/Virtual Action Learning that go far beyond the obvious and these are precisely linked to the virtual nature of the format. Participants very often notice already at the first session that the quality of listening in the virtual environment is of a much higher standard. Due to the fact that participants are not distracted by each other's physical appearance and by the environment, once they have managed to overcome this lack of visual cues and clues, people soon come to see it as a real enabler. They feel that they don't need to pay attention to visual group work conventions (e.g. sitting properly on a chair – they can lie on their bed or walk through the room instead as this might help them to concentrate better) and that they can focus much better on each other. One participant said:

It's much easier to focus in such an intense way with only a notepad in front of me.

For her it was easier to concentrate on what was being said and to make notes without the need to maintain eye contact:

It was easier to get into the key areas...it felt more intense and led to deep insights.

Another participant mentioned to me recently:

Before I thought that I was a good listener but now I know what good listening really means. I cannot hear my colleagues any longer when they claim to be good listeners. They need to attend a Virtual Action Learning session first, then they will know. Also now I struggle with the way we lead our meetings face-to-face; I don't like the way we interact with each other. We don't listen to each other. We truly don't!

These few examples are supported by evidence from other practitioners and researchers.

Val Williams, an experienced virtual facilitator and coach, writes:

> *In fact sometimes we can miss the essence of a person's message while trying to read body language. Body language can sometimes take away from listening'* (2002: 20).

When participants start in an Audio/Virtual Action learning set they often report after the first hour of work in the virtual space how frustrated they are by the lack of visual clues and body language. Some even mention that this type of work goes against popular wisdom of communication and ignores the famous 80 per cent – 20 per cent rule, by which 80 per cent of meaning making is supposed to happen through body language while only 20 per cent through words. It should be noted that this is a major simplification and misinterpretation of findings by Albert Mehrabian (1971) that has developed over time and imposed itself as major wisdom. Albert Mehrabian's research was concerned only with specific situations when people were talking about their feelings and attitudes. On his webpage (www.kaaj.com/psych/smorder.html) Mehrabian clearly states this:

> *(...) Total Liking = 7% Verbal Liking + 38% Vocal Liking + 55% Facial Liking: Please note that this and other equations regarding relative importance of verbal and nonverbal messages were derived from experiments dealing with communications of feelings and attitudes (i.e., like-dislike). Unless a communicator is talking about their feelings or attitudes, these equations are not applicable.*

Further research in the topic emphasises much more the importance of listening as a way to access the other's core.

From a Gestalt perspective, Fritz Perls (1969b: 73) explains how key the voice is as an expression of the essence of a person. He claims that:

> *self-expression comes out somewhere else (other than verbal communication), in our movements, in our posture, and most of all in our voice. A good therapist doesn't listen to the content of the bullshit the patient produces, but to the sound, to the music, to the hesitations... The real communication is beyond words.*

For John Heron:

> *The voice has direct access to this original being* (1999: 236).

The voice:

> *is pregnant with whom you really are* (1999: 234).

Carole Gilligan, who developed the so-called Listening Guide as a method of psychological analysis, also underlines the importance of the voice:

> *Thus, each person's voice is distinct – a footprint of the psyche, bearing the marks of the body, of that person's history, of culture in the form of language, and the myriad ways in which human society and history shape the voice and thus leave their in-prints on the human soul (Gilligan, 1993)* (2006: 253–254).

She then demonstrates that listening to the voice of somebody is a crucial way of entering truly into a relationship with the other person.

When participants start working in an Audio/Virtual Action Learning format they soon realise how much they still need to train their listening in order to hear the several components of the voice (pitch, tone, rhythm, etc.). The role of the Audio/Virtual Action Learning facilitator is to help them learn to listen more carefully beyond the words. Often after three or so sessions participants come to me and tell me that they have achieved a deeper level of listening. For example, when a friend calls they quickly notice whether s/he is well or sick, nervous or tired before even asking how s/he is doing. They would then say what they heard (or what they were 'reading' in the voice) and the friend would react:

> *how do you know?*

Listening in this way in the virtual space is a way to connect intensively with somebody, not only at the intellectual level but at the emotional level, particularly in the virtual environment where there are no visual distracters. Multi-layer listening is like a muscle that can be exercised to become more effective.

Critical success factors

Over the past four years of practice, we have learnt that in order to lead successfully a process of Audio/Virtual Action Learning the facilitator needs to be aware of and actively work on the following parameters:

Leading a process and not only a session

One key difference between face-to-face Action Learning and Audio/Virtual Action Learning is that the facilitator needs to lead the process and also remain present between the sessions in order to keep the momentum going for participants. While in the face-to-face paradigm the facilitator would normally concentrate on the session and make sure that there is a clear date and meeting location for it, this effort does not suffice for Audio/ Virtual Action Learning. It is necessary to remind participants of their learning commitment to each other, of their learning so far and of the next session together. The more the facilitator does this, the lower the chance that participants drop out at the last minute. We have found that the cancellation rate is much higher in the virtual paradigm than in the face-to-face paradigm. There are some practical explanations for this: since no travel or accommodation bookings are involved, there are no cancellation fees and people find it less difficult to cancel. Also there might be a lot of pressure from the environment on the participant and if there is, for example, the need to attend an urgent last minute meeting in the office, colleagues and supervisors find it difficult to understand why the participant is going to spend four hours on the phone instead. For most people, virtual working and/or virtual learning is less real than face-to-face.

Working against the teleconferencing etiquette

Audio/Virtual Action Learning is a powerful learning format when it comes to quickly establishing intimate and trusting connections between participants. In part this is linked to the very nature of the connection. However, there are other aspects that need careful facilitation and awareness. The main challenge for participants and the facilitator in Audio/Virtual Action Learning is to learn to work against the traditional teleconferencing etiquette. Participants need to be encouraged to become spontaneous online, and not to be afraid of interrupting each other. In traditional teleconferences we have learned to work according to a clear agenda and to let another person finish speaking before speaking oneself. There is the expectation of a rather rigid and agenda-based process, which does not allow for the spontaneity of communication and real conversations that are so critical to establishing trust and intimacy (Caulat, 2006).

Trust in the virtual space: An evolving concept

The concept of trust in the virtual space has evolved considerably over the last years. While most people were of the opinion that one needed to have met a person face-to-face first before being able to trust them (Handy, 1995; Lipnack and Stamps, 1997) there are now more and more voices (for example Kirkman et al., 2002) claiming that prior face-to-face meetings are not necessarily as critical as they are claimed to be. This certainly corresponds with our own experience. The factors that do impact on the development of trust in an Audio/Virtual Action Learning session are linked with reliability (do people call at the agreed time?), presence and focus in the virtual space (do people really listen? How dedicated are they to others' learning?) and openness and spontaneity (how open are they regarding their issue, and do they dare say something spontaneously, risking speaking at the same time as somebody else or interrupting?).

Preserving a certain degree of anonymity can foster openness and paradoxically speed up the building of trust in the group. In one experiment with Audio Action Learning (De Haan and Caulat, 2006) a participant declared:

> *In a sense it is better not to know the people at all and to be completely unconnected to them... Then it matters less if they judge you... You have nothing to lose... So I would love to join a fully anonymous Audio Action Learning group.*

The aspect of anonymity and how it helps groups become more open in virtual settings has also been recognised with respect to virtual team work (McFadzean and McKenzie, 2001). As John Suler (2004) explains, people say and do things virtually that they wouldn't ordinarily say or do in the face-to-face world. They loosen up, feel less inhibited and express themselves more openly. Suler (2004) calls this the 'disinhibition effect'. Sometimes people share very personal things about themselves. They reveal secret emotions, fears and wishes.

Group dynamics in Audio/Virtual Action Learning

Also linked to the lack of physical boundaries is the phenomenon of 'confluence' that we have experienced several times over our years of practice of Audio/Virtual Action Learning. We found out that people tend to go more quickly into a kind of psychological symbiosis with others in the Action Learning (Caulat and De Haan, 2006). It is particularly difficult when participants 'go in confluence' with the person presenting the issue: there is 'confluence' when the presenter's issue suddenly becomes someone else's issue as well. In other words the participants have lost the distance to the 'issue holder' and, as a result, cannot help effectively any longer. Needless to say, this is even more risky when the facilitator himself/herself goes in confluence with the issue holder and/or other participants. This might end up with a situation where nobody knows any longer who the issue holder is, who helps who and this might leave the issue holder in a particularly vulnerable position. To avoid this we have developed a focus exercise that enables people to anchor themselves strongly in the physical awareness of their own bodies before we start the Audio/Virtual Action Learning work as a way to counterbalance the lack of physical boundaries and strengthen the sense of one's identity and boundaries.

Working with silences

As Nicki Panteli (2005) observes, unfortunately very little has been done so far to study silence in the face-to-face working and learning paradigm, and even less in the virtual space. What is clear, however, is that silence plays a very important role in Audio/Virtual Action Learning. It is absolutely critical for the Audio/Virtual Action Learning facilitator to learn how to work with silences. First of all silence has a very different meaning depending on the culture of the participants: while it is generally perceived as 'absence' and counterproductive in Western culture, it is often seen as a necessity to preserve harmony and respect in Asian cultures (Gudykunst and Nishida, 1984; Morsbach, 1973 and Sano et al., 1999).

Second, we found out that precisely because the virtual/audio environment leads to slower and deeper sense making silences are often pregnant with a richness of thoughts and emotions that need to be given time and space to unfold at their own pace and rhythm. Hence it is important that the facilitator notices the pregnant pauses, normalises them (by inviting people to notice the silence and be curious about it) instead of wanting to break the silence too fast. Furthermore we have learned that breaking the silence by asking a person what s/he thinks can feel pretty abrupt in the virtual space and people might feel 'put on the spot' in a rather unhelpful way. On the other hand, interventions such as remaining silent, then:

I am noticing the silence and I want to let it unfold

and/or:

I am wondering what this silence tells us: are people feeling tired or unsure whether...?

might lead to powerful insights about the issue presented and/or about the group's current dynamics and perception. In other words, enabling participants to speak about the silence in the group helps draw out, at times, deep streams of consciousness that when shared help the group to enter a deeper level of reflection at a deeper level of connection between members.

Third, linked to the above, I would like to draw attention to Foulkes' (1975) concept of 'matrix', dealing with group psychoanalysis. According to Foulkes, a group is not just a collection of individual's unconsciousness, but has a common unconscious, revealing itself in the 'matrix'. Foulkes speaks of 'resonance' as if individuals in a group would be connected to each other by a web of mental processes which joins them and passes through them. This web would create the social fabric with which each individual would resonate, attuned at an individual specific level but in accordance with the group's shared themes. Hence exploring the silence in the group would correspond to becoming more aware and voicing this web of processes.

Haim Weinberg (2006) builds on Foulkes' concept of 'matrix' and develops the concept of 'social unconscious' on the internet. Weinberg doesn't consider that groups are social systems with a brain, but rather:

> *In the same manner that unconscious forces drive an individual without knowing it, a group, an organisation or the entire society can act upon unconscious forces too* (2006: 96).

He continues:

> *(...) the Social Unconscious is the co-constructed shared unconscious of members of a certain social system such as a community, society, nation or culture. It includes shared anxieties, fantasies, defences, myths, and memories* (2006: 99).

I can strongly relate to these concepts in my own experience of Audio/Virtual Action Learning when I have found myself, for example, overcome by a strong sense of convergence with others and a powerful emotional field that cannot be attributed to single individuals in the group. This sense of convergence is generated particularly in the interplay between silence (or what I would like to call 'pregnant pauses of meaning') and explicit verbal interaction.

As a way to conclude on this important aspect, I posit that this third aspect adds strongly to the need to consider silences and work with them as very precious moments in the Audio/Virtual Action Learning space as they might be the key to uncovering deep levels of wisdom in the group.

At this stage we should also note that these considerations about silence might also apply to face-to-face Action Learning but have not been made explicit so far. However, they appear to be particularly relevant to Audio/Virtual Action Learning. Perhaps this is why these aspects have only become more explicit now.

Implications for the role of the Audio/Virtual Action Learning facilitator

As discussed, the role of the Audio/Virtual Action Learning facilitator is in some aspects similar to the one of the face-to-face Action Learning facilitator, but is different and specific in other aspects. Audio/Virtual Action Learning is a new genre requiring a different facilitation profile. In the following paragraphs we mention selected aspects that appear critical for successful Audio/Virtual Action Learning facilitation.

Providing a safe container

Due to the lack of physical boundaries leading to people opening up faster, potentially also to expressing more intense emotions, it is absolutely critical that the Audio/Virtual Action Learning facilitator learns how to provide a 'container' that is as safe as possible for the work. This will include contracting with participants upfront and making them aware of the intensity and typical characteristics of the work. In practical terms this means, for example, that the facilitator asks participants to plan in a proper buffer time before and after the session to get into the appropriate mode for the work and then to disconnect and come down properly from the intense session before moving on to another meeting or activity requiring dedicated attention. It also means requesting that participants are in a quiet and comfortable place where they cannot be disturbed for the duration of the session.

Providing a safe container also means for the facilitator that s/he is at all times paying extreme attention to participants' mental and emotional states. In practical terms this requires paying attention to silent participants, listening to what is said and not said and listening to one's own intuition and feelings in the virtual group as an important source of data. This also means that s/he makes sure that participants disconnect well from each other at the end of the session, not only technically by putting the phone down, but more importantly mentally and emotionally as we have seen that connectivity can be deep and intense during a session.

Stronger process focus

In the practice of Action Learning there is an ongoing debate as to whether the facilitator should concentrate exclusively on the process of facilitation or whether s/he can both attend to the process and ask questions to the 'issue holder' (see, for example, Casey, 1987). Our current view is that given the highly demanding nature of Audio/Virtual Action Learning facilitation, the facilitator might be better off concentrating predominantly on the process and enabling the participants to best work with the 'issue holder' in the virtual space. However, we would not advocate this as a strict rule, particularly for groups who have no prior experience of Action Learning and start learning in this format in the virtual space as they will also need guidance and modelling of what good questioning in Action Learning means.

Furthermore, as previously mentioned, some specific measures or exercises are needed to work well with the dynamics of the virtual space. We may recall here the 'focus exercise' that we have devised to help people to develop a strong bodily awareness as a way to counterbalance the lack of physical boundaries. In addition we recommend a dedicated process to enable people to disconnect mentally and emotionally.

Working with the voice

We have explored the importance of the voice as a door into a person's true being, thinking and feeling. We have explained why it is important for participants to listen well to each other's voice. For similar reasons we would also argue that it is very important for the facilitator to become aware of his/her own voice in the virtual space. This begins with becoming aware of one's feelings and emotions before a session as these will clearly 'show' precisely through the voice and will impact on the connectivity with other members. This also means becoming aware of one's voice in general and probing whether it conveys what one wants it to convey. Our argument here is not about manipulation of the voice but about a true acquaintance with one's own voice as a way of integrating this essential personal trait and to actively work with this awareness in the virtual space. One concrete aspect of this would be, for example, when one feels that s/he has a nasal voice that might at times generate an impression of tension and even anxiety, hence work against one's best efforts to provide a safe container for the group. In this case, working on breathing techniques and body posture might help the voice to become more grounded and balanced.

Understanding what enables presence

One key challenge for the facilitator of Audio/Virtual action Learning is the capability to develop a strong presence while working remotely.

The facilitator makes him/ herself present to the others in the virtual space by modelling spontaneity and encouraging others to express themselves spontaneously because, as we have already explored, spontaneity is key to the development of trust. As participants cannot check others' reactions in the virtual space it is important that they receive immediate feedback about what they say. A practical and important behaviour that the facilitator might practice is the 'virtual nod' which is about producing noises such as 'mmmh', 'ah', 'oh', or 'I see' as a way to communicate to the other that s/he is well heard. Although one can encourage participants to practice the 'virtual nod' the latter usually feel this to be an odd practice to start with, so foreign to the conventional teleconferencing etiquette. Therefore it is critical that the facilitator models the practice as a way to help the group developing a new culture of engaging virtually together.

Another important component of one's virtual presence for the facilitator is the active work with silences as already explained.

Finally, an additional key aspect of presence is the need for the facilitator to be present, on email and/or phone, between sessions to actively shape and maintain the flow of communication, and hence keep the learning momentum going, and by inviting the members of the set to do the same.

Perspectives for future research

We hope that by now the reader will be convinced that Audio/Virtual Action Learning, if practiced well, offers considerable potential for learning and represents a new genre in its own right. By now the reader might have also realised that some of the aspects explored also apply to face-to-face Action Learning but that for some unclear reasons the latter have not been made explicit in the literature so far. We would argue that Audio/Virtual Action Learning not only represents a new genre in its own right but also offers a good opportunity to revisit and potentially enhance the work that we as practitioners do in the face-to-face version.

We would also argue that Audio/Virtual Action Learning represents a learning format becoming more and more indispensable for future executive education. Not only because of the obvious benefits for the environment and in terms of time savings mentioned earlier but also because of the flexibility and the focus that it offers. Audio/Virtual Action Learning is highly learner-focused. It provides a 'just in time' learning platform where employees can get together as a group on a relatively short-term notice (no travel and room arrangements are needed) and get help from their Audio/Virtual Action Learning Group as they need it.

Unfortunately so far very little research has been done on Audio/Virtual Action learning apart from exploring current emerging practices (Dickenson, M., Pedler, M., and Burgoyne, J., 2010).

We foresee great potential in exploring the following areas:

1. **Audio/Virtual Action Learning for new generations:** From our work with High Potentials in multinationals we know that communicating and connecting with others in a virtual environment is normal for them. However, what about virtual learning? In our experience so far, the key challenge of developing trust virtually so that people feel safe enough to open up and learn at a deep level remains pertinent for younger generations. Furthermore, the challenge of giving priority to slowing down and reflecting above the day-to-day pressure of decision-making also remains and younger generations need to learn this too. We see interesting and important research activities in the exploration of how the virtual social networking that youngsters practice on a regular basis (both asynchronously and synchronously) might promote and/or get in the way of Audio/Virtual Action Learning: What will be 'good' habits to build on for virtual learning and what will need to be learnt differently? Conversely, what can be learnt from youngsters' practice of connecting virtually for the virtual learning formats of the future?

2. **Benefits and risks of 'disembodied' relationships:** Much has been broadcast in the media about the risks and dangers of disembodied relationships and most of us will have come across stories describing how people might

abuse these. So far our experience has shown that actually disembodied relationships represent a true learning potential because, as explained on previous pages, participants sometimes open up quicker and deeper. As Christine Hine (2000) points out: Rather than focusing on how technology enables and might lead to the dark side of disembodied relationships, it is more important to focus the research attention on the contexts in which the technology is used. She advocates, as we do, that we look to the virtual space not only as a formative place where new ways of working and learning are created, but also as a cultural artefact, which is nothing more than a further expression of how specific groups of people think and behave.

3. **The use of technology in helping Action Learning develop**: Experience has taught us the hard way that the choice of the appropriate technology for Audio and Virtual Action Learning is paramount. We strongly believe that the chosen learning format should dictate the choice of technology and not *vice-versa*. However, in the web-based environment that we use for Virtual Action Learning technology offers some interesting features (e.g. the opportunity for participants to chat on a one-to-one basis without others noticing it) that, if well reflected upon and integrated in the learning format, might actually contribute to mature Audio/Virtual Action Learning even further.

Conclusion

With Audio/Virtual Action Learning the future of learning has already started, and practice shows convincing outcomes. The challenge that we see now is not about the didactic approach itself, nor about the technology. It is more about spreading this new emerging format on a wider scale. As we know, and have demonstrated in this chapter, learners have substantial doubts, hesitations or even prejudices when it comes to learning with others virtually and embarking on Audio/Virtual Action Learning and these should not be underestimated. People will overcome their fears only if they have a positive experience of Audio/Virtual Action Learning. While future generations who have grown up in a virtual world of communication might have fewer fears, the basic challenges of establishing trust and setting the right pace for learning in the virtual space will remain. Much will come down to the facilitators of this new format who will need to overcome their own barriers and develop robust skills and capabilities to enthuse the present and future generations.

References

D. Casey, 'Breaking the shell that encloses your understanding', *Journal of Management Development*, Vol. 6, No. 2 (1987).

G. Caulat, 'Creating trust in intimacy in the virtual world', *Converse*, Issue 4 (2006), 8–10.

G. Caulat, and E. De Haan, 'Virtual peer consultation: How virtual leaders learn', *Organization and People*, November, Vol. 13, No. 4 (2006).

M. Dickenson, M. Pedler and J. Burgoyne, 'Virtual action learning – A new frontier?', in S. Voller, E. Blass, and V. Culpin (eds), *The Future of Learning: Innovations and Insights from Executive Education* (Basingstoke: Palgrave Macmillan, 2010).

S.H. Foulkes, *Group Analytic Psychotherapy, Method and Principles* (London: Gordon & Breach, 1975).

C. Gilligan, *In a Different Voice: Psychological Theory and Women's Development* (Cambridge Mass: Harvard University Press, 1993).

W.B. Gudykunst and T. Nishida, 'Individual and cultural influences on uncertainty reduction', *Communication Monographs*, 51 (1984), 26–36.

C. Handy, 'Trust and the virtual organization', *Harvard Business Review*, Vol. 73, No. 3 (1995), 40–50.

J. Heron, *The Complete Facilitator's Handbook* (London: Kogan Page, 1999).

C. Hine, *Virtual Ethnography* (London: Sage Publications Ltd, 2000).

B. Kirkman, B. Rosen, C. Gibson, P. Teshik and S. Mcpherson, 'Five challenges to virtual team success: Lessons from Sabre, Inc.', *Academy of Management Executive*, Vol. 16, No. 3 (2002), 67–79.

J. Lipnack and J. Stamps, *Virtual Teams: Reaching Across Space, Time, and Organizations with Technology* (London: John Wiley & Sons, 1997).

E. McFadzean and J. McKenzie, 'Facilitating virtual learning groups: A practical approach', *Journal of Management Development*, Vol. 20, No. 6 (2001).

A. Mehrabian, *Silent Messages: Implicit Communication of Emotions and Attitudes* (Belmont, CA: Wadsworth, 1971).

H. Morschbach, 'Aspects of nonverbal communication in Japan', *The Journal of Nervous and Mental Disease*, 157 (1973), 266–277.

N. Panteli and S. Fineman, 'The sound of silence: The case of virtual team organizing', *Behaviour & Information Technology*, Vol. 24, No. 5 (2005), 347–352.

N. Sano, S. Yamaguschi and D. Mutsumoto, 'Is silence golden? A cross-cultural study on the meaning of silence', *Progress in Asian Social Psychology: Theoretical and Empirical Contributions*, T. Sugiman, M. Karasawa, J. Liu and C. Ward (eds), 145–155 (New York: Wiley, 1999).

J. Suler, *CyberPsychology and Behavior*, Vol. 7 (2004), 321–326. Available from: www.rider.edu/suler/psycyber/psycyber

H. Weinberg, 'Group analysis, large group and the internet unconscious', *PhD thesis* (Manchester: Metropolitan University, 2006).

8
Virtual Action Learning – A New Frontier?

Mollie Dickenson, Mike Pedler and John Burgoyne

Introduction

Virtual Action Learning (VAL) is an emerging variety of Action Learning (AL), which is usually practised face-to-face (f2f) in small groups known as 'sets'. VAL has been defined as:

> *Action learning which takes place in a virtual environment...via a range of enabling, interactive and collaborative communication technologies* (Dickenson et al., 2008)

Action Learning (AL) evolved from Revans' pioneering work with peer-to-peer management learning in the UK coal industry after the Second World War (Revans, 1982: 30–55). AL promotes experiential learning through the addressing of specific organisational problems and is now increasingly popular as a medium for the development of managers and leaders around the world (Revans, 1980, 1997, 1998, Pedler, 2008). The opportunity for VAL arises from a confluence of three recent developments: (i) a shift towards more work-based and context-sensitive approaches to managerial and leadership development; (ii) advances in communications technologies that enable more collaborative communication; and (iii) the effects of globalisation, including especially the emergence of multi-national and dispersed organisations.

Although there is an established and growing literature in online and networked learning (e.g. McConnell, 2000), and another related one on virtual teamworking (e.g. Kayworth and Leidner, 2000), little exists on VAL itself. Despite the popularity and prevalence of AL, and the increasing availability of enabling technologies to facilitate its virtual variety, the current literature on VAL is anecdotal, sparse and elusive. At the same time, considerable interest is being expressed by business practitioners, educationalists, trainers and facilitators concerning the need and opportunity for VAL, especially in dispersed organisational settings. Currently, various barriers appear to be hindering its uptake, perhaps especially the lack of reliable and widely available technologies and the understanding of how to go about adapting AL to VAL.

The research on which this chapter is based was conducted via a literature review, a network inquiry and interviews with VAL practitioners. This chapter explores what is happening in practice and presents a framework for understanding VAL, its current forms and the skills and capabilities required for its facilitation. We also discuss whether VAL is simply replicating f2f AL or leading to a new form of AL, and raise some of the questions that might usefully be pursued in connection with this emerging practice.

The opportunity for Virtual Action Learning

The opportunity for VAL arises from a confluence of three recent developments: (i) a shift towards more work-based and context-sensitive approaches to managerial and leadership development; (ii) advances in communications technologies that enable more collaborative communication; and (iii) the effects of globalisation, including especially the emergence of multi-national and dispersed organisations.

Work-based and context-sensitive approaches stem from open learning theories (Coffey, 1977) and seek to remove the barriers to learning from time, place and space, to offer flexibility and choice for learners in a supported environment and to give access to those excluded from conventional training. Approaches may be formal or informal (Eraut, 2004) but recognise that 'the workplace offers as many opportunities for learning as the classroom' (Raelin, 2008: 2). Work-based learning (WBL) emphasises 'conscious reflection on actual experience' (Raelin, 2008: 2); involves structured, goal-oriented, social co-participation (Billett, 2002); learning from others in informal learning workgroups as communities of practice (Boud and Middleton, 2003); and can be guided or self-directed (Simons, 2004). WBL is 'embedded in the workplace and is designed to meet the learning needs of the employees and the aims of the organisation' (Sobiechowska and Maish, 2006: 270) with many businesses forming partnerships with education providers to help support the process through innovative learning practices in the workplace (Rhodes and Shiel, 2007).

Technology has enabled new ways of working by breaking down time and place dependence, and supporting the move to a more mobile and flexible workforce, often comprising distributed teams (Birchall and Lyons, 1995). Organisations have embraced the virtualisation of working practices and the acquisition of appropriate skills and capabilities as a business imperative in an increasingly global marketplace where only those businesses able to adapt will survive and flourish.

Bowles and Gintis (1975) have proposed that educational practice mirrors and corresponds to the social, cultural and economic conditions of the day: virtual learning emerges in parallel with the virtualisation of work, just as the rows of desks in the Victorian classroom mirrored those of the clerks in the office. Technology has already facilitated many forms of virtual learning in formal and informal distance learning programmes, in education, business and in social contexts. With virtual working and virtual learning now commonplace, the opportunity for VAL afforded by the confluence of developments, by those who can adapt their teaching and learning approaches, now seems considerable.

Although technology and educational thinking have developed greatly in recent years, educational practice has been much slower to adapt. Changing ideas about the status and nature of knowledge and the access afforded to it from advances in information and communications technologies have outstripped educational practice. Amongst the reasons for this are the lack of experience, training and understanding about the use of active, constructionist approaches to teaching and learning, and ways to use new technology to support such approaches (Hodgson, 2000: 4). In this light, although VAL might seem to be a naturally emerging form of AL with wide applications to managerial, leadership and organisational development, the adaptation of AL to VAL is not straightforward.

The emergence of Virtual Action Learning

VAL's roots date back to the late 1980s where, for example, McConnell and Hodgson (1990) discuss a proposal for introducing 'computer-mediated communications systems' into a range of management programmes at Lancaster University. These included the MA in Management Learning (MAML), which already used AL, and made use of email and the British Universities JANET network. VAL emerges conceptually in the late 1990s (Teare, 1998; Gray, 1999), with examples of practice reported from the early 2000s. However, the term VAL is rarely found, perhaps because VAL appears in a range of different contexts, for example in reports on new ways of working or in new ways of using technology in educational contexts.

The increasing evidence of VAL practice reveals various innovative adaptations, mirroring the tradition of AL, which has demonstrated a mutable versatility whilst remaining essentially as conceived by Revans, a form of learning by doing where 'managers may learn, with and from each other, how to manage in the course of their daily tasks' (in Pedler et al., 2005). AL has been described as a new paradigm: 'a revolution in thinking about management education' (McLaughlin and Thorpe, 1993: 21). Revans conceived AL as a solution to the post-war economic crisis and always resisted a precise definition, acknowledging the scope for experimentation. He recognised the importance of learning for organisational survival: 'In any epoch of rapid change, organisations unable to adapt are soon in trouble, and adaptation is achieved only by learning' (Revans, 1983: 11). The essence of Revans' approach is to develop the capacity to ask fresh questions in order to improve future actions, and AL continues to attract controversy because of its championing of the ideas of practitioners or action learners over those of experts and teachers.

With advancing technology as both the creator and enabler of change and innovation, adapting AL to virtual environments may be regarded as both worthy and timely. Whilst in AL, learning is achieved through active participation in the dialogical and synchronous 'set' process, VAL requires the translation of this process into the virtual context 'via a range of, enabling, collaborative communication technologies' (Dickenson et al., 2009). Whilst this might seem straightforward, the paucity of research evidence suggests that it is not.

VAL assumes a form of viable technology to facilitate virtually the processes typically used in f2f AL, including collaboration and interaction. Some authors question whether current technologies are fit for this purpose (e.g. Dunning et al., 2000), whilst others are concerned with the impact of technology on the learning process (e.g. Arbaugh and Duray, 2002; Jones et al., 2006). There are two streams of work which are especially relevant to our quest for a viable VAL methodology: (i) experience with virtual teams and team working, and (ii) research on e-learning and virtual learning.

(i) Virtual teams

Virtual groups or teams also owe their emergence to the increasing pervasiveness of enabling technologies. They operate across time, distance and organisational boundaries and imply more self-direction, less direct supervision, more diversity and less hierarchical structures (Gill and Birchall, 2004: 2–3). From this rapidly expanding literature, we can conclude that virtual team working offers great opportunities for expanding on approaches and ideas, enables faster knowledge transfer (Kayworth and Leidner, 2000) and more fluid and flexible organisation (Jarvenpaa and Leidner, 1999) but also presents various challenges such as building cohesion, developing synergy and monitoring team work (Paré and Dubé, 1999); developing social relationships due to the depersonalisation effects of virtual communication (Sproull and Keisler, 1986); establishing a team culture and individual affiliation (Pauleen and Yoong, 2001a, 2001b); managing sense-making, information and feedback (DeSanctis and Monge, 1999); achieving shared goals and providing a sense of satisfaction and controlling people and activities (Wright and Barker, 2000).

The facilitation of virtual teams plays an important part in their success but demands new and critical skills: virtual communication skills amongst team members are vital to developing the trust and collaboration to function effectively; whilst learning to initiate, build relationships and generally facilitate virtual teams can be a complex and difficult experience (Pauleen and Yoong, 2004; Gill and Birchall, 2004).

(ii) Virtual learning

Virtual learning has evolved from the early use of electronic technologies such as radio, television, tapes and CDs to support individual learning, but is still generically referred to as 'e-learning' (electronic learning). With the advent of the internet and its associated learning technologies, e-learning now embraces many different forms of technology-enhanced learning (TEL).

Most e-learning has been disseminational (instructional) rather than dia-logical (collaborative) (Boot and Hodgson, 1987), where content is unilaterally decided by trainers or academic staff and designed for individuals working alone. It tends to be 'based on instructional system design principles that do not foster participative learning or critical, analytical thinking' and views learning as a 'passive, linear activity' in contrast to 'the social co-participation and knowledge-building' view of learning, as typified in action learning (McConnell, 2006: 8–11). Yet, there are now many software systems and virtual learning environments (VLEs) that support on-line collaboration and resource sharing amongst groups and virtual communities. These VLEs offer participant choice over the content and direction and management of their own learning and support more constructionist theories of learning (Hodgson, 2000). Extending the disseminational/dialogical model, McConnell proposes a third mind-set of 'networked collaborative learning' based on a self-directed, self-managed learning community model of teaching and learning:

> *Purposeful e-learning that takes place in groups and communities requires a participatory design that involves an understanding of social constructionism and knowledge building; is based on the development of communities of students, draws on understandings of situated learning and the character of practice; (and) is underpinned by problem-based, exploratory, collaborative and critically reflective practice* (McConnell, 2006: 11).

For teachers and developers, this demands a different relationship with learners, away from the focus on teaching, and towards a focus on the facil-itation of learning. This is not a simple shift and involves an understanding of the nature of knowledge and knowledge construction in groups and communities, and also different expectations and skills including:

> *a change in our view of learning, a change in our view of the role of the teacher or trainer as resource person, facilitator, critical observer and co-expert; and our view of learners, as able, self-managing people who can make decisions about their learning, who can learn in virtual social settings where the empha-sis is on negotiation, collaboration, knowledge-sharing, problem-solving and self-assessment* (McConnell, 2006: 28).

Some authors claim that the learning outcomes from e-learning and virtual working are similar to those in f2f situations (e.g. Yoo et al., 2002), whilst others (e.g. Alavi and Leidner, 2001) go further and suggest that computer-based collaborative learning leads to better learning outcomes and deeper levels of thinking.

However, there are unique challenges in working virtually, not least of which is the impact of technology on the learner's experience, where ease of use and familiarity with the technology have been identified as important (Arbaugh and Duray, 2002). Other observers seem to agree that skilful facilitation is also important, if not critical, particularly for online learning groups, as Armitt et al. (2002: 11) note: 'groups do not spontaneously coalesce to undertake effective in-depth synchronous discussions'. Further, Reimann and Zumback (2006) found that verbal exchanges between members of virtual teams differ greatly from those in f2f situations and specific feedback mechanisms, which a facilitator should encourage, enhance interactions, group well-being and problem-solving outcomes. Salmon (2000) offers a five-step model for teaching and learning online which proposes different 'e-moderating skills' to develop the competences of participants in access and motivation, online socialisation, information exchange, knowledge construction and development.

The virtualisation of action learning

There are a variety of synchronous and asynchronous collaborative communication technologies which may be used to support VAL, ranging from single forms such as audio-only telephone conferencing and text-only email, to more sophisticated combinations of text, audio and visual communication such as Cisco's 'Telepresence' (http://www.cisco.com/cisco/web/UK/solutions/tele_index) already in use in virtual group working.

Various authors argue for the merits of using different forms of VAL. Bird (2006) for example, explores the question of whether an AL community can be created virtually through asynchronous text-based computer-mediated conferencing (CMC). On the basis of a literature review, he notes that some authors believe that text-based communication can even be superior to f2f in creating the type of learning communities which are at the heart of action learning. The main challenge to be overcome in the virtual action learning group, he argues, is the loss of 'co-presence', yet, though it may take more time than in f2f, this can be done via personal disclosure and sharing confidences, hopes and desires in an open and honest fashion (Walther, 1996). Asensio et al. (2000) however found that students tend to take more care in emotional disclosures online, but Bird suggests that the online facilitator, as 'online discourse analyst' can support the disclosure process by analysing, unpacking and deconstructing the words where visual clues are lacking.

Table 8.1 shows a six-form classification of the technological possibilities for VAL, based upon the three media of text, voice and visual, and how set meetings take place, either synchronously or asynchronously. It will be used as a starting point for the categorisation of the examples found from practice that follow:

Table 8.1   VAL: A six-form classification

Temporality / Medium	Synchronous (participant interaction is simultaneous, i.e. within the same finite time period)	Asynchronous (participant interaction delayed, i.e. at different time periods)
TEXT	Form 1: Instant messaging	Form 2: Email; Text messaging
AUDIO	Form 3: Live tele/audio conf Discussion forums Chat rooms	Form 4: Audio recordings
VISUAL	Form 5: Video/web-based conferencing	Form 6: Video recordings

However, our literature review, network inquiry and interviews provided evidence of VAL in practice which reveals a complexity beyond the simplicities of the conceptual classification in Table 8.1. First, the three media, text, audio and visual, are not necessarily used in isolation but are sometimes used together. Specifically, where text and audio are typically used alone, visual always includes audio, and often text. This may relate to evidence from the wider literature that different technologies are used for different purposes. For example, one virtual community is reported using asynchronous discussion forums for sharing ideas, telephone conferencing for updates on team progress, synchronous text-based online discussions to promote social cohesion, and other technologies to allow remote workers to participate in staff meetings (Bradshaw et al., 2004). Others suggest that discussion forums help in providing information, weblogs benefit innovation, and wikis enable the sharing of 'wise practice' (Wagner and Bolloju, 2005).

Secondly, whilst the terms synchronous and asynchronous appear clear, the question arises: how synchronous is synchronous and therefore how should we classify response delays in text messaging? To overcome this dilemma, we classed as synchronous all instant messaging and discussion forums where participants were online at the same time and responses were more or less immediate, whereas we classed situations where participants were not online at the same time and responses were delayed as asynchronous, as in email and other forms of threaded text messaging. But it should be noted that as with combinations of the three media, synchronous and asynchronous approaches were also found to be used in combination.

Thirdly, many of the VAL case examples found included some element of f2f meetings, which reflects a view held by other commentators on virtual working and learning that: 'One of the keys to a successful virtual COP (Community of Practice) is an occasional, non-virtual, face-to-face meeting' (Kimble and Hildreth, 2005: 293).

So, from the conceptual six-form classification, Table 8.2 shows an expanded version, populated with the case examples of VAL practice found in the research (NB although theoretically possible, no examples of forms four and six were found).

Table 8.2 VAL: Analysis of cases in an expanded six-form classification

Temporality / Medium	Synchronous	Asynchronous	Plus f2f element	Examples of VAL practice/data sources
TEXT	Form 1 P	Form 2 A B C D E F G H I J N O T	A B C D E F I K N	A Birch (interview)
				B Gray 1999
				C Birchall et al. series of papers 2004, 2006, 2007a, 2007b; Stewart and Alexander 2006; Giambona and Birchall 2008
VOICE	Form 3 H I K L M N O P T U	Form 4 No examples	H M (sometimes but not always)	D Boydell (interview)
				E Asensio et al. 2000
VISUAL	Form 5 N O P	Form 6 No examples	O	F Symons (interview)
				G De Wolfe Waddill 2006
				H Dixon 1998
3 D VIRTUAL WORLDS	Form 7 Q R S V			I Teare 1998; Sandelands 1999; Ingram et al. 2000; Ingram et al. 2002
				J Ridley and Gravestock (emails + questionnaires)
				K Pauleen series of papers 2001a, 2001b, 2003a, 2003b, 2003–4, 2004; Yoong and Gallupe 2001
				L Burns 2001
				M Caulat 2006 (+ interview); Caulat and de Haan 2006
				N Roche and Vernon 2003
				O Powell 2001
				P Henley trials
				Q Sanders and McKeown 2008
				R McKeown (email and telephone)
				S Arrowsmith et al. 2003
				T Yoong et al. 2006
				U Saxton (interview)
				V Wagner and Rachael 2009

Despite the complexities, the six-form classification, expanded to seven forms based on examples from practice, remains useful; it illustrates some distinct alternatives and demonstrates that, as with AL, there is no single practice but many variations of VAL. In terms of our earlier definition, it spells out the 'range of enabling, collaborative communication technologies' whereby action learning can take place in a virtual environment.

The main findings from this examination of cases are:

1. *The efficacy of VAL should not necessarily be measured against that of f2f AL* – different evaluation criteria may be appropriate. It cannot be assumed, for example, that case examples which combine visual and voice forms are necessarily better than single forms just because they more closely mirror the features present in f2f AL. Practitioners of the various VAL approaches frequently assert that there are different potential benefits and costs involved which make such simple comparisons invalid. Some practitioners do however assert that their VAL practices are superior to f2f AL in certain respects (see six below).

2. *Delivery platforms and the requirements for technical competence by both participants and facilitators.* Birchall and colleagues (Birchall et al., 2004, 2006, 2007a, 2007b; Stewart and Alexander, 2006; Giambona and Birchall, 2008) evaluated several trials of VAL with SME (small- to medium sized enterprise) managers in different European countries. They suggest that the role of the facilitator is more challenging than in f2f AL both with regard to initial set-up and the need to communicate with participants almost on a daily basis. VAL requires technical competencies as well as facilitation skills. Participants reported a reluctance to raise confidential aspects of business and personal effectiveness in online discussion forums compared with f2f meetings. Some participants thought this was age-related, and that a younger generation brought up with web-based learning would be more accepting. The authors note that the principles established for effective AL do not immediately translate to an electronic environment and conclude that, as yet, VAL lacks an appropriate delivery platform.

3. *Simpler technologies may work better.* Delivery platforms offering multiple forms of communication are highly attractive but also contain considerable potential for frustration, distraction and de-motivation. Several cases show the benefits of using proven technologies.

   In one of the first published accounts to use the term VAL, Burns (2001) reports on a set using voice-only audio-conferencing (Form 3) in British Telecom (BT). This comprised six facilitated audio-conferences of up to two and a half hours in length over a three-month period and had no f2f element although some, but not all, participants knew each other. Caulat (2006) and Caulat and de Haan (2006) describe 'audio action learning' (Form 3) with participants who sometimes never meet each other or the facilitator. Caulat confirms the validity of audio-conferencing, citing various advantages over f2f AL, and specifies some specific practices, behavioural rules and 'netiquette' to govern the virtual interaction. Birch (interview 21/6/2007) describes the evolution of AL from f2f to e-mail (Form 3) as part of Continuing Professional Development (CPD) programmes for health professionals at the University of Brighton. E-mail-based VAL now forms the basis of an 18-month qualification programme. Like Caulat (2006), Birch notes that participants prefer simpler and robust technologies over more sophisticated but less reliable options.

4. *Combined and sophisticated VAL technologies can work well.* Roche and Vernon (2003) describe a pilot 'Electronic Advanced Learning Sets' project combining f2f AL (Forms 2, 3 and 5) with a range of virtual support processes to create a virtual learning community for remotely distributed health service managers in Western Australia. Clear preferences emerged from participants: although some preferred f2f to virtual working, e-mail and telephone-conferencing were preferred to video-conferencing because of access and technology problems. DeWolfe Waddill (2006) describes 'Action E-Learning' – an online text-based form (Form 2) in which a prescribed format of week-long discussion cycles involved each person posting their issues and questioning other members. The facilitator/teacher supplied resources and information and asked questions about the learning process. Wagner and Rachael (2009) used the 3D virtual world Second Life (Form 7) to provide an action learning environment where students could enact real business ideas. They used the environment to build businesses and were encouraged to plan actions, implement them, and draw conclusions from their virtual experiences. These authors conclude that such virtual worlds show great promise as highly adaptable action learning platforms – providing a rich environment for learning and exploration that encourages students' imagination, draws their interest and leads to positive learning experiences. However, their claim that completing 'real-world tasks' in an environment where failure costs little but success can be rewarding appears to oppose Revans' insistence on the 'risk imperative' in AL (1998: 8–9) where failure is essential.

5. *A crucial role for facilitation.* Although, as in AL, self-facilitated VAL is clearly possible, most of the cases quoted above have the facilitator as a central figure. Overall, the impression is that facilitation is perhaps more important in VAL than in f2f AL, especially during the early days to create a sense of rapport, trust and safety in the virtual space. The facilitation of VAL involves setting up the process with its enabling communication technologies and also running the virtual programme. Although some authors think there is no fundamental difference between f2f and e-facilitation, most suggest that additional special skills are required to

manage the technology and the process within the virtual environment, including helping participants to:

- understand expectations regarding collaboration
- appropriately self-disclose and share confidences online
- build rapport, trust and expertise in the virtual environment
- develop virtual communication skills such as higher levels of listening, the ability to sense what others are feeling without visual clues and the restriction on dialogue caused by a lack of non-verbal cues and a reduction in the exchange of socio-emotional information
- develop reflexivity and social knowledge construction via unpacking and deconstructing the words develop the collective ability to reflect publicly online.

Given the variety of VAL forms, it is perhaps not surprising that some distinctive stances and styles of facilitation emerge from this research. Whilst multiple stances and styles of facilitation also characterise f2f AL, the alternative technologies for VAL may amplify these differences.

6. *Claimed advantages of VAL*. Most case study respondents suggested that VAL had potential advantages over f2f AL. For example:

- the asynchronous online process allows time for to reflection without managers appearing indecisive
- not having eye contact can help with clarification because it enhances the listening
- the slower pace enables the questioner to design and examine a question before submitting it
- the slower and more measured communication gives participants more time to notice the questions being asked, to think, and to write down
- VAL enables individualised attention online from colleagues and the learning coach
- it may facilitate joint working on tasks – it could be useful to do things graphically on screen together and capture it
- VAL requires more discipline in turn taking thus encouraging all members of a set to participate
- participants develop a variety of skills in written expression, reflection and question formation
- the process stimulates the virtual workplace and participants learn how to work in a virtual team with agreed norms and 'netiquette' and by asking questions before making statements.

Conclusions

VAL emerges from this research as a distinct variety of AL with its own strengths and weaknesses. Opinion is divided on whether it is a substitute for AL ('the next best thing to f2f') where this is impossible or too expensive, or whether it is a new and developing variety of AL with advantages that may lead it to be chosen in preference. Practitioners of various VAL approaches assert their benefits but much more research is needed before firm conclusions are reached. On the basis of this evidence, f2f meetings are not essential in VAL, either beforehand or as part of the process, although they may help as part of a rich mix. The cases where VAL exists without a f2f element report as much success as those supplemented by f2f meetings. However, just as VAL should not necessarily be measured against f2f AL, we caution against any assumptions of the superiority of one form over any other.

VAL is currently evolving within five of the seven forms shown in Table 8.2, with a majority of cases in Form 2 (asynchronous text), the only asynchronous form in evidence. There are no examples of Forms 4 and 6 (asynchronous audio or visual i.e. recordings), although recordings of conversations or collaboratively produced documents can clearly add value to otherwise synchronous meetings. The predominance of Form 2 probably reflects its ease of use, the relatively low demands on time and the wide availability of access to appropriate technology. Currently, 'low tech' strategies such as audio conferencing and text messaging, have clearly proved effective. As one respondent puts it, 'Compared to other technologies none have worked anywhere near as well as email...it needs to be easy and to be easy quickly'.

The arguments for 'low' and 'high' tech routes to VAL will continue. Using readily available and familiar technologies, the former maximise access and minimise new technology learning needs. They are easier to assimilate and may 'interfere' less with interaction. Using more recent technologies makes access more problematic and calls for experience or prior learning before VAL can be productive. 'Hi-tech' forms may promise a richer virtual experience but with potentially higher costs of various sorts.

Whilst VAL is a new frontier in the practice of AL, utilising new techniques and requiring new skills, the examples of VAL do not appear to represent a new frontier in existing AL theory, tending to support rather than change or challenge it.

But whilst technology is in general being used to create virtual forms of existing AL processes, an exception to this is *Second Life* and other 3D virtual environments that raise interesting pragmatic and philosophical questions. For example, where 'action' is virtual, in what sense may it be described as 'real'? Does the experience of action on 'real life problems' in the virtual world produce experiences that yield learning that is transferable outside that world? Does, for example, rehearsing the tackling of a conflict at work via avatars help in the resolution of conflict in 'First Life'? And, how can such virtual action meet Revans' risk imperative criteria for action learning, namely that unless action carries a 'significant risk or penalty for failure' (Revans, 1998: 8) then there can be no significant learning? These and other questions merit much more consideration.

Prospects

At the start of this inquiry in October 2006, evidence of VAL practices were hard to find and existing technologies seemed limited in what they could deliver. Three years on there is an increasing amount of activity, not all of it called VAL or set up expressly for this purpose, with advances both in technologies and in varieties of practice.

VAL has an obvious potential in executive education and in the work-place. It promises a more cost-effective form of training and development, especially in bringing together geographically dispersed individuals. It could make a valuable contribution both in education, as part of the move from disseminational to more dialogical teaching and learning, and in business as a medium for dispersed, informal and work-based group problem-solving. However, to make this contribution there are various challenges to overcome, especially those of the misnamed 'softer' variety concerning the cultural practices of teaching and learning.

In terms of technologies, lap-top-based 'net-meeting' software such as Webex (www.webex.co.uk) can offer both a more sustainable delivery plat-form and a combination of synchronous text audio and visual that could presage a rapid increase in educational and workplace usage. If hi-tech technologies become more commonplace and reliable, VAL may migrate more to these forms and away from the lower tech options. Younger gener-ations of users may come to expect no less. As Pascarella notes: 'teachers face a group of learners who have already engaged in the remaking, remix-ing, and renaming of their world in virtual reality and in their everyday one'; and yet such learners conversant in digital media devices and social networking environments such as YouTube, MySpace and Facebook, 'lack the abilities of critical analysis and evaluation of the social and insti-tutional rules, regulations, and norms embedded in those environments and cultural practices' (Pascarella, 2008: 251).

For a future where learners will expect virtual learning technologies, but are not competent in critical analysis, VAL could come into its own.

But technological acceptance and competence alone does not guarantee collaborative virtual learning. Most e-learning has tended to reinforce 'the dominant features of face-to-face classroom structures' (Friesen and Clifford, 2003: 3). Some authors detect a trend in higher education away from more didactic content delivery towards constructionist student-centred models, with an increasing emphasis on the skills that support independent, self-motivated learning (Cullen et al., 2002; Hobbs et al., 2006). Virtual learning environments (VLEs) are increasingly used to facilitate this shift and to support collaborative learning via areas where students can comment, con-tribute and share their learning. For business schools in particular the quality of the learning experience can be a key differentiator and whilst client organ-isations increasingly utilise new and context specific methods such as AL and coaching, many business schools continue to rely upon more traditional methods. Whilst some staff are aware of the newer learning theories that provide the theoretical underpinning for the newer approaches, this is not usually reflected in their practice (Hodgson, 2000; CEML, 2002).

VAL is a comparatively new practice, and one that seems currently to thrive in isolated pockets of both low and high tech forms. Given the considerable expressed interest and with increasing technological advances and competence, VAL appears poised on a threshold of much wider usage.

References

M. Alavi and D.E. Leidner, 'Research commentary: Technology-mediated learning – A call for greater depth and breadth of research', *Information Systems Research*, Vol. 12, No. 1 (2001), 1–10.

J.B. Arbaugh and R. Duray, 'Technology and structural characteristics, student learning and satisfaction with web-based courses: An exploratory study of two on-line MBA programs', *Management Learning*, Vol. 33, No. 3 (2002), 331–347.

G. Armitt, F. Slack, S. Green, et al., 'The development of deep learning during a synchronous collaborative on-line course', G. Stahl (ed.), *Proceedings of Computer Support for Collaborative Learning Conference* (Boulder, Colorado, USA: Lawrence Erlbaum 2002), 151–158.

C. Arrowsmith, A. Counihan and D. McGreevy, 'Development of a multi-scaled virtual field trip for the teaching and learning of geospatial science', *International Journal of Education and Development using Information and Communication Technology*, Vol. 1, No. 3 (2003), 42–56.

M. Asensio, V. Hodgson and K. Trehan, 'Is there a difference? Contrasting experiences of face to face and online learning', *Proceedings of the 2nd International Conference*, Network Learning (2000).

S. Billett, 'Workplace pedagogic practices: Co-participation and learning', *British Journal of Educational Studies*, Vol. 50, No. 4 (2002), 457–481.

D. Birchall and L. Lyons, *Creating Tomorrow's Organization: Unlocking the Benefits of Future Work* (London: FT Pitman Publishing, 1995).

D. Birchall, G. Giambona and G. Alexander, 'Engaging SME managers in a development programmes based on virtual action learning', Conference paper, *IAS Symposium, Lancaster* (2007a).

D. Birchall, J. Giambona, and G. Alexander (2007b), 'Assessing the outcomes of a cross-country virtual action learning programme for SME development', Conference paper, *ICL 2007*, 26–28 September, Villach, Austria (2007b).

D. Birchall, J. Hender and G. Alexander, 'Virtual action learning for SMEs – A review of experiences gained through the ESEN project', Henley Management College (2004).

D. Birchall, J. Hender, G. Alexander, et al., 'An evaluation of SME Development through virtual action learning – A cross country case study', Henley Management College, Working Paper HWP 0614 (2006).

L. Bird, *Action Learning Sets: The Case for Running Them Online* (2006), http://www.coventry.ac.uk

R. Boot and V. Hodgson, 'Open learning, meaning and experience', V. Hodgson, et al. (eds), *Beyond Distance Teaching Towards Open Learning* (Milton Keynes: S.H.R.E./Open University Press, 1987).

D. Boud and H. Middleton, 'Learning from others at work: Communities of practice and informal learning', *Journal of Workplace Learning*, Vol. 15, No. 5 (2003), 194–202.

S. Bowles and H. Gintis, *Schooling in Capitalist America* (London: Routledge, 1975).

P. Bradshaw, S. Powell and I. Terrell (2004), 'Building a community of practice: Technological and social implications for a distributed team', P. Hildreth and C. Kimble (eds), *Knowledge Networks: Innovation through Communities of Practice* (Hershey, PA: Idea Group, 2004), 184–201.

P. Burns, 'Report on a virtual action learning set', *Action Learning News*, Vol. 20, No. 2 (2001), 2–7.

G. Caulat, 'Creating trust and intimacy in the virtual world', *Converse* (2006), 8–10.

G. Caulat and E. De Haan, 'Virtual peer consultation: How virtual leaders learn', *Organization & People*, Vol. 13, No. 4 (2006), 24–32.

CEML Reports (2002) http://www.managementandleadershipcouncil.org/

J. Coffey, 'Open learning opportunities for mature students', C. Davies (ed.) *Open Learning Systems for Mature Students* (Council for Educational Technology, 1977).

J. Cullen, E. Hadjivassiliou, E. Hamilton, et al., *Review of current pedagogic research and practice in the fields of post-compulsory education and lifelong learning*, Final Report to the Economic and Social Research Council by the Tavistock Institute (2002). Available from: http://www/tlrp.org/pub/acadpub/Tavistockreport.pdf

G. DeSanctis and P. Monge, 'Communication processes for virtual organizations', *Organization Science*, Vol. 10 (1999), 693–703.

D. DeWolfe Waddill, 'Action e-learning: An exploratory case study of action learning applied online', *Human Resource Development International*, Vol. 9, No. 2 (2006) 157–171.

M. Dickenson, M. Pedler and J.G. Burgoyne, 'Virtual action learning', *People Management*, Vol. 14, No. 21 (2008), 68.

M. Dickenson, M. Pedler and J. Burgoyne, 'Virtual action learning: What is going on?', *eLearning Papers*, Special edition (2009), 18–24.

N. Dixon, 'Action learning: More than just a task force', *Performance Improvement Quarterly*, Vol. 11, No. 1 (1998), 44–58.

K.A. Dunning, B.S. Vijayaraman, P. Turk, et al., 'Developing asynchronous MBA courses on the WWW', *The Internet and Higher Education*, Vol. 2, No. 2–3 (2000), 135–44.

M. Eraut, 'Informal learning in the workplace', *Studies in Continuing Education*, Vol. 26, No. 2 (2004), 247–273.

S. Friesen and P. Clifford, 'Working across different spaces to create communities of practice in teacher professional development', *Proceedings of MICTE 2003 Multimedia, Information and Communication Technologies, Annual World Conference on Educational Media*, Galileo Educational Network, University of Calgary (2003).

G. Giambona and D. Birchall, 'How to engage SMEs through a development programme based on virtual action learning – a cross country case study', Conference paper, *ICELW June 12013*, New York, USA (2008).

J. Gill and D. Birchall, 'Trust in virtual teams – a framework for management research and action', Henley Management College, Working Paper HWP 0406 (2004).

D. Gray (1999), 'Work-based learning, action learning and the virtual paradigm', Paper presented at the *European Conference on Educational Research*, Lahti, Finland, 22–25 September (1999); Also: *Journal of Further and Higher Education*, Vol. 25, No. 3 (2001), 315–324.

M. Hobbs, E. Brown and M. Gordon, 'Using a virtual world for transferable skills in gaming education', Virtual world environments: http://www.ics.heacacademy.ac.uk (2006).

V. Hodgson, Changing Concepts of the Boundaries within ODL, *Networked Learning 2000 Conference*, University of Lancaster (2000).

H. Ingram, K. Biermann, J. Cannon, et al., 'Internalizing action learning: A company perspective. Establishing critical success factors for action learning courses', *International Journal of Contemporary Hospitality Management*, Vol. 12, No. 2 (2000), 107–113.

H. Ingram, E. Sandelands and E. Teare, 'Cases in e-enabled action learning', *Training & Management Development Methods*, Vol. 16 (2002), 1.27–1.41.

S.L. Jarvenpaa and D.E. Leidner, 'Communications and trust in global virtual teams', *Organizational Science*, Vol. 10 (1999), 791–815.

C. Jones, M. Connolly, A. Gear, et al. (2006), 'Collaborative learning with group interactive technology', *Management Learning*, Vol. 37, No. 3 (2006), 377–396.

T.R. Kayworth and D. Leidner (2000), 'The global virtual manager: A prescription for success', *European Management Journal*, Vol. 18 (2000), 183–194.

C. Kimble and P. Hildreth, 'Virtual communities of practice', M. Khosrow-Pour (ed.) *Encyclopedia of Information Science and Technology* (Hershey, PA: Idea Group, 2005), 2991–2995.

D. McConnell, *Implementing Computer Supported Cooperative Learning*, 2nd edn. (London: Kogan Page, 2000).

D. McConnell, *E-Learning Groups and Communities* (Maidenhead: The Society for Research into Higher Education & Open University Press, 2006).

D. McConnell and V. Hodgson, 'Computer mediated communications systems – Electronic networking and education', *Management Education and Development*, Vol. 21, No. 1 (1990), 51–58.

H. McLaughlin and R. Thorpe, 'Action learning – A paradigm in emergence: The problems facing a challenge to traditional management education and development', *British Journal of Management*, Vol. 4 (1993), 19–27.

G. Paré and L. Dubé, 'Virtual teams: An exploratory study of key challenges and strategies', *Proceedings of the 20th International Conference on Information Systems*, Charlotte, North Carolina, USA (1999), 479–483.

J. Pascarella, 'Confronting the challenges of critical digital literacy: An essay review', *Educational Studies*, Vol. 43 (2008), 246–255.

D.J. Pauleen and P. Yoong, 'Facilitating virtual team relationships via Internet and conventional communication channels', *Internet Research: Electronic Networking Applications and Policies*, Vol. 11, No. 3 (2001a), 190–202.

D.J. Pauleen and P. Yoong, 'Relationship building and the use of ICT in boundary-crossing virtual teams: A facilitator's perspective', *Journal of Information Technology*, Vol. 16, No. 4 (2001b), 205–220.

D.J. Pauleen, 'Leadership in a global virtual team: An action learning approach', *Leadership & Organisation Development Journal*, Vol. 24, No. 3 (2003), 153–162.

D.J. Pauleen, 'An inductively derived model of leader-initiated relationship building with virtual team members', *Journal of Management Information Systems*, Vol. 20, No. 3 (2003–4), 227–256.

D.J. Pauleen and B. Corbitt, 'Using knowledge management processes to develop and implement organizational training strategies for virtual teams: An action learning approach', 7th *Pacific Asia Conference on Information Systems*, 1–13 July, Adelaide (2003).

D.J. Pauleen and P. Yoong, 'Studying human-centred IT innovation using a grounded action learning approach', *The Qualitative Report*, Vol. 9, No. 1 (2004), 137–160.

M. Pedler, *Action Learning for Managers*, 2nd edn. (Aldershot: Gower, 2008).

M. Pedler, J. Burgoyne and C. Brook, 'What has action learning learned to become?', *Action Learning: Research & Practice*, Vol. 2, No. 1 (2005), 49–68.

J.A. Powell, 'Using learning styles and action learning, over the internet, to drive learning for innovation in small and medium enterprises – a case study from construction', Henk J, van der Molen (ed.) *Virtual Universities? Educational Environments of the Future*. Proceedings from a symposium held at Wenner-Gren Centre, Stockholm, October 1999 (London: Portland Press, 2001), 97–111.

J.A. Raelin, *Work-based Learning: Bridging Knowledge and Action in the Workplace* (San Francisco: Jossey-Bass, 2008).

R. Revans, *Action Learning: New Techniques for Management* (London: Blond & Briggs, 1980).

R. Revans, *The Origins and Growth of Action Learning* (London: Chartwell-Bratt Ltd., 1982).

R. Revans, *The ABC of Action Learning*, 2nd edn. (London: Chartwell-Bratt Ltd., 1983).

R. Revans, 'Action learning; its origins and nature', M. Pedler (ed.) 3rd edn. *Action Learning in Practice* (Aldershot: Gower, 1997).

R. Revans, *ABC of Action Learning*, 3rd edn. (London: Lemos & Crane, 1998).

P. Reimann, and J. Zumback, *Supporting Virtual Learning Teams with Dynamic Feedback* (2006). http://zumback.psi.uni-heidelberg

G. Rhodes and G. Shiel, 'Meeting the needs of the workplace and the learner through work-based learning', *Journal of Workplace Learning*, Vol. 19, No. 3 (2007), 173–187.

V. Roche and M. Vernon, 'Developing a virtual learning community of managers in rural and remote health services', *Proceedings of the 7th National Rural Health Conference*, Hobart (2003).

G. Salmon, *E-moderating: The Key to Teaching and Learning Online* (London: Kogan Page, 2000).

E. Sandelands, 'Cyber tutoring and learning: How to facilitate action learning online', *GAJAL Published Papers*, Vol. 3, No. 2 (1999). Available at: http://training.itcilo.it

R.L. Sanders and L. McKeown, 'Promoting reflection through action learning in a 3D virtual world', *International Journal of Social Sciences*, Vol. 2, No. 1 (2008), 50–55.

P.R-J. Simons, 'Metaphors of learning at work and the role of ICT', *International Seminar on Learning and Technology at Work* (London: Institute of Education, March 2004).

P. Sobiechowska and M. Maisch, 'Work-based learning: In search of an effective model', *Journal of Educational Action Research*, Vol. 14, No. 2 (2006), 267–286.

L. Sproull and S. Kiesler, 'Reducing social context clues: Electronic mail in organizational communication', *Management Science Quarterly*, Vol. 32 (1986), 1493–1512.

J-A. Stewart and G. Alexander, 'Virtual Action Learning: Experiences from a study of SME e-learning programme', *Action Learning: Research and Practice*, Vol. 3, No. 2 (2006), 141–159.

R.E. Teare, 'Developing a curriculum for organizational learning', *Journal of Workplace Learning*, Vol. 10, No. 2 (1998), 95–121.

C. Wagner and N. Bolloju, 'Supporting knowledge management in organizations with conversational technologies: Discussion forums, weblogs and wikis', *Journal of Database Management*, Vol. 16, No. 2 (2005), 1–8.

C. Wagner and K.F. Rachael, 'Action learning with Second Life – A pilot study', *Journal of Information Systems Education*, Vol. 20, No. 2 (2009), 249–258.

J.B. Walther, 'Computer-mediated communication', *Communication Research*, Vol. 23, No. 1 (1996), 3–43.

B.M. Wright and J.R. Barker, 'Assessing concertive control in the team environment', *Journal of Occupational & Organizational Psychology*, Vol. 73 (2000), 345–362.

Y. Yoo, P. Kanawattanachai and A. Citurs, 'Forging into the wired wilderness: A case study of a technology-mediated distributed discussion-based class', *Journal of Management Education*, Vol. 26, No. 2 (2002), 139–163.

P. Yoong and B. Gallupe, 'Action learning and groupware technologies: A case study in GSS facilitation research', *Information Technology & People*, Vol. 14, No. 1 (2001), 78.

P. Yoong, K. Thornton and J. Watson, 'Online action learning and knowledge sharing: The case of the Pacific Village', *Asia Pacific International Conference on Knowledge Management*, Hong Kong, 11–13 December (2006).

9

Generation Y and Learning: A Changing World

Carina Paine Schofield and Sue Honoré

Introduction

There is growing concern amongst executive development providers about the changing learning preferences and approaches required to meet the needs of 'Generation Y' (Gen Y) who are rapidly becoming their core clients. This chapter draws on findings from a research project conducted by Ashridge Business School in 2008 to investigate the impact of this generation on learning, with a particular focus on the future of executive development for *all* generations.

There has been a great deal of hype in the media regarding Gen Y, the youngest generation in today's workforce. Over recent years they have been described and discussed at length in opinion pieces in newspapers, in management articles, on websites, in books and in journal papers (Erikson, 2009; Howe and Strauss, 2000; James, Bibb and Walker, 2008; Macleod, 2008; Oblinger, 2003).

Discussions and questions have been raised as to whether Gen Y are fundamentally different to those generations who have come before: do they think and behave differently to previous generations? Do they learn and work differently? There have also been questions around relationships and concerns have been raised about possible intergenerational conflicts in the workplace.

Most of the questions surrounding Gen Y have developed from concerns about a changing workforce. A previous decline in the birth rate in the Western world, combined with the fact that the older, Baby Boomer, population 'bulge' is due to retire from the workforce, is changing the career landscape and is starting to have an impact on UK and global businesses. In the next ten years Gen Y will make up the greatest proportion of the workforce (James et al., 2008): they are the managers and leaders of the future, yet there will be few of them from which to choose. As such, Gen Y is often described in terms of its size and potential effect: 'large in number, huge in influence' (Litmus, 2006: 1).

In addition, concerns have been raised around the changing learning needs of this younger workforce compared to the previous generations they are working alongside: Generation X and Baby Boomers. Learning has changed considerably over the last 50 years since the Baby Boomers were first educated. There has been a move from lectures, books, rote memorisation of facts and essay writing to group projects, electronic information sources, multimedia presentations, informal and rapid learning, with a strong emphasis on technology-driven methods. Recent articles have referred to it as a move from Learning 1.0 to Learning 2.0 (Naish, 2008). Gen Y are typically described as technologically savvy, hands on, interactive and collaborative who want personalised learning (Oblinger, 2003; Pletka, 2007).

Studies have identified that Gen Y value workplace learning. For example, in a recent survey by Ipsos MORI (2008) Gen Y respondents ranked learning and development in their top five important job factors. It is not only Gen Y – continuous learning and development has been identified as important for *all* generations in the workplace, particularly in relation to career development (Deal, 2007). For all generations, what people want to learn is related to what they need, not to their generation (Deal, 2007).

Who are Generation Y?

Generation Y are known by several names including Millennials; the iPod generation; the 'me firsts'; the Internet generation; echo boomers; the Nintendo generation; the digital generation; generation 'why?'; generation next; the 'I' generation and the net generation. There are many definitions of each generation as well as variations on the birthdate boundaries classifying each group. This chapter defines the key generations in today's workforce as shown in the first column of Table 9.1. It should be noted that every generation can be defined by different beliefs, circumstances, value systems and life events. As such, generational theory can be described by some as simply a 'convenient shorthand' (e.g. Eldridge, cited in Matthews, 2008), particularly for analysis. It is important to remember that a generation is made up of individuals who need to be treated as such.

Table 9.1 also summarises some common themes drawn from the existing literature surrounding this generation which relate to their formative years, their attitudes to work, and their relationships with others.

Overall, there is a consensus that Gen Y have grown up in a very different environment to previous generations; that they come to the workplace with different skills, and are motivated by different things; they do think differently about learning and also about relationships. The combination of the differences in generational upbringing alongside changes in the external environment impacting learning have resulted in a rethink of the traditional model of the delivery of material in and outside the workplace in order to reach this new generation, the future learner for executive development. Providers of executive development need to think seriously about

Table 9.1 Generational at a glance (including definitions) (based on various sources including: CIPD, 2008; Howe and Strauss, 2000; Deal, Peterson and Gailor-Loflin, 2001)

Generation	Formative years and influences	Work	Learning methods	Technology	Relationships with others
Baby Boomers 1946–1963 (approx. 30% of UK workforce)	Post war prosperity; booming birth rate; human rights movement; women's movement; inflation; suburbia	*'Committed'* **Start of career:** High competition for jobs **Career progression:** Beating competition; time served; long hours **Value:** Status and job titles **Leadership by:** Consensus	Lectures; books; courses; classroom	Raised with television	**Parents:** Attention lavished on children; opportunities provided parents had not enjoyed **Authority:** Love/hate; suspicious; question
Gen X 1963–1982 (approx. 32% of UK workforce)	Prosperity; globalisation; two earner household; corporate scandals; demand for educational achievement; MTV; AIDS; divorce	*'Balanced; get things done'* **Start of career:** Economic turmoil **Career progression:** Profession rather than employer **Value:** Learning opportunities; work life balance; informality; freedom **Leadership by:** Competition	Hands on; fun; role play; PowerPoint	Technology boom; technologically savvy but *digital immigrants*	**Parents:** 'Latchkey' kids; rebelled against parents **Authority:** Disinterest

Table 9.1 Generational at a glance (including definitions) (based on various sources including: CIPD, 2008; Howe and Strauss, 2000; Deal, Peterson and Gailor-Loflin, 2001) – *continued*

Generation	Formative years and influences	Work	Learning methods	Technology	Relationships with others
Gen Y 1982 onwards (approx. 27% of UK workforce)	Prosperity (followed more recently by a 'credit crunch'); outsourcing; higher costs; strong political leadership; decade of the child; natural disasters; terrorism; drugs and gangs	*'Decisive; individualistic'* **Start of career:** Economic boom; corporate restructures **Career progression:** Career network rather than ladder; profession not organisation **Value:** Guidance; flexibility; self development and growth; making a difference **Leadership by:** Collectivism	Mobile; Web 2.0; collaborative; personalised	Rapid expansion of technology; technologically savvy *digital natives*	**Parents:** Wanted children; parents as role models **Authority:** Respectful; courteous

how approaches to learning are changing and how this may impact their offerings for current and future executives. Gen Y will soon become the dominant group in the workforce: what will they demand from executive development?

It is a concern that many of the discussions in the literature regarding Gen Y are based purely on anecdotal evidence or author opinions without being backed up by evidence, and there has been limited research into learning relative to Gen Y that explores the learners themselves. Furthermore, employee surveys investigating how learning is changing (e.g. Centre for Creative Leadership, 2003; Learning Consortium, 2008) have not considered generational differences, nor fully explored the many drivers and influences surrounding successful individual learning. Therefore, there is a need to explore Gen Y in detail; to provide data which goes beyond the media hype, the existing assumptions and stereotypes and to look at generational differences in depth.

Ashridge research

The Ashridge research explored Gen Y in the context of their environment, separating the myths from the real behaviours and needs of this generation, as well as looking more deeply at the influences on these young people. This information fed into the main research objective which was to investigate Gen Y and learning, in order to better understand how to develop managers and leaders of the future. It aimed to identify the specific development needs and learning preferences of Gen Y compared to previous generations, producing recommendations to assist with learning, teaching and workplace practice in the future. The specific research questions the project set out to answer were:

   i) do young people now learn differently from those who were young in the past?;
  ii) is there something which has specifically impacted Gen Y?; and, most pertinent to this chapter,
 iii) what does great learning look like in the future?

The project began with a synthesis and review of literature selected from a number of sources (including academic publications, leading research organisations, university research centers, leading thinking tanks, websites (including blogs) and news sites). A set of search terms and phrases was developed which predominately focused on: Generation (Y, X, baby boomers, millennials); attitudes/behaviours; learning; and work. The review was confined to materials published between 2000 and present day). Approximately 100 articles were found in total. The majority of the materials found were from practitioner journals and news sites.

Both qualitative and quantitative data collection methods were used. Fifty-nine organisations (both public and private sector) (made up from 133 individuals) took part in face-to-face or focus groups; and 692 individuals responded to an anonymous online survey. Respondents were aged from 16 to over 63 years to ensure data was gathered from multi-generational participants in today's workforce (Gen Y, Generation X and Baby Boomers): to provide an *in-depth, intergenerational viewpoint*. The research was strongly UK-focused although participants in the online survey were global.

A topic guide was developed for the interviews and focus groups based on the literature review. The main aim of the interviews and focus groups was to gain a deeper insight into participants' opinions, beliefs and observations than could be gathered via quantitative data collection methods. Stories and anecdotes were also collected. The key topics covered included: attitudes and behaviours of, and towards, Gen Y; Gen Y's place at work; Gen Y's learning preferences; and the drivers and influences of Gen Y behaviours and needs. The survey topics were based on the existing, relevant literature and on the key discussions from the focus groups and interviews. Using a variety of question formats, the survey explored respondents': personality; attitude towards, and use of, technology; upbringing and school life; ideal learning topics and methods; work life; and communication methods (at work and socially). In addition to describing themselves, survey respondents were also asked about their relationships with other generations and their perceptions of personalities of other generations. Full details of the project's methodology and respondents can be found in Honoré and Paine Schofield (2009).

Research findings

Influences

The interview and focus group research data highlighted a number of external influences on Gen Y which must be taken into consideration when trying to understand the impact this generation is having on learning for all. These key influences are technology, educational experience, the media, world politics and the changing role of the family. Each is considered in turn.

Technology

Technology is embedded in day to day life and rapid advances in technology have been reshaping learning. The influence of technology on learning has encouraged the view that younger generations learn in a fundamentally different way from previous generations. Articles over recent years have referred to a move from 'Learning 1.0' to 'Learning 2.0' (Naish, 2008), with people as active collaborative participants not passive readers. Gen Y are typically described as technologically savvy, hands on, interactive, collaborative learners who want personalised learning (Oblinger, 2003; Pletka, 2007).

However, technology of course impacts on all generations currently in the workplace, and many outside Gen Y experience the same methods of learning in order to fit their working lifestyles, their availability and their experience. Learning and communicating are fundamentally different from 20 years ago.

Education

Governmental policies and availability of information on the Web have had a major influence on education for Gen Y. In the UK in particular there has been a strong drive to increase the number of people in higher education, with current government targets set at 43 per cent (DIUS, 2009). A 'no fail' positive culture has grown within the education world. The instant availability of simple factual knowledge on the internet has, to a certain extent, made memorisation of facts and formulae irrelevant. However the drive to improve exam results has instead resulted in a more modularised exam system and a prescriptive curriculum with memorisation of a different type – how to produce the perfect answer. There is therefore less emphasis on essay writing, in-depth research around a subject or expression of personal opinions and ideas. Exam targets are very important to education providers.

Starting in primary school, the UK education system is built around a 'consumer model', so the Gen Y student demands results and is seen as less responsible for their own learning, holding educators accountable for success. Students expect to be given the 'right' answer to questions and this feeling pervades all the way into the workplace, where many employers in our focus groups commented that Gen Y employees treat them as pseudo-teachers with responsibility to provide correct answers to all business problems and ensure all needs are met in the individual's desired career progression.

The result is that the education system that Gen Y follow is quite different to that of most of their managers and therefore impacts upon expectations of Gen Y by those managers, and on the expectations of their workplace development by Gen Y themselves.

Media

The Western world is now strongly consumer-led and media and communication methods have a major influence on Gen Y. The media portrays a global (generally negative) stereotype of Gen Y (CBS, 2007; Fortune, 2007; Swearingen, 2008) which often hampers their individual success in the workplace and their initial relationship with work colleagues.

In addition, many forms of media developed for young people now deliver in short bursts, resulting in the media fueling the desire for Gen Y to operate with a short attention span. The research shows that some educators are developing increasingly shorter segments of learning because of this expectation that Gen Y groups cannot concentrate. Yet in our interview groups and survey we found that many members of Gen Y can and do focus for long periods. Driven by a media stereotype, the short attention span may become a self-fulfilling prophecy.

World events, political and social landscape

Each generation is partly shaped by the world events around them and Gen Y are a product of increased world terrorism, strong environmental concern and most recently, a credit crunch. The research showed that members of Gen Y may not be keen to move jobs away from their home locality, despite the fact that as a generation they get on well with all different groups of people – far better than previous generations.

The recent recession is beginning to sift out those members of Gen Y who are willing to be very flexible in their ideals and to compromise in the short term in terms of a career. The situation is no different compared to previous recessions, when employment prospects for young (and much older) people take a dip, but Gen Y's high ambitions for themselves and strong self-belief in their employability, as reflected in our survey results, may mean that they experience a bigger psychological setback compared to earlier generations.

Parents and family

Overprotective 'helicopter parents' (Cline and Fay, 1990) are a strong influence on this generation. The research shows that Gen Y are close to their families, emotionally and geographically. For both financial and personal reasons they may live at home well into adulthood and therefore many members of this generation are less self-sufficient than previous generations. Furthermore, many have not developed an innate sense of risk assessment. Variable family structures and less time spent 'as a family' also influence this generation in their relationships with others and their communication abilities.

Generation Y learning characteristics

When it comes to learning, Gen Y were typically described in the focus group and survey data by all other generations as 'confident'; 'honest'; 'demanding'; and 'vociferous'. Such characteristics explain why Gen Y appears to have high expectations, particularly when it comes to learning.

The review of the literature identified typical Gen Y learning preferences. In summary, Gen Y are 'holistic learners' – oriented towards non-linear and non-sequential learning (Faust, Ginno, Laherty and Manuel, 2001). They prefer 'Just in Time' (at the moment it is needed) learning, receiving information from several multimedia sources. They also favour visual (Manuel, 2002) and virtual (Prosperio and Gioia, 2007) modes of learning, valuing interaction, networking and actively participating in learning and staying connected. This generation has a low boredom threshold and no time for delays. They employ a 'trial and error' approach to problem solving (Frand, 2000). Finally, Gen Y value both social and personal learning opportunities within the community context (Pletka, 2007). A fuller description of typical Gen Y learning preferences can be found in Honoré and Paine (2009).

Generation Y's missing skills

Through the interview, focus group and survey data a thread building and shaping Gen Y from birth onwards emerged. There appeared to be certain points at which key behaviours were set, challenges were created, and where adjustments were being made either by Gen Y or by those around them. Gen Y struggle more than previous generations with 'difficult workplace conversations' possibly because of their strongly positive nurtured childhood and an upbringing emphasising technological communication methods which can distance the sender and receiver of messages. They need more support in becoming self-aware and understanding their impact on others. They may lack data validation and comparison skills, although it is unclear whether they are not concerned about accuracy, or because they are assuming most information is by nature accurate (Weiler, 2005). The world of work often comes as a shock to many of Gen Y.

For this generation to be successful as the thinkers and leaders of the future, for the next few years at least, they may have to acquire these

Figure 9.1   Generation Y strengths and weaknesses

missing skills in the workplace as adults. Ideally in time, the educational system will be able to build missing skills in from an early age. For the time being, the positive side of this finding is that the majority of Gen Y want training, and want to learn in the workplace (Sheehan, 2005). They are an ambitious group with a desire to progress rapidly, no matter what field they are in or which subjects need to be learnt.

Figure 9.1 shows the skills which the research found to be Gen Y strengths and weaknesses.

Figure 9.1 shows widespread Gen Y strengths in the top row ('+'), weaknesses in the bottom row ('–') and, where the generation displays a mixture of strengths and weaknesses compared to previous generations in the workplace, in the middle row. Based on information from teachers and employers interviewed in this research, the critical point(s) at which those skills are (or should be) developed are shown along the header row (Home; School; University; and Work).

Overall Figure 9.1 identifies areas to focus on for those responsible for the development of Gen Y in the business world, with the star in the top right hand corner representing where individuals and organisations should be aiming for. The '+' skills (strengths) should be exploited more often by older generations, who often focus critically on the '–' skills (weaknesses). Each member of Gen Y is an individual, so the areas in the middle or bottom rows need to be considered on an individual basis, but some points to highlight are:

IT expertise

It is often assumed that all young people are IT experts and this is not true. Some struggle with technology. However, they do have an ability to pick up new technology very quickly, having grown up in a world where there are rapid technological changes.

Risk

Young people have been cocooned in their lives and many have not developed an innate sense of risk assessment in their brains, whether that concerns crossing the road, conducting an experiment or taking on a new supplier.

Valid sources of information

The challenge to educators and business colleagues is to ensure that young people verify the information sources they have: 'Given the range and volume of information available and the ubiquity of access to information sources and resources, learning strategy shifts from a focus on information as such to judgment concerning reliable information, from memorising information to how to find reliable sources. In short from learning THAT to learning HOW, from content to process' (Davidson and Goldberg, 2009: 27).

The internet or personal contacts are seen as priority sources of solutions to problems by members of Gen Y. Some need to be helped to seek out and use other sources, and to understand the power of relevant experience held by other people in solving specific issues. At the same time Gen Y have an openness to the sharing of information beyond corporate boundaries, which could be better exploited by older colleagues, who have been brought up in an era when all information was kept inside the corporate wall.

Communication

Many young people struggle with face-to-face communication, especially in sending or receiving difficult messages from others. They also need development in understanding which medium of communication is the best for a given situation. Although their intentions may be good, they may cause friction with others because of the methods they use. On the other hand, Gen Y is often very supportive of others with whom they work closely.

Deeper learning

An extension of a lack of curiosity in learning factual knowledge results in a perception that Gen Y have a shallow understanding about the world around them. The acquisition of general knowledge was a concern, particularly amongst university staff and employers as it impacts on assessment of risk and the quality of judgement.

The media and new technology devices have been blamed for the apparent decrease in attention span of this generation (Prensky, 2001; Sheehan, 2005), but although there was debate amongst the research focus group members and interviewees about whether this was a real phenomenon or not, some people are very concerned about the impact on learning. If habits have been developed to gain information quickly, and through trial and error, then as a consequence Gen Y may be missing the opportunity to reflect on that data and to engage in a more in-depth analysis. In the UK the school system is geared to high exam pass rates, and as such is driving a culture of 'know only the minimum to get the grade'. Members of Gen Y struggle with solving complex problems which have 'grey' issues and no clear answers. Their analysis skills often need developing.

The challenge to all educators is to fix any bad habits and develop skills missing from earlier life phases. The issue that employers are finding from this research, is that some of the '–' skills (weaknesses) are not improved by the time Gen Y employees start work and many years of missed learning need to be repaired in the first years of employment. Other skills, particularly those related to 'self' and interaction with others may need to be (re)developed much later by those responsible for executive education. By this time bad habits may be entrenched.

The future: Recommendations

The final, key, section of this chapter builds upon the published literature and all of the research findings to offer recommendations for those people who are concerned with the development of members of Gen Y over the next 15–20 years and for the future of executive development for *all* generations. 'Gen Y is not just a demographic – it is a mindset, a mindset that is permeating all ages and levels of the workforce...their attitudes, demands and desires and spreading' (Sheehan, 2005: xi). Figure 9.2 illustrates a range of solutions for the future produced by interviewees in this research.

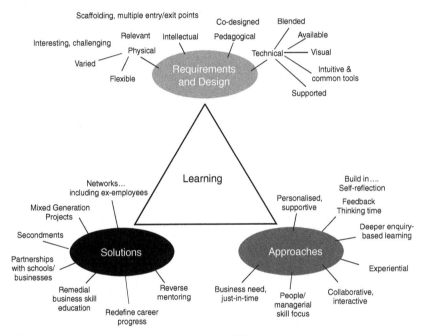

Figure 9.2   Learning solutions and recommendations

Some of the key solutions proposed in Figure 9.2 include:

Remedial education

In order for many members of this generation to advance, as a first step they may need to be encouraged to develop some 'basic' skills that were not acquired in their earlier educational years. Verbal reasoning and written English along with mental arithmetic, and concepts of budgeting were all listed as key items by interview and focus group respondents in the research. Without this foundation further development in managerial roles may be limited.

There are other skills which may need further development at executive education level, including for example, a better understanding of global economics, but mostly the gaps are to be found in the soft skill area.

Although Gen Y have completed many more team-based activities in their youth than previous generations, many need help in understanding team dynamics and how individuals support team goals. Taking the step up from being a team member to a role of team leader can also be challenging for those used to treating people of all levels as peers.

Higher level soft skills such as listening, understanding personal impact, persuasion and influencing were also noted as generic weaknesses of this generation. As mentioned previously, risk assessment and judgement-making based on appropriate validated sources of information need addressing.

In many cases employers are trying to fill these gaps during the first few years of graduate employment, but they may still exist when individuals are further up the ladder and seeking executive development. Given the variability in the Gen Y population, some skills may need to be built into pre-work to ensure all are at the same level. Others may need to be integrated into development programmes.

In order to reduce remedial learning higher up the educational chain, some organisations and universities are looking at partnerships with those institutions which feed them, in order to tackle some of the learning issues at source. Generally this solution works best with local firms, those who have a limited set of feeder sources or where there is a single accreditation body. This model may become more widespread in the future as the cost of employees continues to increase. At a macro level lobbying for changes in the education system may provide longer term benefits.

Personal support

Members of Gen Y demand support in their growth and development. Personal coaching and mentoring are seen by interviewees in this research as successful methods of retaining Gen Y workers and motivating them to achieve higher goals. This generation is used to positive feedback and encouragement, hence a trusted personal coach/mentor is best positioned to introduce critical feedback on performance, which may not have been commonplace in school or home life for Gen Y.

The development of executive educational programmes that incorporate personal coaching where feasible should be encouraged where the audience involves Gen Y, and of course, benefits all generations. Executive coaching is already popular but a shift in emphasis to tackle Gen Y issues may develop.

Inter-generational support and development

Reverse mentoring, where a more experienced employee and a new Gen Y employee coach/mentor each other in different aspects (e.g. office politics and use of new technology), encourages the development of both parties and the sharing of ideas. The two people need to be well-matched in attitude with the same desire to make the relationship succeed. Although in some cases interviewees noted that the HR department acted in the role of match-maker, relationships appear to last longer if the initiative comes from the individuals concerned. Not all partnerships last a long time, but where partnerships worked, they added immense value. A support structure designed for the partnerships and coaching of individuals on how to make the partner-ship work improved success rates.

Equally, mixed generation projects provide learning for all team mem-bers and have been shown to break down stereotypical beliefs about other generations. It may be that in the future the emphasis shifts more strongly to selecting 'culturally matched' candidates and integrating new hires into the corporate culture at earlier stages.

These solutions obviously are better suited to the workplace rather than a formal external educational programme, where the population may be more homogenous. However, it may be advantageous for customised/tai-lored executive development staff to propose building such activities into their clients' environment where appropriate.

Value-added networks

Gen Y have grown up in a society where expertise and knowledge can be obtained from any point in the world, often without ever having a physical meeting. Respect is gained from developing a sense of trust in the knowledge-owner, often through personal recommendation. These wider networks are rarely exploited in the same way by older generations and there is value in learning from Gen Y. The open source IT community is a strong leader in this type of network and the model demonstrated by pharmaceutical and entre-preneurial organisations to encourage innovation from an open community may be worth considering elsewhere. There are of course competitive, security and psychological barriers to opening up the organisation to a wider network, but there are also long term advantages for the learning and development of individuals and the growth of the company.

One consultancy organisation in this research had developed a network which was happy to include ex-employees, knowing that their contribution may continue to be high, and that they may one day return, having gained valuable experience elsewhere.

Learning design

Learning must be well designed, with the right mix of media, learning styles and approaches to retain attention and interest as well as to maximise the learning. High quality learning is not a prerogative of Gen Y, and all good learning designers aim for quality learning solutions no matter who they target, but Gen Y's unwillingness to accept poor learning has raised the profile of learning design once again. Having said that, if Gen Y is the majority of the learning audience then some design considerations may need emphasising to exploit both the strengths and weaknesses of this generation. Gen Y have been brought up on interactive learning and expect learning which encourages their developed skills. Where applicable, sessions should be facilitated rather than taught as Gen Y are more comfortable in this mode and it gives them greater ownership of the outcomes and responsibility for their own learning. They enjoy learning which is discursive and open to their own input. They seek a highly supportive learning environment. The learning interventions should also encourage development of some of Gen Y's 'areas for improvement': deeper thinking, validation of sources, assessment of risk and impact, logical reasoning and problem solving, critical thinking, self-awareness and emotional intelligence.

The research shows that Gen Y demand authentic, applicable learning. The consumer-driven fast-paced environment in which they have grown has highlighted this need. Overwhelmingly the research showed that the use of experiential learning to embed the learning in real life scenarios is critical, especially at executive development level. Experiential learning interventions which involve coaching and support alongside them are seen as a way forward.

A note of caution was sounded though from those with experience of large numbers of Gen Y learners, particularly in the business world. It can be too easy to develop a stereotypical view of Gen Y learners – requiring high technology multimedia solutions, games, designs in small modules, presentations but no writing, non-competitive and so on. Those who focused on meeting the needs of what they believed Gen Y required often did not succeed. It alienated those members of Gen Y who did not fit this stereotype as well as people from older age groups who felt uncomfortable with learning in this way. This type of solution may also have avoided achieving learning in areas where Gen Y were weak. Short attention span and surface skimming may be the exact skills that need development rather than pandering to by designers of learning solutions. Many respondents at tertiary education levels highlighted their frustration at trying to drive 'needed education' at Gen Y when the value may not have been perceived by the recipients, but they also were the people with a true passion for education and development. It is a challenge for educators to justify these approaches, but in the future more people may have to take a stance in order to raise the quality of the educational experience. Both corporate purchasers and individual learners may continue to need to be educated themselves in the value within a learning programme of 'white space' or emotionally challenging experiential learning, yet for Gen Y these elements may be critical for their future development as leaders.

Some learning designers will themselves have to let go of the detailed design of learning interventions and create an outline structure with a looser content as the learners and educators drive the learning jointly, with both contributing to the content and direction. Particularly in the grey areas of business management, the wide experience of all participants is as valuable to learning as more formal theory. Gen Y's educational background will encourage this move.

Ultimately the future of learning design is no different from the past. High quality design appropriate for the audience is what is needed. There are more tools available today and even more that will appear in the future, but the quality of the design and its execution are fundamental.

Redefining career paths

Most learning is now informal rather than formal, and much of that is achieved on the job. Rigid career paths do not suit modern business practice, and certainly are an issue with impatient Gen Y. Focus is turning to finding ways of developing the individual and enriching learning which may not be through a promotion. Some employers quoted involvement in small projects alongside the main role as well as secondments to other areas or businesses to retain and motivate Gen Y staff. Where it makes sense, established programmes such as MBA or other masters degrees or tailored management development programmes may be the answer for selected individuals.

Managing conflict

Because of the vociferous nature of many Gen Y individuals, organisations have found that inter-generational conflict can arise quickly. The most common area involved work-life balance and attitude to work. Just as younger people have been brought up to speak their minds, older people have grown used to 'avoiding the hoodie'. The culture of the organisation dictates expected norms of behaviour and more work needs to be done to encourage managers and employees to deal constructively and swiftly with inappropriate behaviour and unresolved conflict. Many organisations interviewed have some element of management development covering 'respect for others' but the indication from this research is that although it was initially something developed to deal with racial or gender prejudice, it may need reinforcing with Gen Y in the corporate mix.

Conclusion

The positive impact of Generation Y on the future of learning

As described, Gen Y have been vociferous, demanding high quality learning that meets individual needs. Older colleagues have the same needs but often have not asked for support. Technological advances provide new opportunities for learning and communication, but where there may have been pockets of early adopters in previous generations, Gen Y may have the numbers and force to demand more rapid use of appropriate technologies.

Gen Y also question established processes and challenge organisations to move forward in their thinking. They network extensively, accessing a wider group of contacts and bring in a more open attitude to the sharing of knowledge and experience. Having grown up in a supportive culture, this generation also demands coaching or mentoring to help them succeed.

Executive development plays a critical role in this scenario. Like education sectors for younger people, executive education may need to wear many hats. There will be the challenge of getting a level playing field of knowledge, developing missing skills, and working to help individuals unlearn and relearn certain habits and behaviours which may have become entrenched as they mature into managers and leaders. Learning design needs to appeal to a collaborative world and for the co-design of learning interventions. Given the fast pace of the business world and Gen Y's lack of experience in deeper thinking, more than ever before, executive level education needs to provide an environment where real learning and development takes place, a quiet space (whether face-to-face or virtual) for reflection and discussion.

'Generation Z', who are now only at primary school, will be entering the workforce in another decade, and may well rebel against the norms of the generation before. Learning and development moves in cycles, but ultimately high quality learning and development is the goal of people of all ages, not just the younger generation. In the near future Gen Y may be a greater driving force for change than those who have gone before, resulting in benefits for all.

References

Centre for Creative Leadership, *Emerging Leaders Research Survey Summary Report* (2003). Available at: http://www.ccl.org/leadership/pdf/research/elsummary.pdf Accessed 19 March 2009.

CIPD, *Gen Up: How the Four Generations Work* (London: CIPD, 2008).

CBS, *The Millennials are Coming* (2007). Available at: http://www.cbsnews.com/stories/2007/11/08/60minutes/main3475200.shtml?tag=contentMain;contentBody Accessed 25 November 2009.

F.W. Cline and J. Fay, *Parenting with Love and Logic: Teaching Children Responsibility* (United States: Pinon Press, 1990).

C. Davidson and D. Goldberg, *The Future of Learning Institutions in a Digital Age* (United Kingdom: MIT Press, 2009).

J. Deal, *Retiring the Generation Gap: How Employees Young and Old Can Find Common Ground* (United States: Josey Bass and The Center for Creative Leadership, 2007).

J. Deal, K. Peterson and H. Gailor-Loflin, *Emerging Leaders, An Annotated Bibliography* (North Carolina, USA: Center for Creative Leadership, 2001).

DIUS, *Participation Rates in Higher Education: Academic Years 1999/2000–2007/08* (2009) (Provisional March 2009) Available at: http://www.dcsf.gov.uk/rsgateway/DB/SFR/s000839/index.shtml Accessed 12 October 2009.

S.P. Eisner, 'Managing generation Y', *SAM Advanced Management Journal*, Vol. 70, No. 4 (2005), 4–15.

T.J. Erikson, 'Gen Y in the workforce', *Harvard Business Review* (2009), 43–49.

J. Faust, E. Ginno, J. Laherty, et al., 'Teaching Information Literacy to Generation Y: Tested Strategies for Reaching the Headphone-Wearing, Itchy Mouse-Fingered, and Frequently Paged'. A poster session for the *Association of College and Research*

Libraries (ACRL) 10th National Conference, California State University, Hayward (Spring 2001).

Attracting the twentysomething worker, *Fortune Magazine* (2007). Available at: http://money.cnn.com/magazines/fortune/fortune_archive/2007/05/28/100033934/ Accessed: 25 November 2009.

J. Frand, 'The information-age mindset. changes in students and implications for higher education', *EDUCAUSE Review,* September/October (2000), 15–24.

S. Honoré and C. Paine Schofield, *Generation Y: Inside Out,* Ashridge (2009).

N. Howe and W. Strauss, *Millennials Rising. The Next Great Generation* (USA: Vintage Books, 2000).

J. James, S. Bibb and S. Walker, *Generation Y: What They Want from Work* (Newbury, Berkshire: TalentSmoothie Ltd., 2008).

Ipsos MORI, 'Generation Y: The hard facts', *Personnel Today* (2008). Available at: http://www.personneltoday.com/articles/2008/09/14/47463/generation-y-the-hard-facts.html Accessed 12 October 2009.

Learning Consortium, *The Voice of the Learner: How Employees Learn in 2008.* The Masie Centre and Learning Consortium (2008). Available from: http://www.insurancetrainers.org/PDF/Voice-of-the-Learner-070708-appendix.pdf Accessed 19 March 2009.

Litmus, *Decoding the Digital Millennials* (Ohio, USA: Resource Interactive, 2006).

A. Macleod, 'Generation Y: Unlocking the talent of young managers', *Chartered Management Institute,* London (2008).

K. Manuel, 'Teaching information literacy to Generation Y', *Journal of Library Administration,* Vol. 36, No. 1/2 (2000), 195–217.

V. Matthews, 'Debunking the myths about Generation Y', *Personnel Today* (14 September 2008). Available at: http://www.personneltoday.com/articles/2008/09/14/47166/debunking-the-myths-about-generation-y.html Accessed 10 November 2009.

R. Naish, 'Generation X', *E-learning Age.* October (2008), 10–11.

D. Oblinger, 'Boomers, Gen X-ers and Millennials. Understanding the new students', *EDUCAUSE Review,* July/August (2003), 37–45.

B. Pletka, *Educating the Net Generation. How to Engage Students in the 21st Century* (United States: Santa Monica Press, 2007).

M. Prensky, *Digital Natives, Digital Immigrants,* On the Horizon, NCB University Press, Vol. 9, No. 5, October (2001).

L. Prosperio and D. Gioia, 'Teaching the virtual generation', *Academy of Management Learning and Education,* Vol. 6, No. 1 (2007), 69–80.

P. Sheehan (2005), *Generation Y: Thriving and Surviving with Generation Y at Work* (Australia: Hardie Grant Books, 2005).

J. Swearingen, *Workforce Millennials: A BNET Field Guide* (2008). Available at: http://www.bnet.com/2403-13059_23-202118.html?tag=content;col1 Accessed 25 November 2009.

A. Weiler, 'Information-seeking behavior in Gen Y students: Motivation, critical thinking and learning theory', *The Journal of Academic Librarianship,* Vol. 31, No. 1 (2005), 46–53.

Part III
Future Learner

10
Future Learner: Section Editorial

Eddie Blass

This section of the book includes three papers that explore the needs of the future learner in executive education. Interestingly, none of the papers submitted or selected focused on curriculum content. There was no offer of a rewrite of the MBA; no suggestion of new qualifications; and no tick list of knowledge and skills that are predicted as necessary for the future. Instead the papers all take a more reflexive approach to development, focusing on what learners are going to need in order to benefit from a learning experience, and how that experience will need to be delivered in order for them to achieve that learning.

The term reflexivity is normally associated with research. Finlay and Gough (2003) note it as a form of critical self-reflection of the ways in which the researcher's social background, assumptions, positioning and behaviours impact on the research process. If we swap 'researchers' for 'executives' and the 'research process' for the 'leadership and management process' then we have a reflexive approach to executive development.

Being reflexive requires a dedicated and committed effort to identify and interrogate personal and professional practices (*ibid*) and can take individuals on a voyage of self-discovery which they often find uncomfortable when operating at executive levels. Why do we make the decisions we do? What would the impact have been on others if we'd acted differently? Who would have benefited/suffered more from a change in our behaviour? Why do we behave the way we do? This is not a call to complete anarchy. There are good reasons – such as the law – for behaving within certain boundaries, and none of us want to be sectioned for being insane. But there is a huge expanse of allowable and acceptable behaviour that we do not explore in organisations, largely because the culture and systems of the organisation have built up in such a way over time that they dictate what is accepted practice without ever being challenged. In a sense, it is institutional bullying – a term described in a conversation with Professor Ralph Stacey as the organisation bullying you into taking certain courses of action that you might otherwise decide not to take.

The chapters in this section question some of the assumptions and boundaries that learners have previously taken for granted and hence are starting to fight back against organisational control without inciting organisational anarchy.

Chris Breen's chapter explores the discomfort but necessity to challenge what we think we know as right, and open the space of possibility. His session at the 2009 Future of Learning conference was somewhat uncomfortable, and while it made a point, it did provoke a certain degree of hostility in me, and perhaps amongst some other attendees – but then this all contributed to the conversation. The chapter is much more comfortable to read, and I found myself relating to the experience differently when reading about it than I did when I experienced it myself. Somehow vicariously experiencing my own failing through an account of someone else made me take on board the learning more readily than experiencing it first hand. And this is something else for us to consider regarding future learners – we will all have preferred means of learning and for some this may be less social than for others, an idea which contradicts social constructivist theory, unless vicarious learning becomes part of the social construction.

Reflexive analysis encourages us to reveal forgotten choices, expose hidden alternatives and empower voices that may have been suppressed in an oppressive organisational discourse (Lynch, 2000). Such emancipation is also experienced in Breen's chapter as people are given permission to explore the possibility that they might be wrong, they are not perfect, and they may be mistaken. We are given permission to change our minds in light of new evidence – something that many executives find difficult to do in practice. Having started down one avenue of action they continue down that avenue, despite various spectators alerting them to the fact that they are heading down a dead-end.

Breen encourages us to explore what Nightingale and Cromby (1999) refer to as personal reflexivity. It involves us in reflecting on the ways in which our own values, experiences, interests, beliefs, political commitments and social identities have shaped our practice. The other two chapters – Rumboll and Duarte, and Short and Coggan – stray into the realms of epistemological reflexivity (*ibid*) which requires us to engage in challenging our assumptions and how they are limiting what we can find within our practice.

Short and Coggan explore an old concept in a new way – 'place'. They explore the role of our specific environments, including our workplace, and the meaning they hold within our identity. They challenge us to revisit our conception of place and the taken-for-grantedness with which we conceive place. By considering the internal work environment as a place, they give us new insight and meaning to a familiar context, and hence engage us in epistemological reflexivity.

In the final chapter in this section, Rumboll & Duarte challenge the coping strategy many of us have developed to information overload – simply limiting our attention and suspending curiosity. Because we have so much information coming at us so quickly from so many sources and directions, we make quick judgements as to its relevance, giving little if any time to follow our natural curiosity. They suggest ways in which we can become curious again and how this in turn can stimulate learning.

While the style of writing of these three chapters differs greatly, it was not something as editor that I wanted to change. Part of the beauty of this section is the three different presentations. Breen writes from the heart, from his personal experience, and shares the experience of the group. You almost feel you are in the room experiencing the tension. Short and Coggan offer a logical exposition that they later support with evidence. The logic of the argument draws the reader in and encourages them to challenge their own logic, reasoning and assumptions. Rumboll and Duarte combine the two, offering a personal opinion and reflection on practice of a theoretical position. Although the three may lack a coherence in style, this diversity adds to the point this section is trying to make. Perhaps the requirement for conformance as an editor is the wrong premise or assumption to be working from. As an editor, does one have to engage in stylistic issues, or can you have an edited collection that is a *pot pourri* – a range of different ideas coming together to achieve an overall coherent impression?.

This section of the book should be read within the context of the first section, and should be borne in mind when reading about the new forms of learning technologies and methodologies on the horizon. None of these chapters are steeped in technology and ICT. This does not mean that the predictors of technological importance are wrong – it simply means that these authors are exploring a different space. It does not have to be one or the other – that would suggest there is a right and a wrong. If we believe this has to be the case we need to explore our personal reflexivity. Perhaps the future will be both technologically empowered and in need of executive education that finds its roots in reflexivity. Equally, the contexts presented in the first section do not actively promote the need for reflexivity in the workplace, but are more concerned with the delivery process within which such reflexivity may take place. There is no reason, for example, why executives cannot engage in reflexive practice in a virtual action learning set. Generation Y may already engage in reflexive conversations on FaceBook – certainly many of them engage in storytelling and improvising.

The future learner therefore needs to be all things to all organisations – and the message from this section of the book is that this can only be achieved if they start to engage in reflexive practice.

References

L. Finlay and B. Gough, *Reflexivity: A Practical Guide for Researchers in Health and Social Sciences* (Oxford: Blackwell Publishing 2003).

M. Lynch, *Future Learner: Section Editorial* 'Against reflexivity as an academic virtue and source of privileged knowledge', *Theory, Culture and Society*, 17 (3) (2000), 26–54.

D. Nightingale and J. Cromby, *Social Constructionist Psychology* (Milton Keynes: Open University Press, 1999).

11
Re-cognising Learning and Teaching: Opening the Space of Possibility

Chris Breen

> *Oriented by complexivist and ecological discourses, teaching and learning seem to be more about expanding the space of the possible and creating the conditions for the emergence of the as-yet unimagined, rather than about perpetuating entrenched habits of interpretation. Teaching and learning are not about convergence onto a pre-existent truth, but about divergence – about broadening what is knowable, doable, and beable. The emphasis is not on what is, but on what might be brought forth. Thus learning comes to be understood as a recursively elaborative process of opening up new spaces of possibility by exploring current spaces.*
>
> (Davis, 2004: 184)

This chapter will explore some of the implications of the above quotation for the future of learning with a specific focus on executive education. The initial part of the chapter will be located in the author's long past experience as a mathematics educator in the South African context. It will then outline some recent learning and teaching theories that have emerged from complexity science and ecosystemic thinking. With these foundations, the author will ground some implications and possibilities in practical examples drawn from his current work in executive education.

The attempt to do justice to the subtleties and nuances of the topic in a linear piece of writing will not be easy. The challenge will be to remain true to the complex swirl of events and situations that are indicated by the root of the word complex – 'plex' to 'weave' – and try to introduce suitable and helpful threads that will allow the reader to tug gently and uncover the inevitable connections and mutual dependencies.

Insights from an educational past

Everything said is said by an observer (Maturana, 1987)

Maturana's above statement challenges the existence of a detached and totalised knowledge that can be objectively described. This means that, as author, I am irrevocably entwined in the words that follow. This places an onus on me to provide the reader with some upfront access to the sources of my entanglement, especially those from the initial phases of my working career – first as a high school mathematics teacher (seven years), and then as a university mathematics educator (25 years).

As a successful mathematics student at school (regularly winning prizes), I enjoyed the status that success in mathematics gave me. I learnt that the correct way to learn was to follow the teacher carefully and adapt given procedures so as to be fast in getting to the correct answer (Breen, 1990). After school I decided to study chemical engineering – mainly because I was told that it was the most difficult course at university that used mathematics! The reader will be able to recognise a well-developed sense of confidence in personal ability and a willingness to accept the toughest challenge possible. After completing my university studies, this same approach followed me into the teaching profession where I initially endeavoured to produce student clones who could succeed in working quickly, logically and accurately. In this way, both they and I could be seen to be successful high achievers.

Getting complicated

Davis and Sumara (1997) introduce the term 'Complicated' to describe this ego-centred problem-solving world-view and teaching approach which is rooted in the simple mathematical equations of Newton and Descartes' 'I think therefore I am'. They later table additional features of this Complicated paradigm (Davis and Sumara, 2008) as being based on machine metaphors aligned to concepts of input and output; as well as the use of linear imagery as one moves from A to B as efficiently and effectively as possible with the aim of progress. Problems can be solved by reducing them to their component parts. Measurement is an important component which aims to give us stability and control through prediction and routine. Best practice is the target at which everyone aims.

Davis (2004) grounds teaching approaches from this Complicated paradigm as coming from epistemic considerations of rationalism and empiricism where logical procedures are used to see the light of reason and the logic of mathematics is used as the core model. *Teaching as Instructing* or *Telling* (rationalism) and *Teaching as Training* (empiricism) are the main modes for the classroom and what is taught is independent of who is taught (Davis, 2004: 63–90).

During my short high school teaching career, I became aware of some deficiencies in the above approach, but the cracks really started opening up when I was appointed as a university mathematics educator in 1982 in a context of increasing political turmoil in South Africa.

A devastating challenge to the sovereign rule of mathematics in my life came from Julian David (1992), a Jungian analyst, at an open evening talk in Cape Town. As part of his speech, he focused on the damage that he believed that an over-emphasis on Logic has caused in the world. Amongst a great deal more, he said the following:

> *Western worship of intellect goes back to Socrates and Plato. The leading element was Logic – causality in the abstract – and this gave birth to the industrial revolution. Psychologically it conferred power... The founding principle of Logic is that opposites exclude each other. So Logic whips through the world dividing things... Logic classifies, and within classes, everything must be the same. Logic encourages separateness, class war and apartheid. Logic lacks humanity...*
>
> *Logic is crucial in developing effective ego-consciousness. Logic gave Plato stability. Its abstractions offered a more satisfactory world altogether – a world of eternal truths, where there would be no change... The other functions of the psyche – feeling, sensation and intuition – were the dross. Without feeling, thinking is necessarily destructive.*
>
> *Thinking without feeling is not the God Plato thought it would be; it is closer to the Antichrist...*

These were shocking but deeply resonating words to a mathematics educator who on the one hand inevitably privileged Logic as part of his teaching, yet on the other was appalled by the horrors being carried out in the name of apartheid and had been gearing his work towards preparing teachers for a future democratic South Africa (Breen, 1992, 1993).

Further reflection on this theme highlighted the way in which the dominant teaching methodology and context helped shape students views of themselves and their abilities. For example, one of the key features of mathematics learning is the test and the subsequent marking process. The dynamics of achievement and the positioning of students by ability that follows when these 'marks' become public became a growing concern. An example of the insidious nature of this positioning is shown in a piece of research where student teachers wrote a test to examine their knowledge of the school syllabus (Breen, 2004a). Students were asked to predict which of them would achieve the top marks and which of them would do badly. They were quite happy to enter into this artificial game even though they had no evidence other than their verbal class interactions of the past few months. The surprise result was the success of Fred, the only quiet black African student in the class whose silent predisposition did not fit into the dominant expectation of extroversion in class being a good guide to achievement. No-one correctly predicted that he would finish as one of the top three students. More worrying was that Fred had also quite clearly undervalued his own ability and did not consider that he might feature in the top group of achievers. In contrast, Ross, an extrovert white male, was outspoken in class and the whole class consequently deferred to him when he appeared convinced of a viewpoint. Almost everyone placed him at the top of the class when in fact his final result was in the bottom half of the class.

David Henderson (1995: iv), a mathematics lecturer at Cornell University, highlights the loss of intellectual capital that can result from such a limited view of ability and value.

> *I have been teaching a geometry course based on the material in this book for a long time now. One might expect that I have seen everything. But every year, about one-third of the students will show me a meaning or way of looking at the geometry that I have never thought of before and thus my own meaning and experience of geometry deepen. Looking back I notice that these students who have shown me something new are mostly persons whose cultural backgrounds or race or gender are different from mine; and this is true even though most of the students in the class and I are white males... Note that this conclusion implies that I must listen particularly carefully to the meanings and proofs expressed by females and persons from other cultures and races because there is much which they see which I do not see.*

Similarly, experiences with students such as Marissa (Breen, 2004b, 2008a) and Portia (Breen, 2008b) demonstrated the serious damage to self-esteem that resulted from their early and continued failure in mathematics, a subject which has been used as a filter mechanism for career choices. Failing students became withdrawn in class and extremely hesitant to offer an answer.

Into the complex

> *Complexity theorists draw a distinction between the descriptors complicated and complex. This new interdisciplinary field begins by rejecting the modernist tendency to use machine-based metaphors in characterizing and analyzing most phenomena. Machines, however complicated, are always reducible to the sum of their respective parts, whereas complex systems – such as human beings or human communities – in contrast, are more unpredictable, more alive.*
>
> (Davis and Sumara, 1997: 117)

My growing understanding of the above deficiencies of the dominant teaching and learning methodologies arising from a Complicated paradigm and the drastic imperatives of the contested South African context led me to introduce some new innovations to my teaching curriculum (Breen, 1992, 2008b). It was only much later that I found a theoretical basis for many of these ideas in a Complex paradigm. The Complex paradigm is located in the area of adaptive systems and draws on ecosystem rather than machine metaphors. The imagery here is cyclical with a focus on feedback loops that aim at sufficiency and growth and the whole cannot be compressed into individual parts. The key value comes from newness and surprise and the focus is on adaptability and growth through an application of the most appropriate practice for the local context and participants (Davis and Sumara, 2008).

Complexity paradigm discourse stems from two major conceptual orientations (Davis, 2004) – complexity science and ecological discourses – that have their roots in an inter-objective orientation in the world in which attention is placed on both the cultural and the biological as well as to both the announced and enacted (Merleau-Ponty, 1962). Similarly, a strong move is made to bring mind and body together as the embodied mind (Varela et al., 1991). A complexity science orientation leads to a conception of *Teaching as Occasioning* where *occasioning* signals the participatory and emergent natures of learning engagements, pointing to both the deliberate and accidental qualities of teaching (Davis, 2004: 215). Ecological discourses take a different route. While they share with complexity a conviction that all forms and events are intimately intertwined, this conviction has become more oriented to 'questions of meaning, ethical action, spiritual entanglement and mindful participation in the evolution of the cosmos' as it reasserts the role of human consciousness (Davis, 2004: 161). This leads to *Teaching as Conversing* where conversations are 'an emergent form, one whose outcome is never prespecified and (which) is sensitive to contingencies' (Davis, 2004: 177). *Teaching as Conversing* aims to indicate the notion of mindful participation in the unfolding of personal and collective identities, culture, intercultural space and the biosphere. This approach has prompted more of a concern for ethical know-how than the complexity thinking-oriented practical know-how.

Enacted teaching

A key learning theory with its roots in these ideas has variously become known as the Santiago Theory of Cognition (Capra, 1997) or enactivism (Davis, 1996). These terms refer to the work started by two Chilean theoretical biologists, Humberto Maturana and the late Francisco Varela (Maturana and Varela, 1986; Varela, et al., 1991).

One of the key concepts of this theory is one's structure. Varela, Thompson and Rosch (1991: xv) describe the term 'structure' as a fluid and temporal self, which is formed 'by the combined influence of one's biological constitution and one's history of interaction with the world' (Davis, 1996: 9). The enormous influence that this has on the way in which each one of us sees the world is emphasised in the following quotation:

> *In the enactive approach reality is not a given: it is perceiver-dependent, not because the perceiver 'constructs' it as he or she pleases, but because what counts as a relevant world is inseparable from the structure of the perceiver.*
>
> (Varela, 1999: 13)

Since the structure of each individual is so strongly in place at an invisible level, any input from the teacher will be uniquely processed by each learner through the lens of their own structure – a process to which the teacher has no access at all. This means in effect that the teacher can realistically have little impact on the outcome of the lesson so can more usefully focus on paying attention to the input she gives to the session which will aim to perturbate the learner.

> *The perturbations of the environment do not determine what happens to the living being; rather it is the structure of the living being that determines what change occurs in it. This interaction is not instructive, for it does not determine what its effects are going to be.... The changes that result from the interaction between the living being and its environment are brought about by the disturbing agent but determined by the structure of the disturbed system.*
>
> (Maturana and Varela, 1986: 96)

Not only did this theory give me a theoretical foundation for the work I was already doing, but it also gave me permission to move more assertively into new territory. From this perspective, my task as teacher is to become 'a disturbing agent' in the classroom where the changes (which I take to be the learning) will be determined by the structure of the learner. In essence, the theory says that I can only have a limited influence on what actually gets taken up in the classroom and my control over the outcomes is almost non-existent.

These insights gave me the freedom to pursue my interest in becoming a better perturbator in order to challenge the *status quo* in South African mathematics classrooms with relish!

Consciously perturbating executive education

The initial invitation

At the start of 2001, I was invited by Kurt April, one of my past mathematics education students, to teach a few sessions on his MBA module. He knew that I was exploring ideas from complexity and had had first-hand experience of my perturbatory teaching methods! Sitting in on his class in order to get a sense of the students before making my own contribution, I discovered some very familiar dynamics from the class of mainly white male students. Students were seated in a large lecture theatre with fixed seats facing the front. There was overt competition for teacher's attention with a palpable pride in right answers. Fear of being wrong led to a hesitance to commit to an answer. Students from minority groups in the class were generally less vocal. Few seemed concerned about the contributions of others as they tried to be the first to give a correct answer or offer evidence of their superior knowledge and insights.

I decided to try to disturb some of these normalities in my session and so offered the class an activity based on a videotape of people in black and white T-shirts passing around two basketballs (Simons, 2007).

I set the class the challenge for everyone in the class to be able to get the same correct answer for the total number of passes made by the people wearing white T-shirts. The stakes were high as no-one wanted to be the person who let the class down. The focus was absolute. When it came to give answers, there was a surprisingly large range from 12 passes to 22 passes. I asked the class if anyone had noticed anything unusual while watching the film. There were one or two answers such as a shot which bounced off someone's head; or where a black T-shirted person received a pass from a white T-shirted person. Eventually, after the volunteered answers had dried up and nothing new was being offered, I decided to ask Nombeko, the only black woman in the class whether she had noticed anything. Very hesitantly and reluctantly she offered that she thought she had seen an extra person. Intensive further questioning led her to gradually extend this to an extra person wearing black; an extra person dressed up as an animal; as a jungle animal; as a monkey; and finally as a gorilla! At this stage, as she no doubt anticipated, the rest of the class burst into laughter – no way could they have missed a gorilla! No-one believed her.

On replaying the video, someone dressed in a gorilla suit is seen to walk across the front of the screen and beat his chest before walking off screen. The immediate responses came thick and fast. 'You've changed the video'. My response of 'How did Nombeko know there would be a gorilla the second time if it wasn't there the first?' was met with a conspiracy theory of my having cued her during the tea break! Next came: 'We were doing what you told us to do' to which I asked whether they didn't think it might possibly be useful to be aware if there is a gorilla in the room?. And finally when cornered one person said, 'Yes, but what answer did Nombeko get – she probably wasn't concentrating on the task so was one of the ones who let us down!'

And even when it turned out that Nombeko had the correct answer and the questioner the wrong answer, his final statement on going to tea was that he had learnt that he had to be on his guard so that I didn't catch him out again!

The disturbing echoes from my mathematics education past as outlined earlier are frightening. The majority of these business school students who display a comfortable (at times arrogant) regard for their own abilities and a reluctance to turn to others for advice, turn out to have been successful students at mathematics at school. They report that they were rewarded for displaying their abilities in class. There is no understanding that the other presents an ideal additional source of data – especially if their life story is different.

Exploring the literature

A short while after this MBA experience, I was asked to teach on another business school leadership course and these requests started coming with increasing frequency until I eventually decided to make the move from mathematics education to executive education in 2008.

It became important to familiarise myself with relevant literature and one of my first sources was Dee Hock, who had successfully overseen the birth of VISA, and subsequently written a book in which he told his story and outlined the crucial theoretical insights that he gained from the experience. In essence he sets the challenge for future leaders to let go of the dominant mechanistic paradigm and embrace new ideas which he believes belong to what he calls the 'chaordic age' (Hock, 1999). The following two quotes give the reader an idea of his views on two of the topics under consideration – the Complicated paradigm and the ego-drive to succeed:

> *This separatist, mechanistic concept is a powerful way of viewing the world, a useful way of perceiving some aspects of reality and a practical aid in day-to-day activities. Difficulty begins when it is held forth as the best way of perceiving reality. Destruction begins when it is held forth as the only way. It is only one perspective; only one way of perceiving reality. And it is the best way only for narrow, limited, quantifiable purposes.*
>
> (Hock, 1999: 288)

> *Success, while it may build confidence, teaches an insidious lesson: to have too high an opinion of self. It is from failure that amazing growth and grace so often come, provided that one can only recognise it, admit it, learn from it, rise above it, and try again. There is no reason to be discouraged by shortcomings.*
>
> (Hock, 1999: 71)

He also makes a telling comment that speaks to the MBA gorilla experience:

> *Fascinating patterns began to emerge. Most women seemed to understand the concepts quickly, deeply, and intuitively. People raised in Eastern cultures and religions were also swift to understand. Native peoples had no trouble at all... Those who had the most difficulty with the concepts were often Caucasian men from Western societies in positions of power. People like me!*
>
> (Hock, 1999: 199)

The following diagram, adapted from Dalmau (1995) and Kimberley and Fernbach (2006) offers a sharp focus to my experience of the different styles of learning and focus of the Complicated and Complex paradigms as well as their implications for the business world. The diagram associates the rational, complicated paradigm with management and the key areas of structures, systems and processes. This is the territory of traditional mathematics and executive education teaching. It is the section below the line that excites me

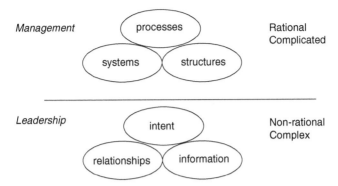

Figure 11.1 Management and leadership, adapted from Dalmau (1995) and Kimberley and Fernbach (2006)

most. Leadership is explicitly linked to a Complex paradigm and the key areas of relationship, intent and information. The challenge for me becomes one of using my insights from complexity and mathematics education to inform my 'below the line' teaching and learning in executive education.

A crucial additional element from the literature came from a book which began to speak directly to my growing understanding of the nature of 'below the line' work in business education (Senge, et al., 2004). Only on my second reading of the book did I notice that the book was dedicated to the memory of Francisco J. Varela, which explained my excitement at the ideas being expressed! This book introduced the concept of the Theory of the U (Senge et al., 2004: 83) which Scharmer later developed in more detail (Scharmer, 2007). A representation of the opening process of the U is given in the figure below (Scharmer, 2007: 37–40).

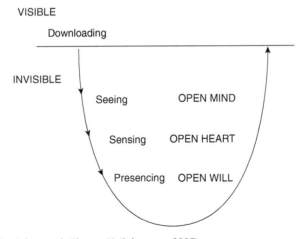

Figure 11.2 Scharmer's Theory U (Scharmer, 2007)

The visible section above the line represents our unconscious responses to situations. We draw heavily on our lived experience which has been strongly informed by our exposure to learning in the complicated paradigm. The result is that we respond by automatically downloading and reacting in a set, unconscious way. He believes that working for change requires one to move into the unconscious or invisible areas and journey through a process where we have to open our minds, hearts and wills as we move down the U.

First challenging steps

The range of what we think and do is limited by what we fail to notice. And because we fail to notice that we fail to notice, there is little we can do to change; until we notice how failing to notice shapes our thoughts and deeds.
(Goleman, 1997: 24)

Repeated work using the gorilla movie with business leaders at all levels showed that the MBA experience was not an aberration. The same features of blind certainty coupled with a reluctance to listen to others – especially if they were not from a similar background – could be found at all levels of leadership.

I decided to take up the task of challenging the download-react unconscious behaviour and attempt to work on Scharmer's first invisible level – that of Open Mind. In doing this, I wanted to work from the enactivist perspective which moves the central position from 'I think therefore I am' to 'I act therefore I am'. I decided to take up the complexity science invitation of *Teaching as Occasioning* and set tasks which would ask participants to work in real time to get a lived experience of the concept under study. In this way they could participate as full subjects in their own learning. By including the ecological *Teaching as Conversing* perspective, they are able to keep a careful watch on themselves in action, and enter into post-activity reflective conversation which would be uniquely personal.

In the South African context, diversity has become the subject of many workshops and participants readily accept theoretical arguments about the need to listen to others to gain new ideas. One of the biggest challenges I face in my initial encounters with new classes is to get participants to become aware of the unconscious negative consequences that inevitably come from an education system that has placed a total emphasis on the rational, complicated world and how these consequences include a general inability to move beyond an ego position and take the views of others seriously. The activity described below gives a brief idea as to how the above ideas from complexity allow me to take an awareness-intending perturbating teaching role.

The class is asked the number of times the letter 'f' appears in a short sentence that is displayed on the screen for a short period. Participants write down their answers without consulting or showing their answers to others. In the crucial

*next step, I ask each person to match their degree of certainty with an ima-
ginary bet in the local currency (in South Africa this is Rand (R)). If they are
100 per cent certain they must bet R100; 50 per cent certainty means a bet
of R50; etc. After the first viewing of the sentence generally only 20 per cent
of the class is willing to bet R100 (10 people in an assumed class of 50).
I show the sentence again and challenge them to be true to themselves and
have the courage of their convictions. The percentage of people who are 100 per
cent certain of their answers generally rises to about 70 per cent at this stage.*

*Now we start exploring answers as I ask those who have seen 0 'f' to come
forward to stand in front of the class, and build this up by one each time. The
first person generally comes up when I reach two 'f's. One can see the look of surprise when they see that there are only 2 of them in the class of 50 who have seen
2 'f's. As they stand in front of the class, I ask them to tell us how much they
bet. They are then asked if they want to change their bet. Those who have bet
R100 and are 100 per cent certain of their answer very seldom change their
answer–even though 96 per cent of the class has seen more than they have! And
they won't even back down when I present them with a logical argument why
they cannot remain 100 per cent sure that 96 per cent of the class can be wrong.
They know what they saw and do not regard their colleagues as data. The only
way they say they will change their bet is if they see what they regard as the data
– the original sentence – again. And of course, when I give them the chance to see
the sentence again, they almost always make the same oversight. They will even
step forward on invitation by me and tell each one of the rest of the class who
have seen more f's than they have, that they are wrong and are stupid! And
the same pattern continues as we increase the number of f's going as high as
some who have seen 8 'f's. Very seldom does anyone seem to learn and accept
colleagues' observations as valid and a possibly superior data source.*

The debrief conversation that they have with colleagues after everyone has
been able to agree on the correct answer allows them to explore the dynamics
that were going on at both individual and collective levels. The implications
of their ego-centred stance and disregard for others highlight the absence of
an open mind. With them thinking they have learnt the lesson, I generally
move on to the gorilla movie mentioned earlier and the shocks continue!
The gorilla serves as an excellent metaphor for threats, weaknesses and opportunities that are around us and that we fail to notice.

A further building block is provided by the following activity (Breen, 2001)
which works with the concept of structure introduced earlier, and the way
in which what we perceive to be reality is strongly influenced by our lived
experience and genetic predispositions.

*I show a brief excerpt from a concert where Hugh Masekela is performing. At the end
of the showing each viewer is asked to select an image that stood out for them and
write down as much detail about that image as they can. The range of differing facts*

reported on a particular image can be seen to be strongly influenced by the individual observer's own particular lived experience and assumptions of that image. It is only when they share their certainties with the rest of the group that the very subjective nature of their 'factual' descriptions of what they saw becomes apparent. For example, there is an image of some policemen standing on a hill looking at the concert. This image has been variously described as consisting of: three bored policemen; four policewomen; four policemen with an Alsatian; or five armed policemen looking for trouble. Each of these descriptions can be shown to have a strong link to the viewer's personal experiences with authority and police in the past!

Once the majority of the class has accepted the deficiencies of an ego-centred source of data and their limited experience, they are ready to move onto activities which highlight the benefits that can come from a careful consideration of those who think differently than they do.

I project a section of the nine times table (up to 10 × nine) on the screen and ask participants to work individually and write down everything that they notice about the table. First attempts are very poor with the maximum number of observations being in the region of four or five. Those who would describe themselves as mathematically able generally have the shortest list that starts with the label that this is the nine × table and not much more.

The second half of the exercise gives each person the task of offering a new observation that has not been said before. Before we start, I ask those who see themselves as being useless at or scared of mathematics to stand up. As non-experts they then take the privileged position of being asked to answer first and, in addition, they are given a wild card to jump the queue whenever they have a new insight. The main instruction given is that they must hide their original answers and not compete with each other, but rather to listen carefully to what each person says and explore the new possibilities that each observation opens up. The class is amazed at the list of over 50 observations that are made, and particularly that it is the self-proclaimed non-experts who often lead the way in creative observations!

These examples have been offered in an attempt to give the reader access to the different type of real life/real time classroom interactions that might be occasioned by foregrounding an enactivist perspective of teaching and learning – they are certainly not intended to be templates for best practice! Each activity is aimed at holding up a mirror that allows participants to observe, think about and discuss their own actions in the moment. This initial work with a group in executive education usually spans one or two full days and my intention is to finish the process where each participant has a new awareness of their blind spots and a willingness to start working on opening their minds to the possibility that they are mistaken and that others may be able to assist.

It is always very sobering to experience the willingness of participants to move to the edge and engage with these ideas and this very different teaching style. The following selection of journal comments from a group of senior executives from a variety of backgrounds and contexts is intended to give the reader an insight into the courage, honesty and responsibility that participants take for their reaction to the experience.

The first session with Chris was brutal to my ego and what I originally saw as strong points. The no.1 MAJOR challenge is to accept that I need to change if I want to learn. (IJ)

I have become aware that the gap between what I may say and what I actually do is big. My insistence, in the face of strong contrary views, that I had seen three 'F' characters has jolted a realization of the extent of my arrogance through the dismissal of any sense that others could in fact have been correct in what they saw. (CD)

Before our session, diversity was a de facto state of my mind as long as I am not racist, anti-gay or anti-anything that is different from my attributes. I didn't know that I was not embracing diversity in the true sense because races and ethnic groups are simply the first layer of diversity. I have been running away from the real world. A world of feelings, relationships, true human values, intents and information that I had forsaken or tried to forget because I programmed myself to be an outcome-driven and performance-driven person. This is why I was associating myself only with people that are like me, who think like me and who see the world like me. (EF)

My career has been pretty remarkable – but I question as to how much of my drive was because I wanted to do it, and how much was because success would impress others? Probably the latter I think. The corporate ladder places great emphasis on the car you drive, the size of the office, the fact as to whether you have a personal assistant or not and so on. (AB)

I take away some wonderful tools as well, that will allow me to self discipline and hence to lead my team better. These include the vision exercises, where I have always argued about being right in terms of seeing the same picture with somebody else, without willing to be disturbed and hence accepting that I could have missed the 'gorilla'. Playing the 9 times table today, it dawned on me that I could have been shutting a whole lot of creativity and value creation out there by being the dominant speaker because I saw quite a number of ways that one can see patterns evolving within a simple exercise like that. Thus an environment needs a leader to create it, to unleash the potential of the whole team. It requires of me to play a critical balance below or above the line. Indeed I have been failing to notice what I fail to notice. (GH)

Digging deeper

The inevitable question that emerges from participants after this type of work is how they can begin working with this new awareness to try to change some of these actions and their taken-for-granted assumptions and unconscious beliefs. This has become the exciting aspect of my current work as it opens up the space for new beginnings and continues the challenge of teaching through *occasioning* and *conversing*. The remaining part of this chapter will try to put down some markers that begin to illuminate a possible path that I have been exploring.

Entering the complex space

> *Man's worst sin is unconsciousness, but it is indulged in with the greatest piety even by those who should serve mankind as teachers and examples.*
>
> Jung (in Hollis, 2003: 21)

Psychoanalytic ideas point to a different understanding of complexity – Jung's concept of the complex – an autonomous, affect-laden idea which has a life of its own and, when unchallenged, puts one's life on automatic pilot. It is a mythological subsystem that is the result of the accretion of personal experience around a certain idea (Hollis, 2003: 15). These complexes are at the root of our patterns of choice and have 'invisible filaments reaching down into history and replicating its dynamics if not its surface appearances' (Hollis, 2003: 21).

Digging deeper involves inviting participants on courses to start paying attention to these complexes which appear as charges or unexpected energies. These charges are 'an embodiment of the invisible' (Hollis, 2003: 26) and provide us with an opportunity to locate and work with what are also known as blind spots or triggers. Wheatley (2005: 212) similarly invites us to be willing to be disturbed and actively pay attention to events that surprise or disturb us and use these occasions as opportunities to initiate non-judgmental conversations about the disturbance.

In similar vein, Varela (1999) introduces the concept of immediate coping as we engage with the world. He claims that we have a readiness-for-action (micro-identity) proper to every lived situation (micro-world). His interest is in the hinge moments where we move between micro-worlds and choose an appropriate micro-identity. If this is generally determined by the 'common-sense emergence of an appropriate stance from an entire history of the agent's life' (Varela, 1999: 11) – a seemingly clear link to Jung's complex – the challenge becomes one of finding ways in which we can become aware and increase our possibilities for action at a hinge moment.

Becoming more aware

I first began working with these ideas in the Researching Teaching module on a taught Masters programme in Teaching at the University of Cape Town at the beginning of the century (see Breen, 2000 and 2002 for the background to the introduction of this course). The main methodology for this work is based on the Discipline of Noticing (Mason, 2002) which asks participants to collect charged situations (critical incidents) in the form of brief-but-vivid accounts-of which removed all emotion, assumptions and personal bias from their reporting and which stopped at the hinge moment. These accounts-of are then offered to others in conversation in what Varela calls 'second person research – an exchange between situated individuals focusing on a specific experiential content developed from a first-person position' (Depraz et al., 2003: 81). This interaction gives the participant access to different interpretations and possible future actions to change the automatic download response. In Breen (2005), I give an extended example of a teacher, Nicky, as she chooses to work on her reaction to students coming to her for extra mathematics lessons who trigger her when they arrive for class without having done the homework that she had set them in their previous session.

In my work with executives, I have streamlined this process to initially focus on incidents where they have lost their temper with someone else – at work or at home. They are asked to re-enter the experience and explore aspects such as: what is happening in their body; whose behaviour from their own childhood are they reminded of as they swing into action; what fear was present in them just before they lost it; and so on.

The task between sessions then is to collect a series of accounts – of situations where they lose it or where they behave in a way that they would like to change. What is going on? What themes and similarities do they notice? This links with Scharmer's advice to enter the unknown and, in the first instance, observe, observe, observe and become one with the environment.

Working on one's own practice, especially when one is trying to change habitual responses, is an extremely difficult task. Participants are introduced to mindfulness practice and body awareness techniques to help them catch the hinge moment as it happens, pause, take a deep breath and then consciously choose a different learning rather than judgment course of action. Once again the willingness of executives to undertake this work and pay attention to their own complexes with honesty and integrity is remarkable. The following two examples come from participants on an extended course who were given an assignment to select an aspect that they wanted to work on and implement some small win change procedures as an action research project.

Freda sees herself as an introvert and perfectionist who is not good with people. At work she runs on autopilot but can feel her body is tense. She is irritated by what she sees as inefficiency in her workers and sees all feedback as being negative criticism. Her collection of critical incidents highlights her sarcastic and defensive interactions with others. She begins a short daily mindfulness practice each day to still the mind after which she prioritises for the day. She introduces open communication sessions with her workers where her task is just to listen to them. She finds herself becoming less tense and less pressurised and stops blocking others. The biggest gain comes from what should have been a tough meeting with union officials where she was able to let go of her defensiveness and fear, listen carefully and ask useful exploratory questions.

John is surprised to discover that nearly all his critical incidents centre around his wife. She is a very capable woman who gave up her career to stay at home and look after the children. She gets rattled when she is under pressure. Looking at his incidents, he recognises that each time he judges his wife as if he is smarter than her. He remembers that his father was very judgmental of his mother and that he grew up knowing that he had to be strong and perfect to be appreciated.

He becomes aware of what goes on in his body as he reaches a hinge moment – his head feels as if it is swelling and his chest expands as if it is going to burst. And then he loses it and the results are devastating. His wife closes off and a thick tension is in the air. The children change behaviour and become tearful and withdrawn. When he gets to work he is already in an emotional state and is impatient and easily frustrated.

He works on becoming more aware of his body and asks his wife to assist him in changing his attitude to her. A new situation arises when he is typing his assignment. His wife is next to him and moves – spilling her coffee over herself and some of his notes. He feels his head start to swell and manages to catch the moment. He breathes in and, instead of following his normal route of blaming her for her irresponsible juvenile behaviour, he tells her that it doesn't matter as he has finished with that information!

John reports that the consequences of his awareness work are immediate and dramatic. He and his wife become closer and the children happier as they sense fewer tense moments between father and mother. Leaving the house in a happy frame of my mind, has led to his having fewer hinge moments with colleagues which has encouraged more cooperation and consultation in decision making. The benefit to the company has been that his project team can now effectively sit around the table and give their individual input to a decision ensuring that it is the best for the company.

Concluding thoughts

I have previously reported (Breen, 1992) how I started this journey into finding a more effective form of teaching in 1986 in the South African context of severe political contestation. The impetus came from my desire to prepare mathematics teachers for an as yet unimagined future with a majority government. Traditional teaching methods that appealed to logic were not working as I saw each student filter the content through their own taken-for-granted assumptions. The challenge was to enter the unknown and explore the possibilities of what was doable and beable. The words of the opening quotation by Davis, written 18 years later, resonate strongly.

Varela (1999: 27) refers to Mencius's comparison of a truly wise person and the village honest person. The village honest person is someone who will know what to do in a specific situation provided that there is sufficient time to think about it and to make a considered decision. The truly wise person, in contrast, does not have to stop and consider what action to take. Through a process which he describes as consisting of extension, attention and intelligent awareness, the truly wise person just acts in accord with the situation.

The traditional Complicated teaching and learning that has formed the majority of school mathematics and executive education instruction seems to be geared towards the development of village honest people. Leaders with this training are able to make excellent decisions when given the time to consider their options. Their default behaviours in familiar situations generally fall into the download-react category and are governed by taken-for-granted assumptions and unconscious complexes.

This chapter has used a theoretical and practical base to explore some of the possibilities that open up when these invisible foundations are explored from a Complex teaching and learning perspective. The move from receptive learning to active participation in real life and real time activity provides the condition for learning in the moment. The perturbations create occasions where the unconscious can be made visible. Once participants have acknowledged their need to notice more, they can choose to take control over the changes they wish to make. The importance of having the space to enter into conversation – especially with those who have different life experiences – is crucial as is a willingness to be disturbed. In this way, each session is co-determined by the participants, the teacher and the context which allows different possibilities to emerge at individual and group levels.

The changes described in this chapter point to the education of more truly wise executives who are aware of their actions in the moment and able to choose to act naturally as required in each situation. The initial results of the work reported in this chapter are extremely encouraging in this regard.

References
(several of the Breen articles listed below are available at www.chrisbreen.net)

C. Breen, 'A cautionary tale about rabbits, moles and choices', *Pythagoras*, Vol. 23 (1990), 20–22.
C. Breen, 'Teacher Education: confronting preconceptions', *Perspectives in Education*, Vol. 13, No. 1 (1992), 33–44.

C. Breen, 'Holding the tension of the opposites', *For the Learning of Mathematics*, Vol. 13, No. 1 (1993), 6–10.

C. Breen, 'Re-searching teaching: Changing paradigms to improve practice', in M.A. Clements, H. Tairab and W.K. Yoong (eds), *Science, Mathematics and Technical Education in the 20th and 21st Centuries* (Department of Science and Mathematics Education: Universiti Brunei Darassalam, 2000), 94–103.

C. Breen, 'Researching teaching: Telling the hole'd truth and nothing but my truth', in A. Rogerson (ed.), *Proceedings of the 3rd Mathematics Education into the 21st Century Project conference* (Palm Cove, Cairns, Australia, August 19–24, 2001).

C. Breen, 'Researching teaching: Moving from gut feeling to disciplined conversation', *South African Journal of Higher Education*, Vol. 16, No. 2 (2002), 25–31.

C. Breen, 'Perturbating the assessment of individuals and groups: Listening for challenges to mathematics teacher educators', *Pythagoras* 60 (December 2004a), 2–12.

C. Breen, 'In the serpent's den: Contrasting scripts relating to fear of mathematics', in M. Høines and A. Fuglestad (eds), *Proceedings of the 28th Conference of the International Group for the Psychology of Mathematics Education*, Vol. 2 (2004b), 167–174, Bergen, Norway.

C. Breen, 'Promising practices in teaching and learning', in C. Kasanda (ed.), *Proceedings of the 13th Annual Conference of the Southern African Association for Research in Mathematics, Science and Technology Education*, January 2005, Safari Conference Centre, Windhoek, Namibia.

C. Breen, 'Tugging at psychological threads in mathematics education', in T. Brown (ed.), *The Psychology of Mathematics Education: A Psychoanalytic Displacement* (Sense: Rotterdam, 2008a), 219–230.

C. Breen, 'The hole is more than the sum of its parts: Mathematics teacher education in a complex world', *Notices of the South African Mathematical Society*, Vol. 39, No. 1, April (2008b), 15–30.

F. Capra, *The Web of Life* (London: HarperCollins, 1997).

T. Dalmau, *The Six Circle Lens* (1995). Available at: http://www.dalmau.com/pdfs/six_circle_lens.pdf Accessed 9 July 2010.

J. David, Unpublished lecture notes on *Plato and Logic*, Public lecture given at the University of Cape Town, July (1992).

B. Davis, *Teaching Mathematics: Towards A Sound Alternative* (New York: Garland Publishing, 1996).

B. Davis, *Inventions of Teaching: A Genealogy* (London: Lawrence Erlbaum, 2004).

B. Davis and D. Sumara, 'Cognition, complexity, and teacher education', *Harvard Educational Review*, Vol. 67, No. 1 (1997), 104–125.

B. Davis and D. Sumara, *Innovation and Complexity Thinking 2.0*, Available from: http://education.alberta.ca/media/890564/innovation%20and%20complexity%20thinking%202.0-brent%20davis%20and%20dennis%20sumara.pdf Accessed 9 December 2008.

N. Depraz, F. Varela and P. Vermersch, *On Becoming Aware* (Amsterdam: John Benjamins, 2003).

D. Goleman, *Vital Lies, Simple Truths* (New York: Bloomsbury Publishing, 1997).

D. Henderson, *Experiencing Geometry: On Plane and Sphere* (New York: Prentice-Hall 1995).

D. Hock, *The Birth of the Chaordic Age* (New York: Berrett-Koehler, 1999).

J. Hollis, *On This Journey We Call Our Life* (Toronto: Inner City Books, 2003).

H. Kimberley and M. Fernbach (2006), *Research in the Middle: The Link between Issues and Actions in Equity Research*. AVETRA conference, 19–21 April. Available at http://www.avetra.org.au/ABSTRACTS2006/PA%200057.pdf Accessed: 8 July 2010.

J. Mason, *Researching Your Own Practice: The Discipline of Noticing* (London: Routledge-Falmer, 2002).

H. Maturana, 'Everything said is said by an observer', in W.I. Thompson (ed.), *Gaia: A Way of Knowing* (New York: Lindisfarne Press, 1987).

H. Maturana and F. Varela, *The Tree of Knowledge* (New York: Shambhala, 1986).

M. Merleau-Ponty, *Phenomenology of Percepti* (London: Routledge, 1962).

Scharmer, C. Otto, *Theory U: Leading from the Future as It Emerges* (Cambridge, Massachusetts: Society for Organisational Learning, 2007).

P. Senge, C.O. Scharmer, J. Jaworski and B.S. Flowers, *Presence: Human Purpose and the Field of the Future* (Cambridge, Massachusetts: Society for Organisational Learning, 2004).

D. Simons, *Gorilla Movie* (2007). Available from: http://viscog.beckman.illinois.edu/flashmovie/15.php

F.J. Varela, *Ethical Know-How* (Stanford: Stanford University Press, 1999).

F.J. Varela, E. Thompson and E. Rosch, *The Embodied Mind: Cognitive Science and Human Experience* (Cambridge, MA: The Press MIT, 1991).

M. Wheatley, *Finding Our Way: Leadership for an Uncertain Time* (New York: Berrett-Koehler, 2005).

12

Place-making: The Executive's Role in Aligning Learning with Work

Tom Short and Susan Coggan

Background

In today's global and competitive society, only a brave optimist would attempt to predict the future of workplace learning and then transfer the ascribed wisdom into a straightforward text. Moreover, the challenge of forecasting how executives might approach learning in the years ahead is hazardous, due to the vastness of the topic and rapidly expanding complexity of how people learn and develop in modern organisations. Nevertheless, in this chapter, we review the environmental context of workplace learning, armed with new findings taken from a qualitative research study in the New Zealand manufacturing sector. We reveal how executives are partnering with in-house HRD professionals to create an innovative strategy for improving performance and employee engagement. This approach focuses on developing a learning culture around an emerging concept of humanistic geography – an activity we have aptly called 'place-making'.

Learning to survive and global turbulence

Since the early 1980s, countless organisations have experienced the effects of globalisation and for some these changes have been overwhelming (Smith et al., 2003; Boxall and Purcell, 2003; Johnson and Scholes, 1993). In parallel with economic challenges, advancements in technology have re-formed the commercial landscape. High-tech environments require less labour and fewer raw materials so the only way organisations can survive is by making radical improvements in the way human capital is managed. In this turbulent environment, survival has become the key imperative, for both the organisation and employees (Cacioppe, 1998). At an organisational level, survival means staying in business by continually addressing gaps between the desired and actual level of performance, but for employees, the instinctive need to survive has stimulated greater flexibility and adaptation to endless programmes of change. Executives have carried prime responsibility for ensuring survival, attaining growth and driving performance improvement, but in addition, managers of today deal with an unremitting range of issues. These include: skills shortages, scarce resources and ever-increasing workload priorities. From a leadership perspective, a defining attribute has become how to survive and create competitive advantage by taking full advantage of human capital. Ongoing research confirms that the development of human capital has a much stronger impact on organisational performance than was previously recognised (Yukl and Lepsinger, 2005).

New practices in management

The introduction of new practices in management, such as total quality management (Oakland, 2004), team working concepts (Williams, 1996), lean production techniques and business process reengineering, has influenced greatly the formalisation of workplace learning, organisational development and employee engagement programmes. Primarily these practices were developed to harness the knowledge and creativity of employees, at the same time building organisational capability to deal with globalisation and change. In America, one estimate claimed over 50 per cent of the entire workforce was affected by at least two new management practices during the 1990s (Smith et al., 2004). In the UK, organisational development frameworks, such as Investors in People, the Charter Mark and Business Excellence added these new management practices. However, critics report the high cost of implementing such projects over long periods of time and claim they rarely delivered on the full promise, leaving the organisation with masses of paperwork, process documents, workplace tension and inflexible systems. In the book, *'First break all the rules'* Buckingham and Coffman (1999) report on two major studies undertaken by the Gallup organisation and state:

> The last 20 years have offered over 9000 different systems, languages, principles and paradigms to help explain the mysteries of management and leadership. This barrage of conflicting, impressionistic and largely anecdotal advice is overwhelming, but it rarely enlightens. It lacks precision and simplicity. There is very little quantitative research and virtually no standards of measurement (p.53).

The notion of alignment

Central to the implementation of new management practices are vertically and horizontally integrated strategies of human resource management that aim to link the performance of people with the longer-term aspirations of the organisation (Anderson, 2009). In recent years, it has become commonplace for managers to borrow marketing-centric jargon to define concepts and 'alignment' is now used to express a desire for strategic integration. This term has grown to accommodate a form of management hegemony, where all training and development activities are subsumed within a HRD portfolio. According to Purlington and Butler, 'Aligning an organisation's strategy with its values, and its objectives with management practices will determine how well the employees perform. This in turn will determine an organisation's successes' (2003: 63). For these reasons, alignment represents an ideology with profound implications. Stakeholders come to the notion of alignment with an emotional blend of excitement and anxiety, looking for ways to advance the *status quo* (Short, 2008). Senge (1990) believes that learning organisations align employees with strategic goals through systematic and sustained programmes of learning. Alignment helps to focus people on the business goals and in doing so minimises the risk of developing strategic drift (Thompson, 1995). Strategic drift is a condition where the cumulative efforts of misaligned people, often small and undetected, produce a resultant energy that shifts the organisation's performance away from its intended direction. Managers say, 'We are aligning our training to the business goals 'or', our training projects are aligned strategically to the business need' but what does this mean? According to Anderson (2009) alignment has evolved to represent 'a dual concept that converges HRD processes on business outcomes' (p.265). Others question whether this idea is possible in an increasingly complex business environment, asking whether it is feasible to align HRD with strategy, given the added complexity that what works today in business may be inappropriate for tomorrow (Bailey and Clarke, 2008; Thompson, 1995). A representation of this concept is illustrated in Figure 12.1.

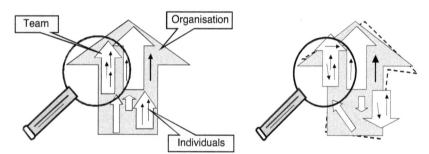

Figure 12.1   Alignment and strategic drift

(Adapted by Short, 2008 from Senge, 1990)

Strategic architecture

An alternative, and perhaps more useful, interpretation of the notion of alignment might be to consider how managers blend the internal demands of the organisation, such as the changing workforce and resource constraints, with challenges from the external environment, such as market, fiscal and ecological pressures. Thompson (1995) refers to this process as strategic architecture and the viewpoint has merit because not only do people become part of and learn from their workplace environment, but the same process happens in reverse – people shape the environment. Aligned organisations with good strategic architecture are thought to be effective and harmonious because learning and performance are crafted around the unique context of each setting.

The emerging paradigms of place and place-making

These notions of environmental congruence, architecture and alignment bring to the surface an emerging paradigm of workplace development that hitherto has not featured in business texts. One based on a more equitable partnership between employer and employee. This is the paradigm of Place. Place offers a reflective platform for evaluating the efficacy of new management practices in the workplace environment, often delivered under the pretext of HRD. Hardy and Newsham observe that 'the physical setting and context for learning within which HRD takes place is often 'taken-for-granted' and rarely discussed' (Elliot and Turnbull, 2005: 96). Elliot also found this 'a curious omission given that we live in an era which debates and discusses about humans' impact on the physical environment, migration patterns, and changing demographics as a daily occurrence' (2005: 504). These insights have an impact on the future of learning and we have defined this process as place-making. In other words, creating and crafting learning environments that provide economic, intellectual, cultural, psychological, emotional and sensory nourishment for the people who will use the place.

The Café
Earnest Hemmingway wrote, "The clean, well-lighted café of the story's title is its central image. This kind of café is a kind of idealised space; in it, even the loneliest most despairing of men can find some comfort. The café represents a space in which one can escape from the troubles – in this case, from the despair of everyday life. The old waiter explains why these specific elements are necessary. In his ideal space; he needs the café to be clean and quiet and most importantly, he requires a lot of light. But why, what does light do for these characters? Why can't the older waiter or old man be content to sit in a dimly-lit bar to drink undisturbed? The answer is simple, light chases away the dark. You know the feeling of insecurity and dread that can creep at night. That's what these characters are feeling...the awful nothingness of life."

This metaphor of the Café by Hemmingway captures perfectly the essence of why place-making is important. It describes an idealised environment where relationships are developed between people, and between people and their place. Place-making strategies are therefore determined through consultation with 'citizens of the settlement' (in this case the employees) and the whole community is engaged towards a fulfilment of their aspirations and needs.

Place and identity in learning

The notion of place has its origins within the spatial tradition of geography and is normally classified as Place Theory, but in recent years there has been an increasing association between geography and philosophy. This phenomenon has grown to acquire a particular relevance for a new perspective within geography, known as humanistic geography (Bullock, Stallybrass and Trombley, 1977). Researchers in geography who focus on people and cultures (known as cultural geography and the sub-field of humanistic geography) see the intricacies of human existence as fundamental to the understanding of cultures (Rosenberg, 2008). In this context, the notion of place goes beyond the rational objectivist paradigm of business and represents the many values, beliefs, feelings, hopes and fears that being human attaches both individually and collectively in certain settlements, environments and landscapes (Somerville, 2008). For example, in New Zealand and the South Pacific Islands, the indigenous populations have a strong sense of belonging to and feeling at home in a certain place. In Maori culture the *Marae*, or meeting place, serves as a community-based conduit in which the spiritual, societal and educational enrichment of a neighbourhood are blended together. People have a desire to feel as if they belong to a social and cultural community and long for a feeling of attachment; feeling in-place with their environment and valuing those people who work within it. Therefore, with foundations in social and environmental psychology, place identity deals with the complex interfaces between the local setting and cultural traditions. It recognises the diversity in educational aspirations and how they influence the choices of lifestyle for people who live within the settlement. In New Zealand, the place of our research, Maori traditionally identify themselves not as individuals, but as members of a set of relations, which include not only relatives but also places and landmarks that are viewed as ancestors (Unitec, 2008). To view oneself through a place signals a collective responsibility to that environment no matter what else transpires. All of these values come together in the *Marae*, or meeting place. This worldview may seem strange in a Westernised society, where one's self interest can often be at the centre of everything. From our interaction with indigenous groups, we found the notion of place had a number of important characteristics:

– It was based on human settlements, communities and unique locations
– It contained all aspects of human existence in a settlement or community
– It relied on citizenship as a basis for security and recognition

- Learning was achieved through the application and sharing of tacit knowledge
- Culture and values underpinned behaviours within the settlement
- The environment was largely qualitative and existential.

Place and work

How then can we transfer these ideas to the workplace? It is part of human nature for people to create and then reside within a place (Fisher, 2006) and the work environment is part of this equation. Many people spend almost a quarter of their lives at work and arrange the environment around their needs. Creating a place identity allows people to feel more in control of their lives and helps them to feel more empowered and safe. The work of Knowles, Holton and Swanson (2005) and others indicates that contextual relevance, individual autonomy, recognition and security are embedded in how people learn. Today, many organisations recognise these 'needs of the environment' by arranging induction programmes at a corporate and local level; encouraging people to feel included and engaged at the earliest opportunity. Therefore, the place has important connections in ensuring learners are ready to learn and embrace what the organisation is asking of people. Place is therefore manifest in several dimensions of an organisation's existence such as culture, climate, employee motivation and employment relations. These emotions are captured frequently with statements such as 'I really enjoy working at this place' or 'this place has changed since we became part of a multi-national group'.

Place and pedagogy

Although mainstream studies on HRD do not address specifically this tradition of geography, the concept of place, and its connections with learning are historic. The pedagogy of place, in relation to employment-based learning pivots on a simple premise with profound implications: our worldview influences our work and our work can influence our worldview. Advocates of vocational learning refer to this concept as the 'the useful citizen' and this notion is grounded in the early work of education theorists such as Kerschensteiner (1912), Dewey (Knowles et al., 2005) and Lindeman (1926). Likewise, Bronfenbrenner (1979) recognised, from an educational and ecological standpoint, how human development is drawn from the settings in which people spend time. The relationship between people and their place of work represents an ongoing and substantial body of research; compounded by the growing complexity of interpreting how the internal and external environments shape workplace learning. According to Gruenwald (2007: 7) education grounded in 'the place' [such as workplace education and training] 'relates directly to the learner's experience of the world and improves the quality of life for the people and their communities'. This statement reinforces an important connection between how the societal outcomes of learning coexist with the learning individual employees experience in the course of their work. The main assertion is that learning employees are also learning citizens and *vice versa*. How organisations recognise this concept, and create a place for effective learning, is central to both employee and workplace development, but there are also important societal connections. Place pedagogy links the employees' worldview with their attitude to learning at work.

The place pentagon

The place pentagon was developed from in-depth research findings to capture the essence of place and define a unique framework against which individuals could evaluate their sense of alignment with the workplace environment, management systems and practices. The employee's self-interest in deriving meaning from workplace development is well documented. Here we suggest that individuals create a cognitive and emotional map of their internal and external environments based on their knowledge, experience and insight. This plan enables individuals to understand and engage with situations, using multiple pathways of learning. In this research, employees within the case study organisations were found to acquire, assimilate and then accommodate learning, reflecting the ideas of Illeris (2004). They drew on five contextual elements from their places of work and many factors were found to influence place. For simplicity, they were assembled into a five-sided tension field called the Place Pentagon (Figure 12.2). Collectively these five dimensions captured the essence of how people created and engaged with

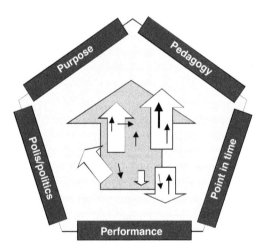

Figure 12.2   The place pentagon

(Short, 2008)

their own learning place. They include: (1) politics/*polis*, (2) pedagogy, (3) place environment at a point in time, (4) purpose and (5) performance.

Place politics and polis: Political awareness and adaptation has become an increasing facet of organisational life (Hartley and Branicki, 2006), but in the context of place, this refers to how employees are able to work together democratically and make decisions as citizens of the enterprise. Through a wide range of formal and informal learning mechanisms, employees assess how managers value participation and distribute power through communication processes and systems that are based on inclusion and involvement. This dimension also considers how the workplace culture aligns with the employee's identity and self-esteem; allowing individuals an opportunity to connect with their work environment and value the organisation's contribution to the wider society in a deeply meaningful way. The toxicity of internal politics was thought to erode cultural engagement in the case studies and employees were looking for authenticity in their workplace, characterised by the need for ethical adeptness, evidence of equity and honesty by the employer. A humanistic/existentialist perspective would argue that authenticity has great importance in the context of delegated authority and the decentralisation of decision-making.

Place pedagogy: Place-based education lacks a specific theoretical tradition, but its practices and purposes can be linked to experiential learning, problem-based learning, constructivism and indigenous education (Gruenwald, 2003). In a learning-centred workplace, the content and context of HRD processes must be congruent with the learners' abilities and geared towards achievement in the work environment. Place-based education values the importance of specific content and tacit skill, arguing that an appreciation of the place increases the value of learning. Place-based education also encourages both trainers and learners to think about how the exploration of the place can become part of how learning content is created and then organised around the organisation's culture. In this study, each case study used the uniqueness of their products and geographic advantage to create bespoke learning environments. In addition, the organisations recognised the unique learning styles and value systems of different cultures towards learning, blending learning activities to meet these needs.

Place environment: From a HRD perspective, a snapshot of an organisation's internal capability at any point-in-time represents a unique synthesis of peoples' abilities, motivations and opportunities. This is sometimes referred to as 'core competency' (Thompson, 1995). However, this snapshot must be seen as a dynamic representation of the internal environment, as sometimes an alignment between the right opportunity, its appropriateness and the right time is not always evident. In the case studies, place-making was linked with an adeptness to identify and craft learning opportunities present in the environment, but these were influenced by the life cycle stages of human resource strategy. For example, the four stage life cycle model suggested by Kochan and

Barocci (1985) of start-up, growth, maturity and decline posed different challenges for local HRD practitioners and learners. In this regard, managers who were more entrepreneurial appeared to be intuitive and had a flare for spotting life-cycle opportunities by positioning both themselves and others in the right place at the right time. In a complex and dynamic working environment what worked today might be inappropriate tomorrow and people could easily become misaligned or displaced as the organisation moved its strategic direction. This suggestion is indicated in the fourth quadrant of Figure 12.3.

Place purpose: The creation of a compelling and meaningful purpose was the foundation of strategic planning and central to place-making. In the case studies, this was communicated to employees through briefing systems, written documents, planning sessions and intranet-based initiatives. Part of this process was to ensure the actions required of people were directed towards mutually acceptable goals. There needed to be a compelling purpose to the place of work and people needed shared commitment to the purpose. How individuals connected with the purpose of the place influenced the extent to which they aligned their behaviours with the organisation's objectives. In this context the place purpose transcended a desire for profit, although most of those interviewed realised the inseparable connection between the two.

Place performance: Finally, we suggest that the well-known synthesis of ability, motivation and opportunity (Appelbaum and Batt, 1994), is a useful predicator of performance improvement. When people felt 'in-place', the utilisation of tacit knowledge and skill was evident and motivation was directed towards favourable results for the organisation. In the case studies, results varied according to the strategy, but included: continuous improvement, attainment of excellence and high levels of sustainability in business performance. Alignment tools, such as performance management systems and coaching techniques, were used to encourage place performance, but the findings indicated that the efficacy of these systems was entirely dependent on the commitment of managers. Equally, when employees' work behaviours were misaligned with the *expectations of the place* their performance diminished.

Place engagement

Our research findings indicated that when employees connected with each dimension of the place pentagon, at a cognitive, emotional and social level, the organisation climate and performance flourished. This was evaluated through employee surveys, customer feedback processes and employment statistics. Borrowing the concept of symbolic convergence theory from Bormann (Olufowote, 2006), place-based alignment was found to be a communication-centric approach to HRD and the five dimensions of the place pentagon represented distinct lenses through which employees, both individually and collectively, evaluated their expectations of the organisation's environment and made sense of how they connected with it. In the main, people were found to adopt three mindsets: (1) feeling 'In place', (2) feeling 'Out of place' and (3) feelings of being 'Placeless'. Two things influenced these mindsets: firstly, the employee's level of awareness in their immediate work environment and secondly, their level of engagement with the organisational ethos. The diagram in Figure 12.3 shows how people engaged with each area of the quadrant box and adopted behavioural characteristics appropriate to their sense of place. Based on an intuitive assessment by the employee of both high (+) or low (–) awareness and connectivity, these lenses converged into an assessment of whether people felt 'in-place', 'out of place' or 'placeless' in relation to the five dimensions of the place pentagon and this affected both the quality of their learning and level of engagement. Importantly, fully engaged employees indicated a strong connection between feeling in place and being aligned with the organisation or team.

Place-based assessment, therefore, became a kind of existential outlook and choice that attempted to make meaning from the complex, and often, chaotic workplace. Furthermore, the notion of place was individualistic and meant different things to different people. For example, long-serving employees saw the workplace as a familiar environment, full of well-known friends who shared in the traditions, team protocols and workplace culture. Newer employees saw these traditions as psychological and/or physical barriers, especially if the new employee was relocating from overseas and had the dual challenge of adapting to a new language and culture; they experienced something akin to existential alienation.

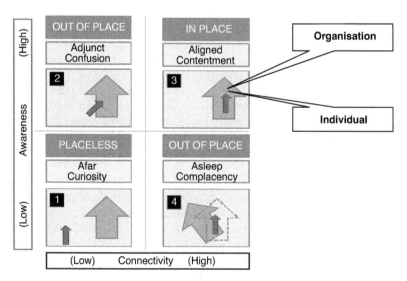

Figure 12.3   Place positioning

(Short, 2009)

Figure 12.3 illustrates a four-stage concept map of place positioning. We suggest the place pentagon offers a framework and tension field on which both leaders and followers can evaluate the sense of alignment with the workplace environment. The employee's self-interest in deriving meaning from workplace development is well documented (VandenBerg, Richardson et al., 1999; Knowles et al., 2005) and the suggestion is that individuals create a cognitive and emotional map of their environments, based on their knowledge and experience of an internal schema. This plan enables individuals to understand and engage with situations, using multiple scripted pathways of learning (Leonard, 2002). This is the essence of the place pentagon and each of the five dimensions can be described as lenses through which employees evaluated their organisation, as a successful settlement, to determine their level of personal engagement and commitment.

Reflections on the research programme

From the outset, we were anxious to know if the accumulated effect of major developments in global strategy, HRM policy deployment and new management practices had led to a confusing state of tension within HRD. We were unsure if the strain of these developments had influenced how managers learnt the important skills of leading and developing people. We questioned if the consequences of this assertion might result in a tired and disengaged workforce, who had become cynical about organisational development initiatives and the concealed management hegemony within HRD. This concern led to our programme of research to determine precisely what was happening in organisations and learn how HRD, learning and strategy were being integrated towards business survival. Importantly, the starting point was to understand fully what was meant by the term alignment. The research programme drew insight from an extensive review of literature, three in-depth case studies conducted in the New Zealand manufacturing sector, feedback from an independent focus group of human resource professionals and observations of current practices in organisations. This research considered the implementation of workforce development projects and practices undertaken to enhance performance improvement.

Approach to research

The chosen research methodology was based on an in-depth qualitative study, drawing evidence from a wide-range of sources, and adopted four important characteristics. First, it was essential to find a qualitative method that accommodated the researchers own experiences of management and HRD; secondly, the researchers wanted to research an environment where their experiences would enable a contextual traction – saving valuable time in learning new jargon and/or processes, thirdly, the researchers sought to understand the US/Anglo centric assumptions and strategies on HRD in a remote and culturally diverse setting; finally, there was a need to include a wider range of stakeholders to build on the initial findings obtained from an extensive literature review.

A case study approach was selected, using an interpretive enquiry, but with a 'splash' of hermeneutics. Hermeneutics is an underused method in business-related research that has been described as the 'art and science of interpretation'. The cyclic nature of hermeneutics analysis allows for the accommodation and examination of our own cultural traditions and expectations, alongside those obtained from the occupational field and wider research community. Hermeneutic analysis is based on the interpretation of pre-existing theories in relation to life experience, which in turn inform the development of new interpretations and theories (Ezzy, 2002). Put simply, as the cycle progresses deeper insights are discovered. Importantly, hermeneutic exploration defines the way new ideas emerge, often tangential from the expected trajectory. An important characteristic of hermeneutic research is how new possibilities become apparent when the researcher moves beyond what is already written (Usher,et al., 1997; Ezzy, 2002). This approach had much appeal and was finally realised with the unintentional emergence of *place making* as a new paradigm for describing an effective HRD strategy. In the main fieldwork, 38 people participated from three organisations,including five different job roles. Organisations were selected because of their size, location and significance to the New Zealand economy. In order to obtain a balance of feedback, nine interviews were held with chief executives, senior HRD practitioners and, where present, trade union representatives. Additionally, six focus groups were held with line managers and worker-learners. Finally, to provide an independent perspective, feedback from an external focus group of HRD practitioners was added. Through a methodical process of analysing and interpreting the literature content and research information, key themes were developed as a basis of the findings. This process was especially valuable in understanding the characteristics of HRD alignment that ultimately led to the significance of place.

Summary

In this chapter, we have focused on the internal and external environments in which contemporary HRD operates and we have questioned, albeit briefly, if new management practices provide the appropriate vehicle for aligning people with business objectives. We have dared to suggest that the implicit management hegemony contained within new management practices may be unhelpful in securing longer-term employee engagement. Through a detailed examination of workplace HRD practices in three successful organisations, we discovered that long-term worker engagement (and success) came not only from the pursuit of overarching alignment activities, such as balanced scorecard frameworks, but from a collection of sub-systems deeply rooted in the discipline of ontology – that is, systems helping employees to learn and develop in order to gain meaning and security from their existence in internal environment. More practically, the paradigm of place was the foundation on which these sub-systems were built. We discovered that the concept of place, as a construct of the physical and psychological work setting, represented a perspective not considered directly in other HRD research, but embodied an innovative idea that encapsulated the essence of what contextual HRD alignment means in organisations. Importantly, the five dimensions of place represented distinct lenses through which managers could evaluate the organisational strategy on HRD and pursue employee engagement. What we discovered in New Zealand was an authentic approach that positioned HRD professionals and managers as the 'architects of place-making' when addressing the highly complex mix of people, place, culture and the environment. Furthermore, the Place Pentagon (Figure 12.2) and an appreciation of place positioning (Figure 12.3) could be assembled into a workable model of gaining employee engagement that recognised the unique challenges for each organisation, but set them in context to each organisation's unique environment. For us, the research revealed that the concepts of 'place' and 'place-making' had implications beyond the bottom line and reached out to the broader well-being of society, helping to define the meaning of learning in the globalised workplace, not just for individuals, but also for the wider community. The notion of 'place' was found to be an underexplored area of organisational development, yet it had a powerful effect on how people embraced learning and served the community in which they worked. As the great educator, John Dewey said, 'Education cannot be detached from the life of the local place it serves.' Every case study organisation in our New Zealand research was part of a multi-national business where the meaning of community was much harder to maintain. In our experience, subsidiaries of multi-national enterprises easily become impersonal and more detached from the local setting (Short, 2008). We suggest that place-making HRD strategies could help managers to avoid becoming disengaged from the life of the local place. Finally, this chapter delved into the complex role of HRD, in a turbulent business environment, and uncovered some of the emerging issues that shape executive decisions about organisational learning. HRD is caught-up in an ongoing debate that challenges the usefulness of its strategic contribution and commentators believe executives and HRD professionals need to get much better at evaluating learning. However, this activity has proved to be illusive, or challenging, at the strategic level. Using research information obtained from the rich bi/multi-cultural work environment, this chapter has discussed how the concept model, based on place, offers an alternative perspective for deploying and evaluating HRD. These concepts contribute to the process of alignment and enhance the strategic significance of HRD. The findings offer a thought-provoking and innovative interpretation of how place-making provides a new platform for executives to arrange HRD. In particular, the definitions of being 'placeless' or 'out of place' in a turbulent workplace draw special attention to how misaligned or context-free learning can impact negatively on the performance of people. This area is a growing issue for those who work outside of their usual place at a physical, psychological, emotional or societal level such as: migrant workers, those forced to make a lateral career transition, older workers facing upskilling programs and people returning to employment after a period away from the workplace. We believe that future leaders can gain much insight from appreciating the paradigm of humanistic geography and develop the skills of place-making, as they strive to improve culture, promote workforce engagement, foster a learning environment and make organisations a better place.

References

V. Anderson, 'Desperately seeking alignment: Reflections of senior line managers and HRD executives', *Human Resource Development International*, Vol. 12, No. 3 (2009), 263–277.

E. Appelbaum and R. Batt, *The New American Workplace* (Ithaca NY: ILR Press, 1994).

C. Bailey and M. Clarke, 'Aligning business leadership development with business needs: The value of discrimination', *Journal of Management Development*, Vol. 27, No. 9 (2008), 912–934.

P. Boxall and J. Purcell, *Strategy on Human Resource Management* (Basingstoke: Palgrave Macmillan, 2003).

U. Bronfenbrenner, *The Ecology of Human Development* (Cambridge: Harvard University Press, 1979).

M. Buckingham and C. Coffman, *First Break All the Rules* (New York: Simon and Schuster, 1999).

A. Bullock, O. Stallybrass and S. Trombley, *The Fontana Dictionary of Modern Thought* (London: Fontana paperbacks, 1977).

R. Cacioppe, 'An integrated model and approach for the design of effective leadership development programs', *Leadership and Organisational Development Journal*, Vol. 19, No. 1 (1998), 44–53.

C. Elliott, AHRD Conference 2005: 'An opportunity to review our learning', *Human Resource Development* International, Vol. 8, No. 4 (2005), 503–508.

D. Ezzy, *Qualitative Analysis – Practice and innovation* (Crows Nest NSW: Allen & Unwin, 2002).

J.J. Fisher, 'Creating place identity: It's part of human nature' (2006) Accessed 10 February 2009 from http://environmentpsychology.com/place identity.htm

D.A. Gruenwald, 'The best of both worlds: A critical pedagogy of place', *Educational Researcher*, Vol. 32, No. 4 (2003), 3–12.

G. Hardy and C. Newsham, 'Place: A (re)source for learning', in C. Elliot and S. Turnbull (eds), *Critical Thinking in HRD* (London: Routledge, 2005).

J. Hartley and L. Branicki, *Managing with Political Awareness* (London: Chartered Management Institute, 2006), October.

K. Illeris, *The Three Dimensions of Learning – Contemporary Learning Theory in the Tension Field Between Cognitive, the Emotional and the Societal* (Frederiksberg: Roskilde University Press, 2004).

G. Johnson and K. Scholes, *Exploring Corporate Strategy* (London: Prentice Hall, 1993).

G. Kerschensteiner, *Der Begriff der Arbeitsschule* (Leipzig and Berlin: Teubner, 1912). Available at: www.faqs.org.childhood/In-Ke/Kerschensteiner-Georg-1854-1932. html Accessed 22 April 2009.

M.S. Knowles, E.F. Holton and R.A. Swanson (2005) *The Adult Learner – The Definitive Classic in Adult Education and Human Resource Development* (Burlington, MA: Elsevier, 2005).

T. Kochan and T. Barocci, *Human Resource Management and Industrial Relations* (Boston: Little Brown, 1985).

D.C. Leonard, *Learning Theories A to Z* (Westport, CT: Greenwood Press, 2002).

E.C. Lindeman, *The Meaning of Adult Education* (New York: New Republic, 1976).

J. Oakland, *Oakland on Quality Management* (Oxford, UK: Elsevier, 2004).

J.O. Olufowote, 'Rousing and redirecting a sleeping giant: Symbolic convergence theory and complexities in the communicative and constitution of collective action', *Management Communications Quarterly*, Vol. 19 (2006), 451–492.

C. Purlington and C. Butler, *Build to Learn* (New York: Amacom, 2003).

M. Rosenberg, *Definition of Geography* (2008). Available at: www.geography.about. com/od/studygeography/a/geographydfn.htm Accessed 10 April 2008.

P. Senge, *The Fifth Discipline – The Art and Practice of the Learning Organisation* (New York: Doubleday, 1990).

T.W. Short, *Strategic Alignment and Learning in Human Resource Development: A Hermeneutic Exploration*, a PhD thesis submitted to the University of South Australia, Adelaide (2008).

T.W. Short, *The Shape and Place of HRD in a Globalised and Turbulent Workplace*, Paper to the 10th International Conference on human resource development research and practice across Europe, Newcastle upon Tyne, 10–12 June (2009).

A. Smith, E. Oczkowski, C. Noble and R. Macklin, 'New management practices and enterprise training in Australia', *International Journal of Manpower*, Vol. 24, No. 1 (2003), 31–47.

A. Smith, E. Oczkowski, C. Noble and R. Macklin, 'The impact of organisational change on the nature and extent of training in Australian enterprises', *International Journal of Training and Development*, Vol. 8, No. 2 (2004), 94–110.

M. Somerville, *Where is 'place' in VET*, AVETRA 11th Annual Conference (2008). Available at: www.avetra.org.au/annual_conference/papers.shtml Accessed 13 June 2008.

J.L. Thompson, *Strategy in Action* (London: Chapman & Hall, 1995).

Unitec, *Maori Pedagogy* Arts (2008) Available at: http://arts.unitec.ac.nz/ask/view_answers. php?question=41 Accessed 6 May 2008.

R. Usher, I. Bryant and R. Johnson, *Adult Education and the Postmodern Challenge: Learning Beyond the Limits* (London: Routledge, 1977).

H. Williams, *The Essence of Managing Groups and Teams* (Hemel Hempstead, UK: Prentice Hall, 1996).

R.J. VandenBerg, H.A. Richardson and L.J. Eastman, 'The impact of high involvement work processes on organisational performance', *Group and Organisational Management*, Vol. 24 (1999), 300–339.

G. Yukl, and R. Lepsinger, 'Why integrating the leader and managing role is essential for organisational effectiveness', *Organizational Dynamics*, Vol. 34, No. 4 (2005), 361–375.

13

'An informed slowness' – Curiosity as an Enabler of Learning in the Attention Economy

Elaine Rumboll and Dave Duarte

In discussion with delegates on our executive education programmes we see mounting evidence of what is a societal trend towards multi-tasking and the uptake of information at speed. Tellingly, the all-pervasive availability of information from mass media channels and the resultant expectation by users to participate in the conversations that are taking place online point more and more to the inadequacy of the one-size-fits-all lecturing model with its focus on transmission-based learning.

Lectures have defined the university learning experience from its outset and are deeply entrenched in the mores of the *academe*. But we are finding our delegates are increasingly expressing frustration with longer, traditional classroom-style lectures and demand almost constant participation in order to remain attentive throughout our programmes. This itself is, in our view, symptomatic of increased complexity in the work context.

Many delegates also express a sense of being overwhelmed by the sheer amount of information they are confronted with daily. There is a certain sense of irony for them in this because, if anything, they come back to university to navigate this complexity more effectively, but instead, they are often presented with more information and complexity, and complete their programmes without a clear idea of what they need to do differently.

Information overload and filter failure

Much has been said about 'information overload' (Lanham, 2007: 6). For most of our delegates the instinctive response is to go faster, or, failing that, put in more hours to keep up. In fact, research on urban behaviour in an international study commissioned by the British Council (2007) suggests that urban populations are walking 10 per cent faster than they did in the last decade; with the greatest changes in the Far East, particularly in Singapore, where the average walking pace has increased by 30 per cent and in Guangzhou, China, where the pace is more than 20 per cent faster. According to Professor Richard Wiseman, who headed the study, as people speed up their lives they neglect diet, exercise and seeing friends and family, thus putting themselves at risk for chronic ill health, heart attacks and self-imposed social isolation.

The misguided belief that time is getting away, that we are starved of it, that there isn't enough of it and that you need to go faster and faster to keep up is known as 'time sickness' (Dossey in Honore, 2005: 3). Saving time and maximising efficiency in a world where information is in over-abundant supply has consequences for the future of learning, specifically in the context of executive education. Already we are seeing organisational requests for contact hours to be shortened significantly on leadership development programmes. Executive education suppliers are invited to design learning interventions which work according to byte-sized chunks able to be digested at speed by delegates. The onus for the uptake of knowledge is becoming increasingly the responsibility of the learner, in their assigned projects undertaken in their own time, for value creation back into the work environment.

It is our contention that this attitude is based on the acceptance of a faulty premise, that may lead to the learner being overwhelmed or perplexed. This premise, we suggest, is the equating of formal learning with the rapid uptake and repetition of information.

We need to understand learning in the context of a more globalised, complex and less predictable economy, which is very different from the kind of economy we have prepared business school delegates for hitherto. In the process we argue that for education to be effective there is a need for our engagement with information to be both different and slower. We suggest designing practices, strategies and principles that deliberately slow the pace of learning down at the beginning of a process, actively engage delegates and help them to apply the learning experiences, ensuring that they are able to filter the irrelevant while remaining open to the possibilities of new learning in even the most rigorously established fields of knowledge.

Clay Shirky (2008) was one of the first to argue that what we are experiencing in our new informational era is not information overload, but filter failure. Information, in Shirky's view, has always been abundant, but given the rise of digitised information, our well-worn info-filters that helped our predecessors to navigate the world of knowledge are no longer in any way adequate. Thus, it is important for educators and facilitators to understand what causes people to engage with new information meaningfully and less stressfully. It will thenceforth be argued that Curiosity is what would provide an effective filter of information, and a means of engaging a higher quality of attention among learners.

Informal polls conducted on various executive education programmes at the University of Cape Town's Graduate School of Business have shown us that the vast majority of delegates on executive education programmes are working longer hours, taking shorter breaks at work, and multi-tasking more, compared to two years ago. Many also agree with the view that there are simply not enough hours in the day to accomplish what they need to at work.

The rise of the attention economy

This sense of working harder and faster, while still falling behind, can perhaps be attributed to the boom in information driven by globalisation and communications technology. Over the last 500 years, civilisation has been shaped by the emergence of at least seven mass media: Print; Recordings; Radio; Cinema; Television; the World Wide Web; and Mobile. The last two, Web and Mobile, will be even more disruptive than the previous five because they bring with them a broad-based publishing boom that has exponentially increased the amount of information available to everyone using them. As educators and facilitators we need to come to terms with the fact that we are now competing for learners' attention with digital content and experiences.

This surely implies that there is a concomitant shift in the value of information. Information in many business fields is now abundantly available online and in the plethora of new books published every month, so the 'price' of certain types of information is plummeting as supply increases. This shift is currently playing out in the news industry, which is faced with an entirely new competitive landscape as a result of the internet. While content may still be as valuable to the consumer as ever, the sheer volume of news freely available online means that many news organisations are struggling to get people to pay for their content. Chris Anderson in his book 'Free: the Future of a Radical Price' (2009) argues that organisations that previously made money from selling information and content need to rethink their business model around giving that content away for free. Ryanair, for instance, has disrupted its industry by defining itself more as a full-service travel agency than a seller of airline seats. Ryanair CEO Michael O'Leary has gone so far as to say that he hopes to one day offer all seats on his flights for free (perhaps offset by in-air gambling, turning his planes into flying casinos) (Chris Anderson, 2008).

If information is freely available, then price or access to information is no longer a driver for consumers. Consumers will be drawn to news sources that are able to add value to the information in ways that enhance their experience of it – through more effective design, accessibility, a larger network of people conversing around it and engagement, for example.

A similar scenario could be playing out in executive education. Considering the growing amount of freely available academic material – accessed via websites such as MIT Open Courseware and Google Scholar, not to mention video talks easily accessibly on websites such as TED.com it may well be that universities need to shift their value proposition away from content. According to the polymath Nobel laureate, Herbert Simon,

> *In an information-rich world, the wealth of information means a dearth of something else: a scarcity of whatever it is that information consumes. What information consumes is rather obvious: it consumes the attention of its recipients. Hence a wealth of information creates a poverty of attention and a need to*

> *allocate that attention efficiently among the overabundance of information sources that might consume it*
>
> (1971: 140–141).

It is the allocation of our scarce resource of attention amidst the abundance of information as a resource which is one of the greatest challenges facing us as learners in the 21st century. According to Sam Anderson (2009), as beneficiaries of the greatest information boom in the history of the world, we are suffering, according to Simon's logic, a correspondingly serious 'poverty of attention'. This poverty of attention, coupled with the rise of information and media that demand it, has been dubbed by Simon as 'the Attention Economy' because it is in this age where attention becomes a scarce and valuable resource to be traded with care.

In the so-called Attention Economy, people become more conservative with their attention resources (Goldhaber, 2009). They tend to notice proportionately less of the total information available to them. Conversely, organisations benefit from the attention of consumers, as evidenced by swelling marketing and branding budgets in organisations of every shape and size in developed societies. This further exacerbates the tension between those that conserve attention, and those that seek it, the effects of which can be seen in the distracted and multi-tasking learner.

The concept of an attention economy sits uncomfortably juxtaposed with the industrial model of knowledge production and education. Information is intrinsically valuable in the industrial model because it is relatively scarce, exclusive and hierarchical. It makes sense then, to build empires around a core of intellectual property, and offer high-priced education and training centred on this scarce information. However, once information becomes freely available on the internet or via mass media it may be easily accessed and shared by anyone who can operate a search engine and send an email. Thus, in sectors where information is abundant and available, the only 'cost' of information is the time and effort – Simon's Attention Economy – that it takes to engage with it.

In order to successfully prepare learners to engage with this new economy, education may need to start emphasising ' Attentiveness', over Information. In other words, the role of education in the 21st century may be to enhance people's ability to navigate and apply new information, rather than to remember it. According to Markova, 'rather than merely accumulating new theories and more information that will be outmoded in a few years, our focus must shift to learning how to learn' (Markova, 2009: 3). It is our assertion that this kind of learning can only happen when the curiosity of learners is engaged, and when they are able to use information to playfully construct and deconstruct their perspectives as befits their context.

This sense-making component of learning may, therefore, provide the key to unlocking the full potential of learners. But this can only be fruitful if we can somehow nurture a state of curious agility in the face of the quantity of information available. This state of curiosity and re-invigoration in the face of new information may even become the key executive survival skill for the 21st century. In fact, a recent McKinsey survey has revealed that 89 per cent of more than 1,500 executives surveyed globally considered agility as either very or extremely important for their business success and 91 per cent indicated that it had become more important over the last five years (Ryan, 2009).

Attention, information and curiosity

If information consumes our attention and attention is a scarce resource, then it would behoove those in places of learning to understand and nurture what it is that improves the quality of our attention. In the same way that it makes no sense to try and speed up the usage of time available, it makes no sense to try and conserve attention as it is a resource, like time, which cannot be saved up for future usage. Mihaly Csikszentmihalyi (2008) observes that our nervous systems are only capable of processing 110 bytes[1] of information per second. We therefore have a limited physiological capacity to process information. Concentration on one person presenting information consumes around 60 bytes of that capacity and it is what makes it difficult for one to concentrate on more than two voices at a time (Shannon, 1948). If we cannot barter in the quantity of this resource then it would be meaningful to engage with what it is that improves the quality of this scarce unit of exchange.

The notion of curiosity sits in a somewhat paradoxical position to attention because it seems reasonable to assume that 'the more curious one is, the more information one acquires' (Harvey, et al., 2007: 44). But according to Simon, information consumes our attention. If curiosity generates more information which in turn consumes our attention which is required for learning effectively, then surely curiosity by the same argument should not be encouraged as it depletes further an already scarce resource? However, as Csikszentmihalyi has demonstrated, attention cannot be stored up for later usage and hence the reaction of many to 'go faster' in order to make better use of their attention is misplaced. It is only meaningful to speak about the quality of its usage as the quantity of our nervous systems' processing power is relatively fixed. It is therefore the *type* of information we are paying attention to which the lens of curiosity helps to filter effectively. 'The more information one acquires [through the lens of curiosity] the more one becomes aware of the gaps in one's knowledge and the more curious

---

[1]When all 110 bytes of attention are consumed by an activity, Csikszentmihalyi (2008) refers to this as being 'in flow'; when there is not enough attention excess to monitor anything else. Hunger, tiredness, even identity disappears from consciousness. High levels of challenge and skill create arousal and in extreme cases, flow.

one becomes about filling them' (Harvey, et al., 2007: 46). These authors termed this 'the spiral of curiosity' (p.46) based on the assumption that engaging in curious exploration can be ineffective and actually spiral our mental capacity down into a deeper morass of information overload and paralysis.

However, we argue that this assumption is based on the generalisation of curiosity. What needs to be acknowledged is that curiosity focuses our attention by filtering information and attempting to identify linkages between particular pieces of information that appear incongruent. Curiosity is 'an internal state occasioned when subjective uncertainty generates a tendency to engage in exploratory behaviour aimed at resolving or partially mitigating the uncertainty' (Walter in Berlyne, 1978: 98). It is critical to understand the nature of what David Berlyne (1978) terms 'epistemic curiosity'. He argues that curiosity is never about general exploration and seldom about overloading the senses with information which would indeed diminish the efficacy of our attention. 'Curiosity is always curiosity about something specific and it is pertinent only to specific exploration and not at all to diversive exploration' (Walter in Berlyne, 1978: 98). Curiosity with its specific focus is thus different from wonder which is associated with the exploration of the general. Perhaps it is rather 'the spiral of wonder' which Harvey et al. (2007) should be referring to, rather than curiosity.

If curiosity is always about the specific, it serves as a cognitive drive to organise (Rahman, 1966), to focus our attention and in this sense improves the quality of our attention by heightening the sense-making components of attending to information. 'It's not about whether we pay attention but how we pay attention to what is in the present' (Kashdan, 2009: 3). This attitude is crucial when it comes to our ability to learn, specifically in organisational contexts where attention is constantly under pressure. Without the necessary lens to filter the quantity of information and raise the quality of our attention in organisational environments which are often the place of anxiety about the amount of information needing to be processed, info-anxiety, the quality of our decision-making and judgment are severely impaired. Curiosity heightens levels of engagement with particular information (Harvey, et al., 2007), which serves as a sense-making tool for our mental models of the world. Cognitive uncertainty leads to increased arousal and exploratory behaviour. When that behaviour leads to resolution of the uncertainty, learning occurs and knowledge is gained (Harvey et al., 2007).

George Loewenstein's definition of curiosity is to our minds the most succinct when it comes to understanding the role of curiosity in the building of knowledge. In this account, curiosity is 'a form of cognitively induced deprivation that results from the perception of a gap in knowledge' (Loewenstein, 1994: 76) or understanding. Here the notion of curiosity is seen as what creates incongruence between a mental model and a referent out in the world containing more information than what we perceive ourselves to have. As our mental models are different so our incongruence will be different and by the same logic, our curiosity will be piqued differently by disparate experiences.

It is therefore our contention that curiosity is a uniquely customised filter for the information we encounter, and a regenerator of our attention or focus in the moment for more effective sensemaking.

Curiosity is 'an appreciating asset' (Leonard and Harvey, 2007: 310). The more one uses one's curiosity the more it grows. As the notion of curiosity emerges when there is incongruence between the mental model that one holds and the perception of a referent in the world holding more knowledge than one has, by implication, the more exposure one has to dissimilar things the more one's curiosity grows. Hence the importance of being exposed to ways of thinking and doing outside one's own discipline of interest or study, and the entailed importance of lifelong learning in order for curiosity to be stimulated.

In an alternative discipline, that of developmental robotics, curiosity is currently being given significant study, because curious robots would be learning robots that could adapt to their environment appropriately. In attempting to teach curiosity to robots, Jürgen Schmidhuber devised a notion of what he has termed 'intelligent adaptive curiosity' (Schmidhuber, 1991). He discovered that by using a process called 'condensation', robots could be equipped with an adaptive predictor to predict future events from the history of previous events and actions. According to Schmidhuber (1991), a reward-maximising, reinforcement-learning, adaptive controller steers the agent and gets a curiosity reward for executing action sequences that improve the predictor. This discourages it from executing actions leading to boring outcomes that are either entirely predictable or totally unpredictable. Instead the controller is motivated to learn actions that help the predictor learn new, previously unknown regularities in its environment, thus improving its model of the world, which in turn can greatly help to solve externally given tasks. '[I]t is called curiosity because maximising the learning progress pushes the robot towards novel situations in which things can be learnt' (Oudeyer and Kaplan, 2005).

The implications of resisting curiosity

This 'pushing towards the novel' is often resisted by delegates attending our executive education programmes and is most evidenced at executive level. Executives generally arrive for a leadership development programme with a very particular way of seeing the world driven by mental models which have served them well in the past. Many lack a learner readiness because of fears around being exposed for not knowing enough or genuinely believing that because their ways of doing things have served them well in the past they will continue to do so into the future. In an increasingly faster business environment the ability to make rapid decisions is seen to be advantageous. However, according to Dawna Markova, 'the first thing we need for innovation is fascination with wonder [curiosity in its particularity], we are taught instead to decide...to decide is to kill off all possibilities but one. A good innovational thinker is always exploring the many other possibilities.' (Markova in Rae-Dupree, 2008). However, due to the increasingly accelerated pace at which people are expected to work and think, the opportunities for 'exploring possibilities' have become increasingly limited and a real resistance to curiosity, which can be perceived as a 'time-waster', develops.

The problem with resisting curiosity in learning, which in its extreme form becomes learner disengagement, is that it limits opportunities for seeing things differently. In fact, according to Kashdan (2009), a lack of curiosity is a breeding ground for stereotyping and discrimination, inflated confidence and ignorance that can actually lead to poor decision making, dogmatism and rigidity of thought. 'Curiosity motivates us to be open to viewing the world, other people, and ourselves from multiple perspectives' (Kashdan, 2009: 26). Furthermore, deeply held beliefs may give us a sense of clarity and confidence, but a curious state of mind aids us in engaging with this tension of conflicting angles and our own deep seated beliefs. For those of us more swayed by arguments of the physical, encouraging people to do something different every day helps with weight loss. Research has shown that when subjects were asked to seek out something novel to do daily, it made them more mindful of other areas of their life and increased the chance of weight loss. Thus, getting out of our routine makes us more aware in general (Ryan, 2006; Fletcher, et al., 2007).

How to create a curious state

We believe that to create a curious state, three things are required: Suspension of judgment, time and stimuli. One of the exercises we encourage delegates to do in order to break down the barrier to curiosity-driven engagement is what we have termed an Attention Audit. In the work of Otto Scharmer (2007), an open mind, open heart and open will are the key drivers for connecting with our deeper selves as well as engaging with more innovative thinking and being. The 'voice of judgment', coined by Michael Ray (2004: 40), the voice of cynicism and the voice of fear are the three voices which chatter in our minds, limiting our ability for growth, self-exploration and engaging with the new. The voice of judgment is the 'inner critic' (Ray, 2004: 41) which criticises the self for not being good enough. It is almost a superego-like state which inhibits the subject from taking the courageous steps often needed for leadership practice. Scharmer connects the voice of judgement to our mental state and calls for a suspension of judgement in order to open our minds. The voice of fear relates to the inability to connect with emotion to what is at hand whereas the voice of cynicism is tied to a paralysis of action which is often a result of not believing that things can be different. Thus an open mind increases the willingness to learn, an open heart the ability to be more receptive to new ideas and an open will generates the appetite for doing something different.

The attention audit

In a two-day reflective process we welcome delegates to undertake an Attention Audit. In this exercise they identify the voices of judgment, fear and cynicism in their own patterns of thinking. The beauty of the exercise lies in the fact that delegates are able to identify when they want to do it. Many choose one day at work and one day at home in order to see if the voices are activated differently in different contexts. We invite delegates to set aside the two days of their choice and to set an alarm which buzzes every two hours. There is a three step process which delegates then follow for the attention audit. First, they identify which voice has been chattering in their head and write down what it is saying.

Second, they are required to undertake a breathing exercise focused on three deep breaths – each breath is a metaphor for ten years forward. Then, after the third breath they are in a place 30 years hence and are invited to write back to the voice from a place of grace and wisdom. The voice of wisdom responds back with advice which is given in the gentlest and most compassionate of ways. This exercise is repeated six times per day for two days. What we have found in the work we have done with six groups across sectors, with artists, designers, publishers, executives, administrative support staff and marketeers, is that the voices become less active with each interaction and that in many cases by the eleventh time, the voice of wisdom is the active guide. For many delegates, it is a surprise that their voices of judgment, fear and cynicism were so prevalent and many realised after having to use the voice of wisdom how often they forgot this part of engaging with themselves.

The use of breath is important in the attention audit. According to Linda Stone (2009), correct breathing cues our attention. Breath is often taken through the mouth which activates our sympathetic nervous system and is associated with fight and flight. When the sympathetic nervous system is activated it is a cue for our bodies to defend themselves and large amounts of cortisol, cholesterol and noradrenalin are downloaded into our blood system. Breathing through the nose however, holding it for two counts and ensuring that the nasal exhalation is twice as long as the inhalation activates our parasympathetic nervous system which is associated with rest and reflection. By activating the parasympathetic nervous system when delegates are called on to exhibit the voice of wisdom allows for ease of access and reflection.

When we speak about time being one of the conditions required to generate a curious state, it is not merely the clearing of space for reflection. It is a conscious decision to slow down one's pace through parasympathetic breathing. According to Carl Honore (2009):

> *Even the workplace is warming to the Slow revolution. Companies such as the Boston Consulting Group and KPMG are goosing [sic] productivity by encouraging*

staff to spend less time on the job. Others are imposing speed limits on the information superhighway with email-free days and cellphone blackouts. A senior executive at IBM has launched a Slow Email Movement to encourage us to check our inboxes less. And that's IBM, not an aromatherapy cooperative.

Human curiosity is often generated when one's interest is piqued by something which is not congruent with one's current frame of reference. It allows one to challenge assumptions, yet at the same time for the curiosity to continue, more interest needs to be piqued.

In the world of augmented reality, designers craft avatars and characters that live not in the full focus of one's vision but to the side – at a glance (Slavin, 2009; Cerveny, 2009). The art of the glance is a useful exercise to practice when attempting to notice things outside of one's normal area of perception. In fact, according to Schmidhuber (1991), humans and other biological systems use sequential gaze shifts to detect and also recognise patterns. This peripheral vision gives rise to residual objects which exist alongside us but which are seldom noticed. Simply put, what are you noticing from the corner of your eye that you would usually filter out, but could possibly give opportunities for seeing differently?

Thus the very nature of curiosity is a paradoxical enabler of learning. It requires the subject to both suspend judgement in the sense of Scharmer's Open Mind (2007) and simultaneously stimulates critical thinking through engaging with what is perceived as incongruent in one's environment in relation to one's own mental model. There has been much debate as to the legitimacy of curiosity as an innate driver in children which is depleted on a linear basis by unstimulating education and repetitive learning. Steven Dutch (2009) goes so far as to say that curiosity is not an innate characteristic but rather a learnt behaviour and that the incidence in children is mere 'tinkering', an exploration of relatively minor variations on known themes. There are other promoters like Todd Kashdan who speak of curiosity as 'hard-wired in the brain', with a specific function that 'urges us to explore, discover and grow' (2009: 6).

Despite the lack of agreement on the origins of curiosity, evidence (Kashdan, 2009; Dutch, 2009) does suggest that it is often the case that curiosity diminishes over time. It has been argued that one of the reasons for this is that the need for exploration and discovery, a sensemaking technique for securing the environment from threat and danger, diminishes over time. Perhaps children have a greater need to secure the environment from threat and danger and as their environment becomes more commonplace, this drive diminishes. Conversely, it has also been shown that curiosity can grow even when these conditions of security are in place (Kashdan, 2009).

How to be a curious learner

There are three mantras which we believe encapsulate the attitude which one needs to adopt to be a curious learner:

1. *Be fascinated by your own ignorance* – Nobel prize winner, Ernest Rutherford supposedly said 'I am fascinated by my own ignorance', and he is believed to have had a practice with his team that they needed to report back daily on what they had observed that they were ignorant of. This activity of noticing what it is we do not know is driven to a large extent by the mechanism of curiosity. For his labour, he and his team went on to split the atom in 1917. Similarly, Albert Einstein, the Nobel Prize winning theoretical physicist, claimed that curiosity was his primary resource, indeed he said, 'I have no particular talents. I am just passionately curious'. He went on to develop the theory for general relativity among many other things. His early work as a physicist was in helping to concretise the existence of atoms. One physicist helped concretise the discovery of the atom; the other split it, driven to a large extent by their own curiosity.
2. *Answers don't change the world, questions do* – Perhaps one of the greatest gifts we can enable our learners with is an understanding that it is not the answers we have which create growth and exploration but rather the questions we develop and the capability for asking. Embracing curiosity as a way of framing new questions is powerful.
3. *Go slow to go fast* – It is by slowing down, such as through our breathing, that we are able to start sensing differently. This capability helps to create fresh insight into issues and problems, develop an ease with others to tackle thorny issues and ultimately makes our learning faster. According to Honore (2009),

> the greatest thinkers in history certainly knew the value of shifting into a lower gear. Milan Kundera talked about 'the wisdom of slowness.' Albert Einstein spent hours just staring into space in his office at Princeton University. Charles Darwin described himself as a 'slow thinker'.

It is the value inherent in slowing down which allows us to starting seeing differently, suspending our judgment of the way the world is and creating extraordinary opportunities for doing and perceiving differently.

Conclusions

In this paper, we have attempted to show how curiosity as a lens for attention is an enabler of learning, especially in the context of the attention economy. Perhaps the origins of the notion of curiosity will always be moot, but whether or not the notion of curiosity is inherent or a learnt capability, we have attempted to demonstrate how it can be developed into a way of being in the world. This would acknowledge that incongruent things have connections and that possibility often comes from the most unexpected places. But harnessing curiosity is always dependent on suspending judgment, engaging with an open mind and understanding that informed slowness is truly the right kind of 'speed' of the 21st century.

In conclusion, it is our assertion that educators should design and present the content of courses in a way that raises the curiosity of learners, rather than simply offering information and answers. The educator of the future will seek to develop mental models that encourage flexibility and curious agility in learners, to encourage the crafting of incisive questions, present incongruities, and allow for the introduction of new informational possibilities from learners. In so doing learners may not only learn and engage more effectively in classes, but may leave the educational context with a sense of invigoration and a desire for deeper engagement in the challenges presented in their working context.

References

C. Anderson, *Free: The Future of a Radical Price* (New York: Hyperion, 2009).

C. Anderson, 'How can airtravel be free?', *Wired* 16.03, Available at: http://www. wired.com/techbiz/it/magazine/16-03/ff_free_air Accessed: 25 February 2008.

S. Anderson, 'In defense of distraction', *New York Magazine*. Available at: http://nymag. com/news/features/56793/ Accessed 17May 2009.

D.E. Berlyne, 'Curiosity and Learning', *Motivation and Learning*, Vol. 2, No. 2 (1978), 97–175.

B. Cerveny, 'Augmented city lab', *Picnic Conference*, 23 September (2009).

M. Csikszentmihalyi, 'Creativity, fulfilment and flow', *Tedtalks Director* (online) September (2008).

S. Dutch, 'Why is there ant-intellectualism?', *Natural and Applied Sciences*, University of Wisconsin – Green Bay. Available at: http://www.uwgb.edu/DutchS/PSEUDOSC/ WhyAntiInt.htm Accessed 13 March 2009.

B. Fletcher, K. Pine and D. Penman, *The No Diet Diet: Do Something Different* (Great Britain: Orion Books Ltd. 2007).

M. Goldhaber, 'Three kinds of money: Industrial, attention and finance'. Available at: http://goldhaber.org/blog/?p=199 Accessed 5 March, at: 2:29 pm 2009.

M. Harvey, M. Novicevic, N. Leonard and D. Payne, 'The role of curiosity in global managers' decision-making', *Journal of Leadership and Organizational Studies*, Vol. 13, No. 3 (2007), 43–58.

C. Honore, *In Praise of Slow – How a Worldwide Movement is Challenging the Cult of Speed* (Great Britain: Orion Books Ltd., 2005).

C. Honore, 'The slow revolution is growing...fast', *The Huffington Post*. Available at: http://www.huffingtonpost.com/carl-honore/the-slow-revolution-is-gr_b_ 310712.html Accessed: 6 October 2009.

C. Honore, 'In praise of slow thinking', *The Huffington Post*. Available at: http://www. huffingtonpost.com/carl-honore/in-praise-of-slow-thinkin_ b_331843.html Accessed 23 October 2009.

T. Kashdan, *Curious? New York, New York* (United States of America: HarperCollins, 2009).

R. Lanham, *The Economics of Attention – Style and Substance in the Age of Information* (Chicago, USA: Chicago University Press, 2007).

N. Leonard and M. Harvey, Curiosity, mindfulness and learning style in the acquisition of knowledge by individuals/organisations, *International Journal of Learning and Intellectual Capital*, Vol. 4, No. 3 (2007), 294–314.

G. Loewenstein, 'The psychology of curiosity: A review and reinterpretation', *Psychological Bulletin*, Vol. 116, No. 1 (1994), 75–98.

D. Markova, *The Open Mind – Exploring the 6 Patterns of Natural Intelligence* (Boston, MA.: Red Wheel/Weiser, 1996).

Near Future Laboratory *Follow Curiosity Not Careers* Available at: http://www.nearfuturelaboratory.com/2009/04/29/follow-curiosity-not-careers/ Accessed 29 April 2009.

J. Rae-Dupree, 'Can you Become a Creature of New Habits?', *The New York Times*. Available at: http://www.nytimes.com/2008/05/04/business/04unbox.html?em& ex=1210910400&en=322198a3861445c2&ei=5087%0A Accessed 4 May 2008.

M.M. Rahman, 'A reinterpretation of curiosity', *Research Bulletin of the Department of Psychology*, Vol. 2 (1966), 15–27.

M. Ray, *The Highest Goal: The Secret That Sustains You In Every Moment* (San Francisco, USA: Berrett-Koehler, 2004).

M.J. Ryan, *AdaptAbility – How to Survive Change you Didn't Ask For* (New York: Broadway Books, 2009).

M.J. Ryan, *This Year I Will...How to Finally Change a Habit, Keep a Resolution or Make a Dream Come True* (New York: Broadway Books, 2006).

P. Oudeyer and F. Kaplan, *Sony Computer Science Lab*, Paris April 2005. Accessed 25October 2009.

C. Otto Scharmer, *Theory U: Leading from the Future as it Emerges* (Massachusetts, USA: The Society for Organisational Learning Incorporated, 2007).

C. Shirky, *Here Comes Everybody – The Power of Organizing Without Organizations* (USA: Penguin, 2008).

J. Schmidhuber and R. Huber, 'Using sequential adaptive neuro-control for efficient learning of rotation and translation invariance', in T. Kohonen, K. Mäkisara, O. Simula et al. (eds), *Artificial Neural Networks* (North-Holland: Elsevier Science Publishers B.V., 1991), 315–320.

J. Schmidhuber, 'Driven by compression progress: a simple principle explains essential aspects of subjective beauty, novelty, surprise, interestingness, attention, curiosity, creativity, art, science, music, jokes', in G. Pezzulo, M.V. Butz, O. Sigaud et al. (eds), *Anticipatory Behavior in Adaptive Learning Systems, from Sensorimotor to Higher-level Cognitive Capabilities* (LNAI: Springer, 2009).

F.F. Schmitt and R. Lahroodi, 'The epistemic value of curiosity', *Educational Theory*, Vol. 58, No. 2 (2009), 125–148.

C.E. Shannon, 'A mathematical theory of communication', *Bell System Technical Journal*, Vol. 27 (1948), 379–423 (July), 623–656 (October).

K. Slavin, 'Augmented city lab', *Picnic*, 23 September (2009).

L. Stone, 'Start breathing', Keynote Talk at Picnic 09, Amsterdam, 25 September (2009).

What walking speeds say about us (BBC News: Wednesday 2 May 2007) Available at: http://news.bbc.co.uk/go/pr/fr/-/1/hi/magazine/6614637.stm Accessed: 1 January 2010.

Wikipedia Biography of Earnest Rutherford. Available at: http://en.wikipedia.org/wiki/ Ernest_Rutherford Accessed 27 October 2009.

14
Concluding Thoughts

Shirine Voller, Eddie Blass and Vicki Culpin

We started this book by discussing the future context for learning: The environment, influenced by political, economic, social, environmental and technological change, in which learning will take place. We then moved on to future learning, presenting emerging tools, techniques and approaches to learning which we anticipate will grow and become established, or perhaps be eclipsed by newer variants. In the final section of the book we introduced the future learner and discussed the capabilities and characteristics she or he will need to thrive.

All three sections of the book are oriented to the domain of executive education, where the audience comprises managers and leaders who themselves will need to grapple with what the future holds for their respective industries and professions. With this in mind, perhaps there are two areas with which the executive education business should concern itself above all else. First, developing individuals' capacity to learn and respond to unpredictable circumstances and, second, raising managers' awareness of their personal agency – their role and influence on the world around them. These themes are reflected in many of the chapters in this book. If the executive education industry is to play a leading role in shaping the future, and not merely hang on to the coat tails of change, then we believe it is through developing the innate capabilities of those who will be leading us into the new world.

Shirine Voller
Eddie Blass
Vicki Culpin
June 2010

Index